"There are numbers of memoirs written about the radical politics of the 1960s but Stephen Mann offers an important new perspective to the historical record. While still serving in the Navy he went on anti-Vietnam war demonstrations and attracted the attentions of Whitehall and the Special Branch. The book is both highly readable and an important addition to our knowledge of the history of the 1960s from someone who played a part in them." **Dr Keith Flett, Convenor, Socialist History Seminar, Institute of Historical Research, University of London.**

"Having worked with the National Council for Civil Liberties I enjoyed reading Stephen Mann's personal experiences of the NCCL campaign for justice for boy servicemen. Although the subject matter is serious Stephen manages to make his book an entertaining and amusing read, taking us through his adventures in the Navy. This is a story of despair but then hope for a reluctant serviceman who made the mistake of joining the armed forces at the age of fifteen without realising that he had signed away the next twelve years of his life. I thoroughly recommend you to read this book." **Hilary Kitchin, former Lawyer NCCL.**

"Stephen's story should be required reading for all those, whatever their political persuasion, who claim that enlisting at 16 is a "good thing" for young people. He reveals how easily a child is manipulated by exciting recruitment materials, how little they understand or consider the legal implications of their terms of service until it's too late, and how desperate many are to get out once the boredom and bullying begins. Half a century since the NCCL campaign, Stephen's cautionary tale is still all too familiar among child recruits today." **Rachel Taylor, Research and Advocacy, Child Soldiers International**

ISBN-13:978-1497404434
ISBN-10:1497404436

Author - Stephen Mann

Title - Sadism, Songs and Stolen Liberty

Cover Design by Martin Grimshaw

Follow Stephen on Twitter
@stephenmann12

Follow the "Sadism, Songs and Stolen Liberty" Blog
http://stephenmannblog.wordpress.com/

Stephen Mann

Sadism, Songs and Stolen Liberty

Dedicated to Clare and Kevin

CHAPTERS

PREFACE

I was in the Royal Navy for five years and ninety three days, which is five years and ninety two days longer than I had wanted to be.

The day I joined the Navy I didn't know it but I was to become a reluctant sailor. It was the day after I signed up that the penny dropped and I wondered what I had let myself in for. Despite the fact that I was only fifteen years old I had been allowed to sign up for twelve years which the Ministry of Defence had stipulated was the minimum period of service. I was laughed at by the people in charge of me when I asked if I could leave and go home. This was the1960s which was a great decade for young people in Britain. The music was fantastic, the fashion fabulous and revolution, freedom and equality were at the top of the political agenda. The era was dubbed the swinging sixties and the youth were out to sweep away the old systems and in the process enjoy themselves. However, it was also a time when working class boys were encouraged to join the armed forces at the age of fifteen. What many of these boys didn't realise fully was once they had signed on the dotted line there was no way out. For them the 1960s were not so great and a brutal and sadistic regime awaited them in their first year of training. Whilst some boys accepted their fate others tried to escape. The people I served with did so in a variety of ways, by pretending to be daft, punching Officers, deliberately disabling themselves or they just deserted. As the political and anti war movements of the 1960s began to influence me, my way out of the Royal Navy would take a different and surprising course. My adventures include my brief war with Iceland and my twenty minutes as the last line of defence of the British Empire in Gibraltar when Franco's Spain threatened. The story tells of encounters with the Secret Services, my conversion to socialism and my part in the National Council for Civil Liberties campaign for justice for all servicemen.

My struggle was for freedom and this story tells how some of us achieved it. Please sing along to the songs in the book as I did throughout my adventures, it was these wonderful songs of the 1960s that lifted my spirits, kept me sane and allowed me to mentally escape the worse times. I will be indebted to them forever.

Sadism, Songs and Stolen Liberty

CHAPTER ONE

MY BOY LOLLIPOP

It was June 1964 and I was standing outside Holloway Women's Prison in North London waiting for Christine Keeler to be released.

I had decided it was only right that somebody was there for her when she came out. Christine Keeler was involved in the Profumo scandal in the 1960s, a story of sex, spies and intrigue. John Profumo was Minister for War in Harold McMillan's Conservative Government and Christine had an affair with him at the same time as allegedly sleeping with a Soviet naval attaché, known to the British Secret Service as a spy. It was the days of the Cold War, when the West had nuclear missiles aimed at Moscow and the Soviet Union had theirs aimed at Washington and London.

The United States had almost invaded Cuba the year before after the Soviet Union had installed missiles there. This had resulted in the Cuban missile crisis where the world was on the brink of nuclear war. The idea that the War Minister of America's main ally was sleeping with a woman who was having an affair with a Soviet spy was headline making material. Following various court cases Christine had been jailed for nine months in 1963 for perjury but today was the day she was to be released and I was waiting outside the gates of the prison to see her.

Well, the fact was most of the worlds press and half a dozen of my workmates from a local factory, Holloway Engineering, who had skived off with me were there too.

I had recently left school at the age of fifteen and made the decision to join Her Majesty's Royal Navy. My start date was in October so I was marking time, and making a few bob producing televisions at the factory near the Nags Head in Holloway. Working there didn't have much going for it so a bit of history taking place just up the road at the prison made for some relief from the tedium of working on an assembly line putting ten rivets into a television chassis every minute.

Standing outside Holloway Prison an hour went by and we had already exceeded our break and were about to leave when the gates opened and a Black Maria swept out. Straining our necks we tried to peer inside the darkened back window but could see nothing and the vehicle was gone in seconds. We assumed it was Christine and left. We had to wait until the news on the TV that night to see her posing outside her London flat and later to read her exclusive story she had sold to the News of the World.

Arriving back at the factory the foreman was waiting for us at the gate in order to administer a ticking off for being late. He said he wanted to acquaint us with the rules on having money deducted from our wages for such a misdemeanour, the rules were displayed on the main notice board by the front gate and the foreman lined us up to read them in turn.

When I reached the front of the queue my eyes immediately went to a handwritten letter on the notice board from Millie Small who had worked at the factory but had recently left as she had made the big time in pop music. Millie Small? Yes Millie of "*My Boy Lollipop*" fame, she had worked here and I had just missed out on working with her! I thought the letter was a wind up but was assured by all, including the foreman that she had indeed worked here and the letter was genuine. If she really had worked here she must have viewed Holloway Engineering the same as I did, somewhere to make a living until something better came up.

Millie! My mind wandered back to a recent trip to Ravens Ait, an island on the River Thames at Surbiton that was owned by the sea cadets. The island was kitted out to look like a real ship with all the trimmings. I went there at weekends and also during school holidays, to practise rowing, sailing, tying knots and other naval tasks.

After one Saturday of arduous rowing on the river I was lying exhausted in my bunk after lights out trying to get to sleep. I never had a problem nodding off to sleep but some of my fellow young sailors were still awake and had decided to tell jokes which they were laughing out loud to. The head sea cadet, who was a year or so older than us was known as "Anchor" because he was a Leading Hand which gave him the right to have an anchor badge sewn onto his uniform, called out angrily:

"Pipe down you lot and get to sleep you woke me up from my dream. I had Brigitte Bardot, Sophia Loren and Millie with me, they'll be gone when I go back to sleep again."

"I've heard of the first two but who the bloody hell is Millie?" Sparky Hayes called out from the darkness of the mess. Sparky was a cadet who came from Walthamstow and was called Sparky as he loved everything to do with electricity and repeatedly told us that one day he wanted to be an electrician.

"The beautiful girl who sings the song *"My Boy Lollipop,"* you must have heard it," replied Anchor.

I had actually bought a copy of Millie's record a month ago but being up to date on pop music was not one of Sparky's strong points. He was soon to be acquainted with the lyrics though as the next day when my group were messing about on boats on the River Thames everyone was singing *"My Boy Lollipop"* over and over again.

There I was, just a few months later, standing at the notice board at Holloway Engineering reading Millie's letter of resignation. In the letter she thanked her fellow television set makers for making her time at the firm so enjoyable and regretting that she had to leave but she did now have a career in music to follow! Never mind I thought I'll be out of here too in October and in the Royal Navy preparing for a life of travel to exotic ports around the World.

My only concern with working at Holloway Engineering apart from the boredom was my personal safety which was highlighted one day when my rivet machine was provided with a guard to stop the rivets going into my hands. The foreman came up to the assembly line to make an announcement:

"Right, listen up everybody, you will notice that the machines you use now have very expensive guards on them and you will all make sure that they are in place before you start work each day!"

He shouted this information out whilst looking around to check that he had the attention of everyone before continuing:

"You all know that old Fred is no longer on the assembly line but is now working in the packing section because he lost two fingers on one of the machines recently. Stupid sod, he should have been looking at what he was doing instead of chatting. Because of his lack of concentration we have had to put these guards on the machines to stop you chopping your fingers off as well."

He finished off with a swipe at the Factory Acts that were there for our protection:

"Bloody health and safety gone mad I know but just make sure you use the guards!"

With that rant out of the way he went off to a place he called his goldfish bowl, a room made up of windows that was elevated above the shop floor where he could keep his eye on the workers.

"I could have lost my fingers too!" I cried out to no one in particular.

For the rest of my time at the firm, along with a lovely sixty year old Jamaican woman named Hyacinth who worked next to me on the assembly line, we couldn't get the words of Millie's song out of our heads and every day we joyfully sang "*My Boy Lollipop*." Hyacinth though would make me blush when she looked into my eyes as she serenaded me with the song.

CHAPTER TWO

CARRY ON JACK

I had thought long and hard about my future. All sorts of jobs had been tossed around in my head such as a train driver or maybe playing on the left wing for the Arsenal Football Club.

I had actually been offered an apprenticeship in Kings Bakery on Stroud Green Road which I seriously considered but when I reached the age of thirteen I decided that I wanted to become a chef with the aim of owning my own restaurant one day. To further this goal I took up cooking lessons, in fact I was the only boy who studied domestic science at Tollington Park Comprehensive School and when I announced to my teacher that this was my wish I was summoned in by the Headmaster who was not pleased with my decision and told me so in no uncertain terms

"I didn't become Headmaster of Tollington Park School to encourage Nancy Boys," he told me.

In spite of this discouragement I was single minded and I was going to become a chef so against his advice I started my lessons in domestic science where I learnt the rudiments of cookery. At home I baked cakes and made everyone my own culinary invention: spicy fluffy eggs. This was a sort of omelette made by beating an egg and some milk together, adding a pinch of curry powder to spice it up and frying in margarine, we never had butter but if we had I'm sure they wouldn't have tasted as good.

Throughout 1963 my dreams of owning a restaurant had developed in tandem with my desire to join the Navy. The Daily Mirror had run an advertisement for months showing two young boys standing next to a shiny ship in an exotic foreign port with the caption:

"These boys are seventeen years old and they are in Singapore."

Singapore! Outside of the Armed Forces I didn't know anyone who had been abroad in the early sixties and the job prospects for fifteen and sixteen year old boys leaving Comprehensive schools were to join firms like Holloway Engineering or W. Britains toy factory in Lambton Road where they made soldiers and farm animals with lead or if you passed GCE O levels in Maths and English you could become a bank clerk or a GPO telephone engineer.

Having a job that took you overseas therefore was alluring, almost an impossible dream in the early 1960s. There were plenty of jobs in North London that involved manual labour but there was no social mobility and there were no foreign holidays.

I reasoned that if I spent some time in the Navy I could save my money and come out as an experienced cook with enough capital to buy a restaurant in North London that would serve up delicious meals. That was my future sorted then.

**

I had been in the sea cadets for over a year and that had been fun and I always looked forward with excitement to spending weekends with them. Because of this I knew that I would get on very well in the Navy so in the autumn of 1963, although I was still only 14 years old, I decided to call the number on the Daily Mirror advertisement and I asked the person who answered if the Navy trained chefs.

"Of course we do son," a friendly voice at the other end of the line assured me and after giving the man my details an application form duly arrived in the post. I filled this in and sent it back and another letter soon arrived asking me to attend an interview at the Royal Navy Recruitment Offices in High Holborn, London.

My body tingled with excitement at the thought of the great adventure that I was now on the verge of.

If I was accepted into the Royal Navy I was told in the letter, I would be sent to Her Majesty's Ship Ganges which was the shore training establishment for boy entrants into the Navy at a place called Shotley Gate, near Ipswich in Suffolk. I read more of the information sent to me in the letter and it told me that all entrants to HMS Ganges were boys of 15 years of age who signed on for 12 years, which is 9 years from the age of 18 plus the three years from the age of 15.

It occurred to me that this was rather a long time but if I didn't like being in the Navy there must be a get out clause.

My Dad came along with me to the interview and reluctantly I had accepted his idea of wearing what he called sensible and smart clothes that would impress the people at the recruitment office. My attire consisted of an eye catching turquoise blue woollen suit and brown brogue shoes that my parents had bought for me in the one shop in North London that:

a) Specialised in unfashionable clothes and

b) Allowed customers to use provident cheques instead of cash which was a way of getting credit in the 1960s. I would certainly stand out from the crowd!

As we travelled on the Piccadilly Line from Finsbury Park to Holborn I was oblivious to the stares from the commuters who must have been wondering why I was wearing such strange clothes. In the packed underground carriage people puffed away at their morning cigarettes and as the thick smoke swirled in front of my eyes I was lost in my thoughts and rising excitement, today I was going to join the Royal Navy! What I didn't realise until sometime later was that I must have resembled a docile trout swimming aimlessly in a lake. An angler had cast his rod and line and I had swallowed the bait, the hook was firmly secured in my mouth and I was about to be reeled in.

Alighting from the train at Holborn my Dad and I shuffled slowly along with the massed ranks of city workers trying to escape from the underground station and as we approached the bottom of the escalator a loud voice shouted out:

"Onward wage slaves!"

My interview was with a Chief Petty Officer who was very enthusiastic and reassuring about how much I would enjoy being a member of Her Majesty's Royal Navy where they would take me in as a boy and make me into a man. Following the interview my Dad was given some forms to sign whilst I was taken into a room where an elderly grey haired man in a white coat asked me to read some letters that got increasingly smaller on a wall several yards away. I then had to take all my clothes off and stand in front of a bed where the man proceeded to cup his white gloved hand under my testicles and asked me to cough.

I did so and felt my balls do a little dance in his palm. This procedure seemed to indicate that all was well down below.

He continued with his examination by putting a little wooden stick into my mouth and asking me to say "Ahhh." Next I was hit on my knees with a rubber mallet, both my chest and back were listened to with a stethoscope, my abdomen was tapped and a torch was shone into my eyes and ears. I was questioned on what illnesses I had succumbed to in my fourteen years on this earth and all the time I was naked and shivering in the freezing cold room. Eventually I was told to dress and was sent to another room to take some written tests. The tests were fairly straightforward, one for colour blindness involving electrical wiring, some simple Maths and English and a sort of intelligence test. This consisted of a sheet of paper with pictures of various tools and what you might use them for.

For instance, a picture of a screw and four options as to what tool you would use on it to join two pieces of wood together. This was:

a) Hammer;
b) Spanner;
c) Screwdriver;
d) Saw.

I guessed a screwdriver would be the appropriate tool so that was the box I ticked. Next was a nail with the same four options. Now this proved a little trickier. Most households would possess a tool box with an assortment of tools for various jobs. In our house we had a draw in the kitchen with a flat handled screwdriver in it. So, when any job needed doing the screwdriver was always the answer. I thought back to the last time my Dad put a nail in the wall to hang a picture and it was the flat handle of the screwdriver that was the method used to tap the nail in. Was I to be truthful and say that in my experience it was a screwdriver you used on a nail or should I say hammer? I pondered this for a minute then decided to tick hammer. My family's peculiarities were not something I wanted to explain to the Royal Navy.

Completing the tests I returned to the interview room where I was handed a book by the Chief Petty Officer. The cover showed a picture of a young sailor in his uniform at HMS Ganges looking happy.

The pages within told of all the sports and leisure activities awaiting us new recruits when we began our naval career at Ganges. The book was called "*All work and no play make Jack a dull boy.*"

We were informed that it would be an hour before I got the results of my tests and medical so we decided to go for a cup of tea in the café next door. As we sat down I was amazed to see Bernard Bresslaw and Sid James on the next table, household names from TV and the Carry on Films, they were eating their breakfast and chatting. I was an enthusiastic autograph hunter, living in North London I had the autographs of the entire Arsenal, Tottenham, Barnet and Crewe Alexandra football teams, (I know that Crewe is nowhere near Islington but I had a pen pal in Cheshire and I would get him Arsenal autographs and programmes and he would send me Crewe ones in exchange). I offered Sid the blank back page of my "*All work and no play make Jack a dull boy*" book for his autograph. Sid looked at the front cover first.

"Joining the Navy are you son, how long for?"

"Twelve years." I replied.

"Twelve years! That can't be right; you must be able to sign for less than that."

When I told him twelve years was the minimum he told me that I must be barmy but he obligingly signed the back page and giving a loud and fruity laugh he passed the book to Bernard who also signed and returned the book to me with a worried smile before concentrating again on his breakfast. Blimey! I'd just met two famous people; this joining the Navy thing was already broadening my horizons, but I was sure that Sid must have been joking about me being barmy to join the Navy for twelve years as they must let me go home if I didn't like it, of course they would.

Returning an hour later from the café with my book duly autographed by the two celebrities I noticed a poster outside the recruiting office that said:

"Join the Navy, see the world and meet interesting people."

Someone had written at the end of this:

"And kill them!"

Back inside I was informed that I had passed all the tests with flying colours.

I now just had to wait for a letter informing me of the exact date for joining which would be sometime after I had left school. The Chief Petty Officer shook my Dad's hand and patted me on the head as he said:

"Well done lad, we look forward to having you in the Navy, just make sure that between now and when you join up you keep your nose clean."

My nose clean! Would a dirty nose affect my ability to be a sailor? This thought troubled me for the next few weeks and I made sure that I washed my face with soap and hot water several times a day. It was sometime later that I was told that "keeping your nose clean" was a way of saying "keep out of trouble." I was to discover that Navy speak was a whole language of its own. I asked the people in the sea cadets for more words and sayings and I learnt that the floor was the deck, the wall was a bulkhead, the toilets were the heads, a rumour was a buzz, being in the Navy was being in the Mob, rubbish was gash, the kitchen was the galley, a Vicar was a Sky Pilot, that your friend was your Oppo and many more.

Soon after the interview a letter arrived which informed me officially that I had been accepted as a member of the Royal Navy and my joining date was to be Monday 26th October 1964 when I was to report at 07.30 to the Royal Navy Recruitment Offices in Holborn and carry a small empty suitcase that my clothes could be packed into so that they could be sent back to my family.

**

Eleven days before I was to join up a great event occurred when the Labour Party won the General Election. On 15th October the nation had gone to the polls and in the early evening, when both my Dad and I had returned from work, we walked from our house in Lennox Road into my old Primary School, Pooles Park where the hall was being used as an election polling station.

I was too young to vote, you had to be 21 years old but I went to take in the atmosphere and when I asked my Dad who he would be voting for he replied:

"Labour of course. They're the only Political Party that working people can vote for."

The next day the newspapers proclaimed a Labour victory with Harold Wilson as the new Prime Minister and people at work felt more hopeful for a better future.

On Friday 23rd October I packed up working at Holloway Engineering and my only regret came when Hyacinth gave me a hug and started crying as she announced to the rest of the factory that:

"My Boy Lollipop is joining the Navy; he is running away to sea!"

After saying goodbye to my work mates and collecting my final wages of £6 I walked out of the factory gates for the last time and looked forward to a lovely weekend at home with my Mum and Dad and brothers, Geoff and John.

CHAPTER THREE

ALWAYS SOMETHING THERE TO REMIND ME

I loved the music from my childhood; my favourite singers had been Eddie Cochran and Buddy Holly.

As a young boy, earning pocket money delivering milk and newspapers, I had used my wages to purchase the latest pop records and also buy tickets to see as many shows as possible.

I felt lucky living in London and from the age of twelve years old I had seen acts at the Finsbury Park Majestic Ballroom as diverse as Gene Vincent and Freddie and the Dreamers. At the Finsbury Park Astoria I had seen Joe Brown and the Bruvvers and the Beatles and at the Tottenham Royal I had seen the Dave Clark Five. I also paid visits to music shops in Denmark Street or Tin Pan Alley as it is known, to buy the sheet music of the songs I liked so that I could learn the cords and strum along on my old acoustic guitar.

On my last Sunday afternoon at home before I ran away to sea so to speak, I listened as usual to "Pick of the Pops" on the radio in my bedroom. Alan Freeman was telling us pop pickers that the number one record this week was Sandie Shaw's *"There's Always Something There to Remind Me."* Alan told us that we would all fall in love with Sandie and this song was a cracker: "Not 'arf!"

I had already bought Sandie's record so that evening I played it several times on my record player and memorised the words as I did with all my records.

Just singing a song in my head, or out loud if no one was around, was something I enjoyed doing.

As I packed my bag and hung my clothes out for the morning and prepared myself to leave home for my great adventure I sang along to the words of Sandie Shaw's song.

Next morning I set off again with my Dad to the Royal Navy Recruitment Offices in Holborn. As I had been a wage earner for a while I had been able to buy some fashionable clothes. My attire consisted of a brown fine corduroy jacket, a red and white gingham shirt, Wrangler jeans and light brown hush puppy shoes. I was also wearing trendy boxer shorts and yellow socks. Importantly my hair was worn in the style of the Beatles. The lyrics of Sandie Shaw's number one hit were still going through my head as I made the trip to my new life. Walking along the city streets of Holborn I sang the song to myself as I watched workers disappear into their offices. I was suddenly pulled out of my day dream as I considered Sid's warning to me; was he right? Was I really mad joining the Navy for twelve years? A cold chill ran down my spine and suddenly I had second thoughts about my decision to join up.

Putting these feelings to one side we arrived at the Recruitment Offices and the excitement of my new adventure returned. We were early and there was time for a quick cup of tea with Dad in the café but although I looked, Bernard and Sid were nowhere to be seen. From Holborn, along with a half a dozen other excited embryonic sailors, we took the short tube ride on the Central Line to Liverpool Street Station where we were to catch a train for Ipswich.

"Harwich for the Continent," proclaimed a British Rail poster in large white letters on a wooden panel inside the station.

"Frinton for the Incontinent!" some wag had written underneath.

On the platform I waved goodbye to my Dad and boarded the train for the journey to Ipswich. I was already beginning to feel home sick but the cheery Royal Navy Petty Officers who had met us on the platform opened the doors for us to get onto the train and during the journey they filled us with stories of travel and adventure that the Navy was to offer us.

During the journey one thing the Petty Officers warned us about was the Ganges mast.

"Everyone has to climb it and when you first see it the size of it will scare you but don't be too worried we will show you how to climb it safely," they assured us with knowing nods and winks to each other.

Arriving at Ipswich we got off the train where we were met by a blue coach with the words "Royal Navy" painted in white on the side that took us onto Shotley Gate and HMS Ganges.

This is going to be nice I thought, these kindly Petty Officers will look after me and I will be given a lovely uniform and taught how to tie knots, play games and cook chips and roast dinners and then be let loose on a ship to go to faraway places like Singapore, places that the mates I left behind could only dream of. I had warm feelings of excitement and happiness at these thoughts.

The eleven miles of country road from Ipswich to Shotley Gate took about thirty five minutes when all of a sudden I saw the enormous mast of HMS Ganges looming before me. However, the coach ignored the main establishment and drove into a much smaller place a quarter of a mile away which one Petty Officer told us was called the Annexe. Another Petty Officer on the coach informed us this was to be home for the next four weeks. At this place he said we would have Civvy Street "knocked out of us." What on earth could he mean?

The Annexe was a small training compound with three low tin roofed huts called messes which all had a sort of outside conservatory without windows or walls attached to them called colonnades. I looked around and saw a Parade Ground and a much smaller mast than the one in the main establishment. Other buildings were pointed out to me including the dining hall, a clothing store, administrative block, a laundry, wash rooms and the heads as the toilets were known in the Navy. As the corrugated iron gates of the Annexe closed behind us with an ominous loud clunk the kind and cheery Petty Officers who had accompanied us on our journey suddenly changed. They were transformed into shouting, unpleasant people who screamed and barked orders at us. They swore and told us to hurry up out of the bus and "fall in" on the Parade Ground. The chill that had run down my spine returned and something was telling me that the excitement of leaving Finsbury Park for the Navy and the big wide world had started to evaporate.

I was taken to my mess, a long dormitory with iron framed beds lined up on both sides of the room with a locker next to each bed. The mess was cold and the windows were open and had no curtains allowing a cold wind to blow in. We were told to choose a bed and then stand to attention next to it.

A brutish looking man in a Petty Officers uniform who I hadn't seen on the train marched into the mess. He had a square jaw and looked to be in his forties. He stood rigidly to attention before he started to rise and fall on the balls of his feet. He had a stick in his left hand that he stroked with his other hand. Words were starting to come out of his mouth but stopped before they did. He looked mean and hostile.

Then a much younger man in ordinary Navy uniform appeared next to him. The Petty Officer glanced at the sailor next to him and then glared at us, making eye contact with us one by one, and then he began:

"I am Petty Officer Craddock, my friends call me Johnnie but you will call me Sir at all times. This fine young man next to me is Junior Instructor Hitchcock who you will also refer to as Sir at all times. Do I make myself clear?"

A few of us mumbled: "Yes."

"I said DO I MAKE MYSELF CLEAR?"

"YES!" we all replied, loudly.

"YES FUCKING WHAT?" he barked back.

"YES SIR!" we responded in terrified unison.

I had never had people in authority swear at me before and this was the second time in a matter of minutes. I was beginning to get the idea of what life was to be like, at least for the next four weeks. Little did I know that this was how people would speak to me for many years to come!

"If I ever ask you what your name is boys, I want you to give me your full title. If you are a seaman you will say Junior Seaman Second Class Blogs or whatever name you took from your Mummy and Daddy," demanded the Petty Officer.

After a few days when we talked about Petty Officer Craddock we referred to him out of his hearing not as Johnnie or Sir but as Fanny and Junior Instructor Hitchcock was soon named Psycho although we never told him to his face for obvious reasons.

A Junior Instructor was assigned to each mess in the Annexe. They were boys who had completed their year at Ganges and had apparently shown leadership qualities which meant they could instruct new recruits in all things to do with the Navy while we were in the Annexe. Psycho was our Junior Instructor and he also slept in our mess with his own special bed nearest to the door.

There were three meals a day at HMS Ganges, all substantial and all good; breakfast at 07.00, dinner at 12.00 and tea at 17.00. This was my first day in the Navy and dinner was to become my first meal as we were taken to the dining hall and joined a queue. I was surprised how much I enjoyed the food. It was similar to school dinners but better quality and more of it. There were plenty of chips and a choice of apple crumble or spotted dick with lashings of thick hot custard for pudding. After dinner and with a full and satisfied stomach, we were taken to a part of the dining hall that had been screened off where we were given a document to sign committing us to the Royal Navy for the next twelve years. I thought about not signing but this would mean I would have to return to my friends and family in Islington a failure, not even getting over the first hurdle of life away from home; I signed but I was not given a copy of the document.

The signing ceremony was followed by the worse moment of my life so far, a Navy haircut. We were lined up like sheep and taken to the man who was called the demon barber of Shotley Gate one by one. When it was my turn I sat helplessly as my lovely blond locks fell to the ground as electric clippers painfully and ruthlessly made their way back and forth over my balding skull. I went to the heads and looked in the mirror. I was unrecognisable from the person I used to be, I looked like a convict. If I was given the document to sign after the haircut I would not have done so.

Whilst I was in the heads I noticed there were no doors on the cubicles. I later spoke to some boys about this and they said they had heard the rumour that there had been attempted suicides in the Annexe in the past so this was to prevent boys doing themselves in! I shivered at this thought

Following my dreadful haircut I was summoned into a room that had medical people in it and made to strip off while my body was probed, examined and measured.

Afterwards I was given a copy of my details that had been recorded; I was five feet, five and a half inches tall, my hair was fair, my eyes were blue, my complexion was fresh and my chest measured thirty one and a half inches.

The medical examination was followed by a dental check up before I was told to line up at the clothing store where I was fitted out with my various uniforms.

I was given a kit bag, working clothes called number 8s, a serge blue Navy suit called number 2s which had enormous bell bottom trousers, a raincoat called a Burberry, a cap, gaiters, deck shoes, blue woollen socks, striped pyjamas, underpants, vests, white sailors tops and blue Navy jumpers that were made of the roughest wool known to mankind. In fact for the rest of my time in the Navy I had a deep red rash on my chest that was the exact dimensions of the woollen jumper. I was then handed a piece of blue cloth called a housewife. This unrolled to disclose needles, cotton, wool, a darning mushroom, thimble and scissors. Lastly an enamel mug was thrust into my hand that contained toothpaste and brush and a razor. I had yet to start shaving so I doubted if I would need to use the razor but Fanny would have other ideas about that.

Back in the mess I put on my unflattering naval underwear, the underpants hung to the knee and were a yellowy off white colour and made from a hard cotton material. Over these went my Number 8s. Once dressed in my uniform I was told to pack my civilian clothes into the suitcase I had brought with me. To this I attached a label on which I had written my home address and I placed the case outside the mess on the colonnade. I felt wretched as I watched all of our suitcases being packed onto a lorry to be dispatched back to our homes.

We were fed again at 17.00, another large meal; I had sausage and mash with peas and gravy followed by a slab of fruit cake and a cup of strange tasting tea. I picked up an extra piece of cake to take back to the mess to eat later but a Petty Officer who I didn't know saw this and screamed to tell me that no food was to be taken from the dining hall.

As a punishment for this misdemeanour I was taken out onto the Parade Ground and made to run around it five times.

This physical exertion immediately after eating a large meal had the effect of making me sick; I just made it to the heads before I emptied my meal into the pan.

Back in the mess we had to make our beds, properly stow our new kit into lockers and were given various cleaning materials to clean the decks, windows, heads, dustbins, everything in fact that didn't move. I was given a tin of metal polish and told to buff up the mess dustbin until I could see my face reflected in it.

As I rubbed and polished away at the dustbin the radio was on and Sandie Shaw was singing her song, "*There's Always Something There to Remind Me*" but for me there was nothing there to remind me anymore. My clothes, my last link with the world I had left behind, were making their way back to London on the back of a lorry and my hair had been swept up from the barber room floor and thrown away.

My new mess-mates and I were told to go and wash before going to bed and as we did so I was wondering what I had let myself into. The sea cadets had been fun, this certainly was not. It was lights out at 21.00 and five minutes before the mess was plunged into darkness I put on my striped naval pyjamas and lay down on my new bed for the first time. I thought about my plight, I was fifteen years old and I had just signed away the next twelve years of my life, that was almost as many years as I had already been alive, I had signed up to a life that I thought I had known everything about but I now realised I didn't really know what it had in store for me. I would be twenty seven years old when I left the Navy, an old man! I did some mental arithmetic and concluded that twelve years came to another 4,379 more days! As far as I knew they could all be like the one I had just endured. My dream had been taken away and I was living in a nightmare.

As waves of homesickness and fear washed over me in the darkness of my new home in Suffolk I could hear the boys in nearby beds sobbing into their pillows. I joined them and cried myself to sleep, as I would many more times during my year at HMS Ganges. Before I drifted off to sleep I made up my mind to ask Petty Officer Craddock in the morning if I could leave the Navy and go home, I would do this as soon as I got a chance to talk to him.

I was awoken next morning at 05.00 by a loud noise over the tannoy speakers that I discovered was a bugle playing Reveille. This was followed seconds later by the sound of a stick being run along the iron beds in the mess by Petty Officer Craddock.

"Hands off cocks, on socks!" instructed Fanny.

"Get out of your stinking pits right now!" screamed Psycho.

I swung my legs out of the bed and sat on the edge with my feet touching the cold floor. As I rubbed at sleepy eyes the feeling of homesickness welled up inside me again.

I was obviously taking too long to wake up as I sat on my bed so Psycho came over and kicked me in the shin. I tried to hide the pain as I got to my feet.

"I'll get you for that one day you bastard," I muttered under my breath.

I really wanted to leave this place now. Yesterday had been bad enough but to start my first full day with being shouted at and kicked stiffened my resolve. Communications with the outside world were impossible, no one in my family had a telephone and anyway, there were no telephones in the Annexe so I had no one to help me get out of the Navy, I had to do this myself. After getting washed and dressed I met Fanny coming back into the mess and bucking up courage I asked him the question.

"I'm sorry Sir, I don't like being in the Navy and I would like to go home."

I saw in his face a mixture of anger and amusement as he looked at me for quite a while before he burst out laughing saying:

"No son, you've signed up for twelve years and there's no way you can get out of that, now go and get your breakfast, we have a full day's work ahead and there's not a moment to lose."

I was stunned; was there no way out for me, was this really to be my fate, twelve years of misery in a job I now realised I didn't want to be in?

CHAPTER FOUR

SURVIVING THE ANNEXE

At breakfast my appetite returned despite an overwhelming feeling of disappointment and I again found the food was very good with plenty of crispy deep fried bread and a portion of a smooth light yellow slab the cook called scrambled eggs. I was to discover that this was made with lots of powdered milk and not many eggs but nevertheless it was delicious.

As good as the food was however, I was deeply unhappy. I went back to the mess and made sure I was in my correct working uniform before being herded out again onto the Parade Ground along with the boys from the other two messes. We were lined up and told to stand to attention whilst we awaited further orders from a Chief Petty Officer who seemed to be in charge of the various Petty Officer Instructors.

It was cold and miserable standing on the Parade Ground and a fierce north easterly wind was almost blowing us over. The Chief Petty Officer went through what we were going to do that day, basically marking our names onto our uniforms, sewing on badges, learning to iron and polish boots and how to apply Blanco to plimsolls. We would also start to learn how to march around the Parade Ground properly.

As I looked up at the corrugated iron fences and to all corners of the compound I was reminded of the exercise yards in the American prison films I had watched at the cinema.

The prisons must have been modelled on the Annexe.

We were then subjected to what was to become a daily ritual, an inspection. The inspection of the boy sailors from my mess was carried out by Fanny. He found fault with everyone and when it came to me he looked at my face and said:

"You spoke to me earlier, remind me of your name boy?"

"Junior Assistant Cook Second Class Mann, Sir," I replied.

"Right then Junior Assistant Cook Second Class Mann, have you heard of a pop group called Manfred Mann?"

"Yes Sir, I have and I particularly like their song Pretty Flamingo."

"Yes, well never mind that, you may not have realised that they share the same surname as you so from now on we will call you Manfred."

I looked at Fanny incredulously as he continued.

"Tell me something Manfred what is that stuff on your face?"

"I'm not sure Sir," I replied.

"I will tell you what it is Manfred, it is what we call Bum Fluff, it is what little boys grow before they become men and have whiskers. You were issued with a razor which you will use to shave it off; you will do this every morning, DO I MAKE MYSELF CLEAR!"

"Yes Sir" I replied.

He then barked to us all:

"Now get back to the fucking mess and listen to what Junior Instructor Hitchcock is going to tell you about how to mark your name on your bloody uniforms!"

This was the second day of my naval career and I now knew that I had made a big mistake and had to get out of the Navy. How big a mistake it was and how it took me over five years to achieve my freedom is my story.

During this quest and whilst I wondered how I could get out of the Navy, others did so in a variety of ways, by pretending to be daft, punching Officers, deliberately disabling themselves or they just deserted. As the political and anti war movements of the 1960s began to influence me, my way out of the Royal Navy would take shape.

Although I didn't yet know it yet, my escape route would even surprise me. For the time being I made the decision to survive the Annexe and then see what my options were for getting myself out of the Navy. I stopped feeling sorry for myself. Instead I decided to try and have no feelings at all until the nightmare I was in was over.

**

The misery of my four weeks of hell in the Annexe continued though. We were shown how to sew, and march and clean and were shouted at and punished for any perceived misdemeanour. Each day saw our individuality drained from us as we became a frightened body of boys who when asked to jump would do so without question.

After a few days we had amassed a small pile of dirty clothing so it was time to be shown how to do our laundry. We gathered up our soiled clothes in our bed sheets and were marched to the laundry block wearing just our shorts and plimsolls. We were all given a huge sink to stand in front of and told to strip naked. Junior Instructor Hitchcock issued each of us with a large yellow slab that resembled the smooth blocks of scrambled eggs we had for breakfast. However, this turned out to be soap; "Pussers Hard" to be precise. Everything in the Royal Navy was called Pussers. Our long baggy yellowy off white and ill fitting underpants with our names now stamped on the side were accurately nicknamed Pussers passion killers and green pulse peas were called Pussers peas.

We were instructed how to rub the Pussers Hard on any stains on our clothes in order to get them clean. We rubbed and scrubbed all of our clothes in tepid water and rinsed them off in cold water. The technique was to rub as much soap as possible onto the stains and fiercely knead the material between your knuckles. Very soon the skin came off my knuckles and I don't think it grew again properly until I eventually left the Navy.

One enhancement I was to discover was when I was paid my wages in the main establishment I would be able to buy my own washing powder, known in the Navy as dhoby dust, which was much better for cleaning clothes than Pussers Hard.

I would still have raw bleeding knuckles but much brighter looking clothes. For now though Pussers Hard had to suffice and after much scrubbing our clothes were inspected by Psycho.

Anyone who still had stains was told to get into a giant circular bath that was filled with icy cold water as a punishment.

They had their head held under the water for several seconds before being told to go back to their sinks and try again at removing the stains.

After an hour or so of washing and humiliation where we were all in turn subjected to the head held under in the cold bath treatment, we were marched back to the mess naked. Well, we did have a flimsy towel around our waists but that blew off in the wind so we held our blocks of Pussers Hard over our bits to protect our modesty as we crossed the freezing cold Parade Ground back to our mess where we hung our clean washing up in the drying room.

**

Most of my mess-mates I spoke to felt they were being treated badly and couldn't really understand why they were not allowed to go home if they wanted too. Surely a fifteen year old couldn't make a decision that bound them to a job for the next twelve years without the chance to leave? This was Britain after all, what about that song, *Rule Britannia*, with the words: "*Britons never, never, never will be slaves?*"

Many of the boys were fed up, scared and homesick but we were all in this together and from our common sense of injustice friendships were beginning to be formed in the mess. A boy who always sat next to me at mealtimes who I got on really well with was Barry Bond. He was from a naval family living in Plymouth and he told me that his Dad was an Officer.

Barry was nicknamed 007 by some and Brooke Bond by others but I called him Odd Job from the character in the Bond Film, Goldfinger. Barry was certainly odd. It wasn't because he spoke with a posh accent; he was odd in a number of ways. For one thing he was the only boy I knew who never drank tea. Also, whilst at breakfast we had cereal followed by eggs and bacon and other savoury stuff he did it in reverse, having his cornflakes last.

At dinner he would eat his pudding first before his main meal, he did this every day. He once told me that his ambition was to become an Officer in the Navy himself. Out of all the hundreds of boys who joined Ganges that year he was the only one I knew who professed to this ambition.

After several months Odd Job didn't seem to be around anymore. Maybe he had been discharged, lucky sod, although someone had heard he might have been sent off somewhere else to train as an Officer.

I thought that if this was true then maybe it was because he was idiosyncratic and different, well a bit barmy really, either way it worried me that Officers were in charge of ships full of guns and rockets. I made a mental note to keep an eye on them in future. I would miss Barry though when he left. He was odd but we always had a laugh together and I knew he acted as he did to see how others responded to his peculiar habits. I thought that Barry was funny, others that he was off his trolley, and maybe the powers that be that he would make a good Officer. For now though, in the Annexe, he was good company.

Until I joined the Navy I'd only really heard Cockney or BBC accents. Now I had to train my ear to understand the many and varied accents of the British Isles. There was one person in my mess with an accent I really liked. Cyril Jenkins had a real country twang when he spoke and sounded to me like the farm labourers in the Archers. His family worked on farms mainly producing sugar beet and they also had their own pigs and chickens. In the Navy you wouldn't survive with a name like Cyril so in the hope of getting a reasonable nickname he told us that at school he was called CJ. Being that he was from a country background most townies in the mess called him a swede basher so it didn't take long before this was shortened and he became just "Basher."

Basher joined me and Odd Job at mealtimes and he also became a good pal. Basher was also very odd too, he had a habit of doing everything arse about face. We were taught to salute Officers with our right hand but Basher would use his left.

When we began marching we were told to lead off with our left foot, Basher started with his right one and so on and so on.

His co-ordination was poor and some of the answers he gave were almost beyond belief. Basher was a good lad though and we spent many an hour chatting together.

Basher was the first farmer boy I had ever met and I told him that at Primary School my favourite song had been *"The Farmer's Boy"* which he said he liked a lot too.

We swapped stories about our schooldays and it transpired that both our schools had been very strong on singing folk songs and also promoting English country dancing and we had both been taken on trips to Cecile Sharpe House in North London to learn about our folk heritage.

I told Basher about how both my Primary and Secondary Schools joined in the annual performances of country dancing at the Islington Town Hall where we would perform the various country dance sequences such as stripping the willow and do-si-do. One day Basher and I used our collective memories to recall the words of our favourite folk song and when it was just us two together polishing our boots or cleaning our gaiters on the colonnade we would revive our schooldays and gustily sing:

"To reap and sow and plough and mow to be a farmer's boy."

After singing the song together for the first time Basher confided in me that he was unhappy and not enjoying being in the Navy and he wanted to go home. I told him that I wanted to as well and I let him know that when I asked Fanny if I could leave he said I would have to complete my twelve years service. Over the coming weeks most people I spoke to wanted to go home but one of those who didn't was a strange and rather manic looking lad from Manchester who always seemed to want to pick a fight with everyone for no particular reason. He was given the name Mad Man by the rest of the boys in the mess and I made a point of keeping out of his way.

One evening after tea we were cleaning the mess as usual when Fanny entered with an Officer who had two and a half gold rings on his sleeve signifying that he was a Lieutenant Commander. We had been told by Fanny that on ships there was always a First Lieutenant often with the rank of Lieutenant Commander and they were referred to as Jimmy the One.

This particular Lieutenant Commander had a very upper class accent so we all, including Fanny, called him Jimmy the Toff.

Fanny got us to fall in and stand to attention in the mess and he introduced Jimmy the Toff to us who, he said, had a very special message to announce. Jimmy coughed into his hand before he addressed us in a very haughty and affected manner and we realised that he had a speech impediment as he said:

"Boys, I have to tell you that I am visiting all messes today to inform boys of an important and special honour that has been bestowed on us at HMS Ganges. A small gwoup of four newly twained sailors will wepwesent Her Majesty's Senior Service, i.e. the Woyal Navy, at an event to take place in the New Year at Buckingham Palace.

If you boys show the cowwect attitude, a smart appearance and do exceptionally well in your work you will be in with a chance of being one of those taken to the Palace. You will be in competition with a lot of other boys at HMS Ganges so it is up to you to do your best and show me that you are worthy."

He smiled and looked at us one by one allowing time for us to take in this piece of news before he pointed at Basher.

"You boy, who do you think has invited us to this event?"

Basher looked perplexed and did not answer.

"Well, who lives at Buckingham Palace?" asked Jimmy still smiling,

Basher went red and looked flustered.

"Huwwie up boy, we haven't got all night!" urged Jimmy the Toff.

You could see that Basher was deep in thought, then at last a look that said he had the answer came into his face and he shouted out:

"Cinderella Sir!"

"CINDERWELLA!" said Jimmy.

"CINDER – FUCKING - WELLA!"

After a few moments with his jaw in a dropped position Jimmy turned to Fanny and I could hear him say:

"Is this boy taking the piss Petty Officer Cwaddock?"

Jimmy the Toff then turned on his heels and departed from our mess leaving Fanny to exact some awful punishment on us. When Jimmy was out of sight Fanny walked over to Basher and you could see that Fanny looked a broken man and there was a tear in his eye as he whispered into Basher's ear:

"Were you taking the piss matey?"

If Basher was taking the piss it was a cracking joke which he would pay for but it turned out that Basher remembered his Mum reading him stories at night when he was young and the only person he could think of that might live in a palace was Cinderella! His family weren't up on current affairs.

Unsurprisingly, no one from my mess was selected to visit the Palace. Basher's punishment for being stupid was to hold the mess dustbin above his head for half an hour with fully outstretched arms.

After ten minutes he couldn't hold it any longer and the dustbin fell onto his head almost knocking him out. He had to keep holding the dustbin though until the half hour was up which Psycho signified by further threats of similar retribution to anyone who stepped out of line. During the coming weeks everyone in the mess, including me, committed some perceived crime or other against the Navy that meant we had to perform this punishment.

CHAPTER FIVE

MORNING GLORY

It had become the norm that for part of our evenings we would sit out in pairs or small groups on the colonnade.

Although it was cold this was a place where we could have a fag and a discussion while spitting onto our boots and applying polish to get a shine that would please the Instructors. One evening a small group of us were polishing away when someone mentioned they had no thoughts about sex since joining the Navy. This prompted another boy to suggest:

"We should be but we're not and I know that it's a medical fact that all young men should wake up every morning with a hard on. This is called Morning Glory and is perfectly normal, it's not normal if you don't."

Another boy said he had wondered about this but had put the lack of any erections down to being physically and mentally exhausted and in a state of constant fear and terror of the various punishments that were regularly administered.

"It's the Bromide," offered Odd Job.

"What's Bromide?" we all chipped in.

Odd Job continued, "Apparently Bromide is a substance they slip into the tea that numbs your sexual feelings and stops you getting an erection, my Daddy told me this before I joined. Daddy said he got this information from the family G.P."

He continued: " Bromide is used in hospitals for people who have operations on their penises and it prevents an erection and the stitches coming undone. They give it to us though to stop us being distracted by erotic thoughts. That's why I don't drink the tea."

"I thought Navy tea tasted funny!" said Basher.

I enjoyed our discussions on the colonnade and although the Navy wanted us to become unthinking cogs in their machinery, we were individuals, albeit young and inexperienced, and we did posses intelligence and our own spirit and our own thoughts.

We would frequently chat about why people joined the Navy and although some had seen the same Daily Mirror advert as I had and been lured in by promises of exotic travel some were from orphanages where they were encouraged to join the Navy once they became fifteen. Others said that there simply were not enough jobs where they came from. The lads from the industrial cities told me of the lack of jobs at home so they saw the armed forces as a way out for them. Odd Job said he had once read a book about press gangs, where in the old days groups of sailors would go around the pubs of British ports and bang people over the head with a cosh. When these unfortunate individuals woke up they were at sea and in the Navy. He said that nowadays having no work in some areas meant this was a form of economic press ganging that got young people into the Navy and probably as many joined the Army for the same reasons. As we chatted I thought about the different methods of recruitment into the armed forces and that my form of press ganging was enticement by propaganda, not a cosh over the head. The result was the same as I was no longer a free man. I was effectively press ganged but in a more sophisticated way than was practised in earlier times.

Many of my current mess-mates expressed a desire to leave the Royal Navy if they could but some now actually accepted their plight. Basher had told me about the chickens his family kept and the phenomenon that when a chick escaped out of its shell it attaches itself to the first chicken it sees.

We pondered on the fact that a lot of these boys had a hard life as children; some told us they had parents who had beaten and neglected them or walked out and left them to cope, to be looked after by older siblings or an Aunt and also the fact that some actually were orphans.

Coming to Ganges was their first step out of childhood and into adult life and as such they accepted it, as hard and as brutal as it was, it was the first thing they had experienced after leaving home. For some boys, being at Ganges was the happiest time of their lives. More than one boy had told me that they had lived with alcoholic parents and had dreaded hearing them come home from the pub at night as this meant they would be subjected to verbal abuse and a beating just for being alive. At least at Ganges they did not have that fear anymore.

The next evening sex reared its head again. After tea we were told to go to a building next to the dining hall and we were led into a small room with a projector and screen. Once we were seated the lights went out and we were shown a graphic American film about the dangers of going off with girls and catching venereal diseases. The film was in colour and was set in a fairground where a group of sailors were enjoying themselves. A good looking young woman walks up to one of the sailors and starts talking to him. After a while they kiss and walk off together and apparently go into a bedroom. The next scene is a doctor in a white coat pointing to pictures of penises with all sorts of scabs, boils and rashes on them. The doctor informed us that these were pictures of real American sailors penises after they have gone off and had sex with women. In the next scene the same group of sailors are out having a good time in a bar some months later when a different woman walks up to one of the other sailors. The "victim" from the previous scene runs over and tells his friend to have nothing to do with this woman as he could end up with the same diseases inflicted on his manhood as he had. They rudely tell the woman to go away and not bother them before they leave her and go to the bar to order another round of Pepsi Colas. The moral of the film seemed to be; don't have sex with women. No mention was made of having safe sex and using a condom. Anyway, being only fifteen years old and not very wise in the ways of the world this information went over our heads to a large extent.

When the lights were switched on again a Chaplain appeared along with a Doctor and we were lectured on what they described to us as the birds and the bees which in fact was some basic sex education.

The Chaplain added at the end that as good Christians and upstanding citizens it was our duty to save fallen women. No one knew what he meant, particularly as we were incarcerated and wouldn't even see a fallen woman let alone be able to save one.

As well as our sexual health being taken care of great emphasis was placed on our cleanliness. We had to wash, shower, clean our teeth and shave every day and all of our clothing and bedding as well as our mess had to be spotless. We were inspected every morning at Parade and every evening our mess was scrubbed, polished and inspected during the Officers rounds.

Also, our kit had to be laid out each evening according to the regulations with our name showing in the centre of each item of clothing. If anything was out of place, or even if it wasn't, Psycho, Fanny or Jimmy the Toff, depending who was doing the inspection would kick our clothing all over the mess and sometimes throw it out onto the colonnade or out of the window in a fit of rage.

As for personal cleanliness a scapegoat was found who hadn't quite managed to appear clean enough according to our Instructors. A boy from Blackburn called Tony was adjudged to have been smelly at evening inspections. His mess-mates were encouraged by Psycho to drag him into the showers and scrub him with brushes, brooms, wire wool, Pusser's Hard and any other cleaning materials that could be found. He was left a bleeding, crying, quivering wreck on the floor of the showers and Psycho told us this would be an example that we were never to allow our standards to fall.

A few nights later further punishment was meted out for another heinous crime: someone in the mess spoke after lights out! It was in fact five minutes after lights out. I lay in my bed in the darkness, trying to work out what the day had been about, we had done a lot of marching around the Parade Ground, this time with rifles on our shoulders for the first time. We had tried to march in straight lines and we had right wheeled and left wheeled and come to attention, we had learnt how to present arms, stand at ease and stand easy and also we were taught how to fall out properly. Fanny and Psycho did not seem too pleased with our efforts. During the day we had been screamed at and on two occasions Psycho and also a Junior Instructor from another mess had kicked my shin to make me stand in the correct way and the bruised area on my leg made by the kicks now throbbed.

As I pondered on the injustice of my situation I heard someone from the far end of the mess say something funny. No one replied but a few boys laughed. Within seconds the lights were switched on and Psycho was out of his bed and walking along the centre of the mess. In a very loud voice he screamed:

"So, you think you lot are comedians do you? You certainly aren't sailors; the way you marched about today was a disgrace. Everyone get out of your beds and roll up your mattresses tightly, take your pyjamas off and put just your socks and boots on and fall in outside on the Parade Ground with your mattresses held on your back."

So there we were, my entire mess, in the middle of nowhere bollock naked, in the dark, freezing cold and with a sadist in charge of us.

"You will now march at the double around the Parade Ground ten times," ordered Psycho.

"If you drop your mattress you will have to do it another ten times."

Off we went running around the Parade Ground with just boots and no clothes on with light snow fluttering around us. It was agony trying to keep the mattress on my back from unravelling and falling to the ground but all of us somehow managed it. Coming back into the mess exhausted I saw Psycho give Basher a push for being a bit slower than the rest of us.

The next morning we were lined up, in our clothes this time, on the Parade Ground for morning inspections. It had been three weeks since I had my hair cut and it was beginning to look a little more normal. It was really very short still but I could almost pass for a respected member of society, like a bank clerk with a short back and sides rather than someone on a chain gang. Fanny came over to me and stood with his nose two inches from mine.

"Is your hair hurting you boy?" he shouted. Spit came out of his mouth and landed on my chin.

I was puzzled by this question but I thought I would give the honest answer.

"No Sir." I replied.

"Well it bloody well should be because I'm standing on it!" bellowed Fanny.

An exaggeration I thought but I kept quiet.

"Visit the barber as soon as you have had breakfast and report to me immediately afterwards so that I can see that it has been done."

**

It was our last week in the Annexe before we were to be transferred to the Main Establishment down the road and there were still surprises in store for us. On the Friday evening we were told to put on our blue sports shirts, shorts and black plimsolls and fall in outside the mess. We were marched at the double to the dining hall where the tables and chairs had been replaced with a boxing ring. I had never boxed before and I had no inclination to do so now. However, a group of PTIs in their white vests and tight sporty trousers were waiting for us and began pairing us off. We were all to fight someone over three, two minute rounds. I sat in trepidation as I watched my mess-mates pummel one another until it was my turn. I protested to one of the PTIs that I wasn't really cut out for this type of thing but my pleas went unnoticed. Boxing gloves were tied to my hands and I was placed into the ring with a stocky boy from Glasgow who looked like he had done this sort of thing before.

As the bell rang and we squared up to each I tried to remember what the boxer Henry Cooper had looked like when I had seen him fighting on the TV. I pulled the gloves in front of my face for protection but suddenly felt a sickening blow to my abdomen. As I bent over in agony leaving my face exposed a punch struck me on the nose. I decided to jog backwards and dance around a bit to kill time. My opponent sprinted towards me so in desperation I started swinging punches in his direction. Luckily, a couple of these caught him and he retreated to reassess his tactics. He came again and as I had a longer reach than him a punch caught his head and he fell to the ground. After a count of six he was up again and then the bell went. In the next round he had me on the deck with a combination punch to the head but I got up again straight away. In the third round a stinging punch to my face resulted in a bloodied tooth coming out and hitting the deck.

The final bell sounded and we were sent to our corners. A PTI, who was acting, in boxing parlance as my second, sponged my face and uttered encouraging words. I had blood coming out of my mouth and running from my nose.

There was no doubt that my adversary had hit me more times than I had hit him and his arm was held high by the referee as the winner. This suited me because if you won a fight you went on to box again until a Champion was declared. We spent the next hour or so watching people batter each other before being sent back to the mess where I had a shower and turned in. As I lay there in the dark I wondered how many more such surprises the Navy had in store for me. I lay awake for several hours that night trying to make sense of what I was doing in this place. I thought about my life back in London and my family and friends and the people I had left behind. To make myself feel human I recalled as much as I could of my family history. I knew that several generations of my family had lived and worked around the Holloway Road and Finsbury Park areas of North London, it was my patch. My relations had worked on the railways, the buses and in factories, garages and one uncle had owned a shop in Hornsey Rise. My Dad had no sisters but he did have one Brother who was tragically killed at the age of fourteen when he fell off a lamp post he was playing on in Durham Road.

My Dad and his Dad had both served in the Royal Navy so it was a bit of a family tradition I supposed. My Dad had joined in the Second World War and he even got married to my Mum dressed in his Navy uniform! As he was a naval storeman, called a Jack Dusty, his best uniform was similar to one worn by a Petty Officer and he looked very smart.

As for my Granddad he was a ships stoker and I was to find out that every time he came home on leave the police had to come and take him back, he hated the Navy and didn't want to return but he had signed for a long term and couldn't get out. My Grandmother on my Mums side was the newcomer to London. She had come up to London from Gloucestershire as a young girl between the wars and had worked in service for a well to do family in a large house in Birnam Road.

My Dad now worked as the store's manager in a garage on the Holloway Road that conveniently for him had a pub, The Half Moon, situated between the stores and the garage.

Working in the garage didn't pay very much so to make ends meet he would get up at 04.30 each day and clean the windows of most of the shops in Seven Sisters Road before starting his real job at 07.30 at the garage. My Mum had worked at a variety of jobs ranging from a conductress on the trolley buses, a doctors receptionist and serving in the Land Army in the war where she drove a tractor. She had recently been an usherette at both the Savoy Cinema in Holloway Road and the Astoria in Finsbury Park shining her torch to help people find their seat in the dark. She would also open the back door for me and let me see films without having to pay to get in.

I was born in Islington and I came into the world in the upstairs front room of number 4 Lennox Road, a rented top floor of a house opposite Pooles Park Primary School which I later attended as a young boy. Most housing in London in the 1960s was multi occupancy and there was also no electricity in my house until I was seven years old. We were kept warm by a single coal fire in the front room supplemented by portable paraffin heaters which created so much condensation that everything in the house dripped with water. Our lighting was from gas mantles on the walls that we lit with matches and the street lighting was also gas, a man came around every evening just before dark with a flame on the end of a long pole with which he lit the street lights. We had no television so all of our entertainment was reading, conversation or playing games.

There were hardly any cars on the roads in Islington and most people had no need of them, buses and trains were our transport if we needed to go anywhere. I remember though a time when my brother Geoff was a patient in a remote hospital in Hertfordshire and a good friend of my Dad, a man named Leslie Compton, came to the rescue as he was the only person we knew who had a car. Leslie was an Arsenal legend having played centre half for them over a 22 year period but on his retirement he became the landlord at the Hanley Arms pub in Hornsey Road, one of my Dad's watering holes. Leslie always told me to play football whenever I could as it would keep me fit.

So, as a young boy in Islington, my playgrounds were the car free local streets, the fields of Finsbury Park where we used our jumpers as goalposts for endless games of football and of course the wonderful Hornsey Road Swimming Pool. Several of the streets near where I lived were bomb sites from the Second World War. They were dangerous but I loved playing in them. Campbell Road ran parallel with Fonthill Road and stretched from Seven Sisters Road to Lennox Road and every house in the street between Biggerstaff Street and Lennox Road had been destroyed by the Luftwaffe. This bomb site was our main playground that we called "the Bunk." The boys and girls of the area pretended to be British or German soldiers. With pieces of wood as our guns and broken bricks as hand grenades we would scramble in and out of the shells of blown up houses shooting at each other and being occasionally chased by real Islington policemen who would smack us around the head if they caught us to warn us off playing on our Bunk. I remember being caught once which improved my running skills thereafter.

The great steam trains of the day, the Flying Scotsman and the Pacific A4s known as Streaks including Mallard and Golden Fleece could be seen from the viewing platform at Finsbury Park where the drivers of these magnificent trains would look out for you and wave as they made their way from Kings Cross Station north to York, Newcastle, Leeds and Edinburgh. On Sundays I would walk to the railway yards at Kings Cross with friends and climb the walls into the vast sidings where trains were rested and we would illegally clamber in and out of the engines of these trains to our huge enjoyment.

On Saturday afternoons in the football season, when they were at home, my friends and I would walk up St Thomas's Road to Highbury to go and watch the Arsenal play. I also sometimes got the bus to watch Barnet Football Club who played in the Athenian League in a lovely little ground called Underhill.

Another way I passed the time was to stand outside number 304, Holloway Road where record producer Joe Meek had set up his studios and where many famous songs of the sixties were recorded - in his bathroom!

We would wait and hope to see and get the autographs of the Tornados who had a hit with Telstar and other pop stars including the Honeycombs, Tom Jones, Heinz and Rod Stewart. This was my childhood and between being born and entering Tollington Park Comprehensive School at the age of eleven my family had moved from number 4 to number 12, Lennox Road where we now rented the whole two storey terraced house. There was a break of three years when I lived outside London, from the age of seven to ten which I spent in a New Town called Harlow in Essex where my Dad had got a job in the glass works.

In my early teens I had spent many enjoyable evenings at a youth club in St Mark's Church. Most of the time there was taken up chatting to mates, playing table tennis and snooker and listening to pop music. Saturday nights were best when everyone could be seen dancing around to the music of the time. *"Let's Dance"* by Chris Montez was a favourite to leap about to. The club also organised great trips and one unforgettable holiday was a week on a narrow boat on the Grand Union canal, what happy memories!

It was about that time when I fully realised that I had been born under Clement Attlee's post war Labour Government which had created the National Health Service and had nationalised major industries and utilities including the Bank of England, coal mining, the steel industry, electricity, gas and inland transport. Until Labour formed the NHS millions of people in Britain had little or no proper health care. I can remember having a cup of tea one day with my Aunt who was a bit left wing and called herself a socialist and she told me that until the formation of the NHS women who could not afford it were offered no pain relief at childbirth. My Aunt went on to tell me that before the NHS most working people could not afford health treatment and those who were unfortunate enough not to be able to get work or had disabilities had no chance. When she went on to tell me that the Conservative Party opposed the NHS and voted against setting it up it I was shocked. When I heard about these things I thought that one day I would become a socialist too.

Lying in bed that night in the Annexe at HMS Ganges recalling my childhood I was feeling more homesick than ever as I nursed my sore mouth and nose.

The photograph we had on the mantelpiece at home of my Mum and Dad on their wedding day with my Dad wearing his uniform came into my head and I wondered if he had been made to box when he joined the Navy. As I closed my eyes I told myself that I should have listened to Sid!

Mum and Dad

CHAPTER SIX

THE MAST

On Monday 23rd November 1964 the boys in my mess packed their belongings into kit bags, put on their blue serge bell bottom uniforms, their Number 2s, and marched out of the Annexe, along the roads of Shotley Gate village and into the main establishment of HMS Ganges.

What struck me was the size of the place. The Parade Ground appeared ten times the size of the one in the Annexe and across it groups of well drilled young sailors doubled here and there with commands being shouted out from their Instructors.

As well as Instructors barking orders I noticed members of the dreaded Regulating Branch going about their business. These were the Navy's own Military police who were responsible for discipline and as I was to find out kept order at Ganges by coming down heavily on any recalcitrant young sailors. Across the Parade Ground I could see the living accommodation which was divided into ten Divisions, all named after Admirals. At one end of the Parade Ground were the Green Mansions. This was where the green corrugated iron mess deck of Hawke Division was situated; a two storey building that was to be my home for the next eleven months.

Opposite was Nelson Hall which we were told would be used for drill and Divisions in wet weather.

There was a block that housed school rooms, a wardroom for the Officers, a gunnery school, a cookery school and schools for all other naval professions, a gymnasium, swimming pool, sports fields, athletics track, a pier, a NAAFI shop, Fisk's photography shop and a barber's shop. There was also a laundry block, the Sick Quarters and there were Faith, Hope and Charity the infamous steps that were to cause us much pain as one of the punishments of HMS Ganges was to double up and down these steps over and over again. As we marched along I glanced to my left and spotted the most important building, the CMG, Central Messing Galley, where we were to be fed three times a day.

Then we stopped under the dreaded and gigantic mast. I looked up and at such close proximity it was a most terrifying sight to behold. Fanny proceeded to tell us the history of the mast and said it was originally the foremast of HMS Cordelia and was over 143 feet tall. He told us that only one boy had died falling off the mast but another had fallen head first and went through the safety net taking all of the skin off his back.

"So the chances of any of you being killed climbing it are very small, but if you do fall make sure it's not head first!" he reassuringly advised us.

This close up the mast was already scary but it became more so when Fanny told us these stories, he also added that part of our training would be to climb the mast on a regular basis! As well as climbing for exercise and punishment there was a formal event known as "Manning the Mast." This would consist of us climbing the mast in a choreographed manner to the accompaniment of music played by the band of the Royal Marines. When doing this some of us would be told to walk out onto the yardarms while others would hang on to the rigging and at the very top a Button Boy would grip the lightning conductor between his knees whilst standing to attention and saluting. I made up my mind there and then never to volunteer for that job!

Leaving the mast we reached an area called the short covered way where we were met by a number of Petty Officers from the various Divisions and as our names were called out we were allocated to our different classes in the Divisions.

To my dismay, whilst I was assigned to Hawke Division, Odd Job was sent to Collingwood and Basher to Keppel Division. Once we were handed over to our new Petty Officers, Fanny and Psycho said their farewells and turned and marched off back to the Annexe to make preparations for inflicting more pain and misery on the next unsuspecting entry of raw junior sailors. Entering our new mess we were told to select a bed and stow our kit into lockers while caps and Burberrys were to be neatly hung on hooks at the end of the mess. Our new Class Instructor introduced himself as Petty Officer Stewart to be called Sir at all times which we did but among ourselves we just called him Andy. He gave us a talk on the routine at Ganges.

"Your time will be divided between school work, seamanship and technical training for your trade whether it be a Seaman, Electrician, Engineer, Signal Operator, Cook or whatever," he explained.

My ears pricked up as I took in the information that at last I would be learning to be a Cook, doing what I signed up for I thought. Andy continued:

"The rest of your time will be taken up with physical and recreational activities, also looking after your kit and learning about the Royal Navy."

Andy informed us that we were to be allowed ashore on Saturday afternoons to Ipswich or Harwich and this news cheered me up. Our Divisional Lieutenant Commander then appeared and was introduced to us, he told us his name was Jones and he gave us a short lecture on what was expected of us; basically, be smart, work hard, do as you are told and keep your nose clean. Her Majesty's Ship Ganges, he explained, has been the shore training establishment for boy entrants into the Royal Navy since 1905 and in that time over 130,000 recruits had passed through its gates so we were following a fine tradition he told us, unconvincingly I have to say.

I was to have very little to do with the Officer in my time at Ganges but after my treatment by the nasty people I met in the Annexe both the Officer and Petty Officer Stewart seemed quite decent chaps.

Following the introductions our new Petty Officer instructor marched us, his new class in Hawke Division, around HMS Ganges to show us the sights and explain what we would be doing for the next eleven months. He took us into Nelson Hall which was the size of a huge aircraft hanger to keep us out of the cold weather whilst he gave us a lecture on the place. On the wall was a picture of an Admiral, Sir Philip King Enright, who Andy proudly told us had started his naval career as a Ganges boy in 1910.

"That picture is placed there as an example that you all have a chance to get to the top in the Royal Navy if you try hard enough," beamed our new Petty Officer who added that over the years Ganges had been opened three boys had gone on to become Admirals.

I thought of the numbers of boy sailors who had come through Ganges that had been mentioned to us by the Divisional Officer earlier.

"That means three boys out of 130,000 became an Admiral, those are not very good odds," I said to the boy standing next to me.

Following an extensive tour around the training establishment we were marched into the CMG for dinner. As we patiently queued for our food it must have been obvious to the seasoned older boys of HMS Ganges that we were a new class fresh from the Annexe as there was much thumping of tables and loud shouts of derision and insults were hurled at us by these old timers.

Back in the mess I bumped into Mad Man. This was the manic angry boy who had, I noticed, chosen the bed nearest the rear door. His inclination to fight first then ask questions later had, I now found out, increased with his move to the main establishment. I had decided to have a look out of the back door to see what was behind our living accommodation and as I passed his bed I was caught by a swinging punch that landed on the cheek of my face. Mad Man was dancing and prancing around me with his raised fists in front of him and as he did so he evoked the image of the lion with no courage in the film The Wizard of Oz.

"Come on put them up, put them up," he said.

I ignored him and tried to walk past but he punched me in the face again. This time I kicked him hard in his testicles and walked out of the door. I noticed though that he picked a fight with everyone in the mess over the coming weeks.

"He is clearly mad enough for the Navy," I said to myself.

The first evening in Hawke Division was taken up with the usual scrubbing, cleaning and polishing of everything in sight that I had got used to in the Annexe. I was given the task of cleaning the windows so I armed myself with a bucket of soapy water and a cloth and got to work. Cleaning windows entailed balancing on a step ladder and for me it was a close second to cleaning the heads as my least favourite job. My first efforts to clean windows in Hawke Division ended up with me leaving smears of soap on the window panes which resulted in much shouting and anger aimed in my direction by instructors and Officers.

The next morning after breakfast we were told to get into our white sports gear and were marched at the double to the foot of the mast. As my eyes slowly made their way from the bottom to the top of the mast, 143 feet into the sky, we were joined by a boisterous group of Physical Training Instructors, PTIs. It was explained that the PTIs would supervise small groups of us as we were told we would have to climb most of the way up the mast although not to the button on this occasion. For many of us this was a very scary experience. We tightly grabbed each piece of taut rope as if our life depended on it and we slowly ascended with a PTI climbing next to us urging us on. When we got to the platform called the Devil's Elbow we had to climb out on this with our backs to the ground at almost a 45 degrees angle hanging on for dear life, which was both physically exhausting and terrifying at the same time. Once over this platform we climbed to the Half Moon and went over it and then returned to the bottom by sliding down a rope. I managed to climb the mast, just, but some of the boys froze at the Devil's Elbow. These lads were told to climb through an escape hole in the platform named the Lubber's Hole and make their way up to the Half Moon, swing over it and descend the same way. Those who were too scared to climb to the Devil's Elbow though were told they would have to try this every morning until they had mastered the art of climbing the mast to the required height. For all of us though, mast climbing became a frequent activity that we were forced to do regularly.

At 10.30 we were introduced to what was to become a welcome daily break with a mug of Kye and a sticky bun.

Kye was a thick sweet cocoa drink made with evaporated milk and was both delicious and revitalizing. This was followed by school work. The first day's lesson was about the history of the Royal Navy and was almost entirely taken up watching grainy Ministry of Defence films showing British ships that had been attacked by German U – Boats in the Second World War and were in the process of sinking.

The films showed sailors sliding down the sides of capsizing ships or jumping into oily waters to escape burning hulls. I have to say that this did not fill any of us with much enthusiasm for our chosen careers.

**

That afternoon we were taken to the Ganges Pier and introduced to the boats used for sailing and rowing. There were boats called Whalers and there were also clinker built Cutters. We were placed into a Whaler and given oars. After some elementary instructions we cast off and before long we were pulling our way up the River Orwell.

I had mentioned to Andy my experience in the sea cadets and was given the position of Stroke Oar. This meant that everyone else followed my lead in how often they made strokes with their oars. After a number had "caught a crab", a term for an error where the rower is unable to remove the oar blade from the water and the oar acts as a brake on the boat, we were finally pulling in unison and making steady progress up the river. Although it was freezing cold I really enjoyed messing about on the river in this way. In fact I enjoyed it so much that I enlisted into a rowing club which meant that if I got up an hour early I could spend some mornings before breakfast rowing up and down the rivers Stour and Orwell and for much of my time at Ganges I did this several days a week.

During my first week at HMS Ganges main establishment I received my pay. As a Junior Assistant Cook Second Class I received £1 per week rising to £2 per week when I achieved the rank of Junior Assistant Cook First Class. We were mustered in Nelson Hall and were taught that when our name was called out, (this did not come as a complete surprise as we were lined up alphabetically), we were to march up to the Pay Officer, salute, call out our rank, name and pay number, hold out our left hand and receive a little packet with a pound note inside.

Then we had to bring our saluting hand down to grasp the packet and return it to our side before doing an about turn and marching smartly off. I got the call and marched over to the desk:

"Junior Assistant Cook Second Class Mann P083270, Sir!" I shouted and received my first Royal Navy pound note.

Once outside the hall I ran over to the NAAFI shop and bought cigarettes and sweets to last me for a few days. When I looked at the few pence change I received it occurred to me that my dream of saving enough money to buy a restaurant when I left the Navy was seriously threatened by such low wages. Why hadn't I asked what my pay would be before I joined?

That same evening we had our first full blown kit muster in the main establishment. This involved displaying all of our belongings including bedding and underwear, on the deck by our lockers. Everything had to be laid out in a certain way with our names displayed in the centre of each item. If anything was not spotless or folded in the exact way we were told we would be in trouble. As far as I could see everyone had put out their kit in a pretty decent display of naval precision and cleanliness. As the duty Officer came in he walked up to Tony's neat pile of clothes and immediately started to scream about what a disgrace it was before he kicked it in all directions. Still red faced he walked up to my kit and picked most of it up and threw it out of the window! Everyone in the mess suffered a similar treatment that evening. I must have given an ironic laugh as I said under my breath:

"That's bloody unfair we worked hard to get our kit cleaned and displayed correctly."

My laugh must have been picked up by the Officer who screamed at me:

"So you think having filthy kit is funny do you?"

"Pick up the dustbin and hold it above your head until I come back and tell you to put it down."

I did as I was told but the dustbin was heavy and made my arms ache so that after fifteen minutes, with no sign of the Officer returning, my arms gave up and the dustbin fell on my head and I almost passed out.

When I came round some kind souls in my mess had collected up my clothes along with their own from outside the building where they had been thrown.

Everyone in the mess spent their spare time over the next couple of days up to their arms in hot water and dhoby dust cleaning mud off their kit. The kit muster farce was repeated every week for the rest of my time at HMS Ganges.

CHAPTER SEVEN

THE DAY WE STORMED RADIO CAROLINE

A saving grace of life at Ganges was listening to the radio.

There seemed to be a radio positioned in each mess and during our so called leisure time, when in fact we were cleaning, polishing, ironing and sewing, music played. The radio was nearly always tuned to the pop music station Radio Caroline which had been founded earlier in 1964. Radio Caroline was broadcast from the Motor Vessel Caroline which was unlicensed by the Government and was considered a pirate radio station. Amazingly the ship was anchored three miles off the coast from HMS Ganges just outside British territorial waters.

One day we were told that we would sail around the Motor Vessel Caroline as part of our training and the rumour grew that as we were Royal Navy sailors from HMS Ganges and agents of Her Majesty's Government we would form an armada to storm Caroline and take it under Government control. After all it was a pirate radio station! Amazingly, we were then officially informed by our Gunnery Instructor that we really were all part of the boarding party! Although the idea that we were actually going to see real action, which for a fifteen year old had a lot of glamour attached to it, we were still sceptical.

Nevertheless, six sailing boats from Ganges, each with five juniors and a Petty Officer onboard set off and sailed up to the Motor Vessel Caroline.

When we were close to the ship it had the appearance of the Mary Celeste and no one was to be seen onboard. They had probably heard the rumour too and were hiding below decks. However, we were not ordered to board the radio station but instead we were instructed to sail back to the River Stour to practise our sailing manoeuvres in the calm of the river. On the way back the Petty Officers on all of our boats were laughing heartily and it seemed that the idea that we were to storm Caroline that day was made up by the Instructors to wind us up for their amusement.

I was really glad that Radio Caroline was never closed down; the songs they played kept me sane. No matter the hardship I was asked to bear, if I could sing the words of the latest pop tune in my head I was able to cut everything else out. Listening to and singing along with the songs gave me contact with the world I knew, magical sounds that I allowed to fill my imagination, words of love and hope and dreams of better times. The songs humanised my senses which were being debased in this alien and cruel place. I couldn't get physical escape from Ganges but music from Radio Caroline gave me mental escape. Many songs will place me exactly where I was when I first heard them. For instance I can't hear the song *"Baby Love"* by the Supremes, which was number one in the charts during much of November 1964, without remembering being on my hands and knees scrubbing and polishing the deck in my mess in the Annexe with Fanny and Psycho bellowing orders and insults at me. That song was the first of many that saved my sanity at Ganges as I had closed my eyes and allowed it to transport me somewhere better. Thank you Radio Caroline!

Apart from music the other saving grace that kept me sane at HMS Ganges was that in the main establishment we were able send and receive mail. I received letters from my Dad, Uncle Ben, my Brother Geoff's girlfriend Christine, from my school mate Mad Frank and best of all a weekly letter and parcel from my best friend Dave Charie. Dad's letters were pretty matter of fact, about what was happening in the family back in Islington and encouraging me to keep my chin up.

Ben's were humorous and very knowing about the military life style; he had served in the Queen's Dragoon Guards, mainly in Aden and was now a Prison Officer.

He lived in a three story house in a road called Tollington Place. Ben had a one bed roomed flat with his wife and my Grandmother lived in another flat on the same floor. My Aunt Babe and her husband Chalky lived on the top floor. There was a family on the ground floor and everyone in the house shared a single cold water tap and a solitary toilet. On the back of the envelope Ben would write his return address as: The Right Honourable Benjamin Hall, Tollington Towers, London.

I think that my brother's girlfriend, Christine, felt sorry for me particularly when she heard about my hair cut and she wrote lovely, kind and cheery letters sympathizing with my plight and letting me know about the latest films, music and the pop groups that she had recently seen performing at the Majestic Ballroom in Finsbury Park. Mad Frank and I (he referred to me as Mad Steve,) corresponded in the same outrageous manner as would befit the two subscribers to "Mad" magazine in North London. We both would get a fit of the giggles reading letters from each other. On the back of his letters he always wrote: "Wot, me worry?"

Dave though would send me food parcels or, to be more precise, Cadbury's chocolate biscuit parcels. To explain; during 1963 and early in 1964 we both worked for Mr. Edwards Dairy in Windsor Road near the Nags Head. I would knock at Dave's door at 05.00 every morning and we would walk along Seven Sisters Road to the Dairy together. Mr. Edwards was a good advert for those who said that smoking was bad for you.

As we rang his doorbell he would signify his presence with a cough so loud and rich that we thought his lungs would be coming out of his mouth. When he opened his door to us a freshly lit cigarette would be between his lips as he gave us the key to open up the dairy to start loading the milk bottles onto the cart. We would go around with Mr. Edwards and his electric cart delivering milk on the doorstep and also ride the bicycle with a crate on the front delivering milk to shops and businesses around the Holloway Road areas. We would finish our milk round in time to get to school before the first lesson.

At a department store called Selbys I would park the bike outside and carry a crate of milk to the store's kitchen on the top floor.

The cook was a lady called Edith and I would always stop and chat and tell her of my dreams to be a cook and own a restaurant and how I was joining the Navy to learn the trade and save up money. She would give me tips on making pies and other dishes but best of all she would not let me leave the kitchen until she had made me coffee with hot milk and given me a packet of chocolate biscuits. As I sat there cupping the warm mug in my cold hands and dipping my chocolate fingers into the coffee and sucking the melted chocolate I would watch Edith at work. She always had a cigarette in her mouth and the ash would get to over an inch long before she would avert her face from the cooking and blow it off onto the floor. One day as I watched her making a steak and kidney pudding the inch of ash from her cigarette fell onto the meat. Unperturbed she stirred the ash in, put the top crust on the pudding and popped it into the steamer.

"I'll get people asking me how I got that smokey flavour in the pudding," she laughed.

Dave stayed on at school for another year after I had left to study for his GCE O' levels and he continued delivering milk during that time. When he visited Selbys kitchen each morning Edith would give him extra chocolate biscuits to send on to me and thankfully that is what he did.

So at HMS Ganges I would expectantly await the arrival of the parcel of chocolate biscuits each week and I don't think Dave or Edith will ever know how thankful I was to receive them.

**

At Ganges I was soon re-introduced to the hyper individuals called Physical Training Instructors. This time it was on their territory, in the gym. We were marched in wearing our smartest sports gear and made to stand to attention while we were first of all inspected for any crease not sharp enough in our shorts or plimsoll not whitened enough or hair too long or a whole list of reasons to be given extra press ups or circuit training as punishment. Then we awaited instructions on what we had to do that day in the way of physical exercise.

At the far end of the gymnasium, either side of the stage, I was struck by two huge paintings of Rudyard Kipling's poem "If."

I had never read this poem before but today I had ample time while the Chief PTI went on and on about the benefits of physical education and discipline. Allowing his words to wash over me I started to read the poem on the wall and I thought that one sentiment in particular was a bloody good philosophy of how to get on in life:

"If you can meet with Triumph and Disaster, and treat those two impostors just the same."

I was shaken out of my thoughts by the scream of another PTI who ordered me to climb to the top of one of the ropes that was hanging from the deck head. Luckily, I had climbed similar ropes at school so I knew the drill. I shinned up the rope and was then instructed to let go of my hands and adopt a pose like a flying swan holding on with just my legs. I actually knew how to do this so for me there was no problem. For a couple of others new to this rope trick as soon as they let go they fell to the coconut matting below with a painful thud. After we were put through everything the gym could throw at us we left exhausted and with our ear drums throbbing from the close proximity of PTIs when shouting orders at us. The PTIs though were still wide eyed and it appeared they couldn't keep still. They bounced up and down, ran on the spot, did star jumps, launched themselves at each other bouncing off one another's chest and generally looked athletic. The boy next to me, Tony, wondered if these PTIs were on Purple Hearts, a recreational drug of the 1960s. I doubted this as I had read that these drugs gave you an up for a day and a down for some time afterwards. The PTIs were always up so I guessed it was adrenalin that kept them hyper. Although we thought the PTIs were bullies we had to admire their level of fitness and physiques which Tony and I agreed we would like to emulate one day.

CHAPTER EIGHT

SANTA IS AN ARSENAL FAN

The next few weeks continued relentlessly with Parade Ground drill, school lessons and gymnastics, climbing the mast and doing things in boats.

There were plenty of collective and individual punishments dished out which mainly entailed having to march at the double up and down Laundry Hill or the dreaded uneven steps called "Faith, Hope and Charity." There was much shouting and ticking off for various deemed failings of us boy sailors and many hours were also spent cleaning and polishing the mess and keeping our kit clean. There was still no hint yet of learning how to cook the Navy way but the main thing on my mind was the thought that I would soon be able to go on Christmas Leave and get home.

Then the day arrived! It was a week before Christmas when we were given an early breakfast and told to muster in our best uniforms at 07.00 in an area called the Long Covered Way. We were being sent home on what was called Long Leave, hooray! Rail passes were issued and our bags were packed. We had our final inspection to make sure we looked good enough to be let out and then we were loaded into buses and dispatched to Ipswich Rail Station. It was snowing as the train made its way through the East Anglian countryside towards London where on arrival I left the train and got onto the underground to Finsbury Park.

In the short time I had been in the Navy my parents had moved.

The lower end of Lennox Road was demolished under so called slum clearance even though there was nothing wrong with the houses and we were moved into a new block of Council flats built on the Campbell Road site. I rang the bell to my new flat, 133 Haden Court and my Mum answered the door with the question I had been dreading to hear:

"Hello Steve, when are you going back?"

I went into my new bedroom that I now shared with my Brother John and changed into my civvies. I had a cup of tea with Mum and chatted about things in general and when she asked me how I was enjoying life in the Navy I lied, as I did to everyone who asked that question over the next few weeks and said it was OK. I still didn't want to appear a loser who had made a big mistake, especially as I now knew that I couldn't get out anyway.

On leave I wanted to catch up on the news I'd missed out on being at Ganges so I read as many newspapers as possible and discussed current affairs with my family and friends. I read that the world was becoming worried that trouble was brewing in the Far East. I was getting worried too as I didn't want Britain to enter an unjustified war alongside America, especially as I was now a member of the Armed Forces! The papers said that the USA was increasingly involved in backing the South Vietnamese Government in its fight with North Vietnam. The USA had over recent years sent hundreds of military advisors to Vietnam and now America had committed huge funds to what it called the war against communism. I read in the Daily Mirror that the United States had conducted major air strikes against the Vietnamese National Liberation Front and that 8,000 American troops were being sent to Da Nang to secure the US Airbase there.

Christmas Day was spent in my parents new flat. I woke up to find a pillow case that my parents had placed at the end of my bed, something they had always done, stuffed with presents from my family. These included the traditional orange, a Football Annual, a pair of socks, a pair of slippers with two left feet, pyjamas that were too small for me and a bottle of bay rum for grooming my hair. "What hair!"

Dad cooked the turkey and my Mum the vegetables. We had Christmas pudding with custard that Mum had made with sterilised milk. Custard always tasted better when it was made with sterilised milk. As usual shops and pubs were closed on Christmas Day so we spent the evening watching television. On Boxing Day I went to see Arsenal play Stoke City where I took my usual position in the North Bank behind the goal where I really enjoyed watching Arsenal winning by three goals to two. It was great to be a part of the Highbury crowd again and singing:

"Jingle bells, jingle bells, jingle all the way, Santa is an Arsenal fan and at Highbury today, hey!"

The rest of the day was spent mainly in the Kings Arms in Durham Road playing darts and cards with my mates and drinking lemonade as the landlord knew I was underage for drinking alcohol. My Mum regularly sang in the pub and on that day she did a range of Doris Day songs, her favourite singer and the entire pub joined in with *"Que Sera Sera."*

We all had a good time. During the course of the day my Dad had managed to surreptitiously slip a few half pints of Whitbread's Best Bitter my way so as we walked home together we were all in a merry mood and gave the neighbours a loud rendition of Jingle Bells.

During the rest of my leave I went to the cinema and to several parties my old friends had arranged, but I felt like the odd one out as everyone else's hair was growing longer while mine had almost disappeared. I went to W.H. Smiths bookshop in Holloway Road and browsed the books as I was now allowed to take reading material back with me to Ganges. I had been recommended George Orwell as an author by one of my teachers at Tollington Park Comprehensive and in particular his book *"1984."* I bought a copy and took it home to start reading it and if it was any good I would take it back to HMS Ganges with me. It was very good. My friend Mad Frank had moved to Crystal Palace, the far side of London so I got a train out to him one day and we spent our time reading pages from Mad magazine out loud and laughing.

On Saturday 2nd January I went to the Arsenal again, this time they played Wolverhampton Wanderers and we won by four goals to one and being at the football match gave me the feeling that I had returned to the real world.

Walking home along Seven Sisters Road reading my match day programme I started to think about my collection of memorabilia and autographs that I had amassed as a young lad. I had spent many a long day standing outside the famous marble halls at Highbury as players came and went and I would ask them to sign my book. I had even spent time outside the Spurs ground in Tottenham High Road getting the autographs of their players. Bobby Smith, their big centre forward was always helpful and would take my book into the dressing room and get other players to sign and then come out and return the book to me, what a gentleman. During the summer when I was thirteen Jon Sammels, Geordie Armstrong and other young Arsenal players, after finishing their training sessions at Highbury would take me into the Arsenal Café in Gillespie Road and buy me cups of tea and rock cakes and talk to me about football and also sign autographs for me. I think that the lady who served us in the Arsenal café must have been the sister of the cook at Selbys as she also always had a cigarette between her lips and blew the ash sideways rather than take the cigarette of her mouth. The rock cakes often had a dusting of ash over them which gave them a distinctive appearance and taste. Another favourite haunt of Arsenal players when off duty was the snooker hall above Burton tailors in Southgate where I was allowed to sit inside whilst they played snooker and the players would even buy me a coca cola whilst I gawped at them.

Walking back from the Wolves game I decided I would have a look through my collection when I got home. With this thought a feeling of trepidation came over me. Everyone I knew who had been in the Armed Forces had come home to some sort of loss or disaster. My Uncle Ben had a budgerigar named Joey that had the freedom of his Mum's flat in Tollington Place. Whenever I visited as a young boy it would fly onto my shoulder and talk at me for hours on end. Ben loved Joey more than anything else in the world but arriving home on leave once he asked where Joey was only for my Nan to start crying and having to inform Ben that she had accidentally trodden on the bird and killed it. I knew that my budgie was alive and well but a premonition of some sort of loss suddenly came to me. Arriving home I asked my Mum where she had put the cardboard boxes with my football programmes and autographs I had lovingly assembled since the age of seven.

"Oh I didn't think you wanted that old rubbish anymore so I threw them out when we moved," was the reply. I was dumbstruck for a few moments before I got my voice back and asked:

"What, my colour photo of the 1963/64 Arsenal team with the autograph of every player on it?"

My Mum nodded.

"My photograph of the Tottenham Hotspur's double winning team with all their autographs too?

"I think so."

I was in full flight now.

"My signed photo of Eusébio I got when the Portugal National team visited Highbury and my Navy book with Sid James and Bernard Bresslaw's autographs and the photo of me and the Arsenal and Wales goalkeeper where he wrote on it 'good luck for the future and I look forward to seeing you playing for the Arsenal one day, best wishes Jack Kelsey'?"

"Yes, they've been dumped too."

"My collection of every Arsenal, Spurs, Barnet and Crewe Alexandra programme from 1960 to 1964?"

"Yes, I'm sorry, but I'm sure you can get them all again if you really want to," my Mum replied reassuringly.

I was again speechless and I don't think I ever got over the loss.

In the evening after eating my post match meal of egg and bacon I was drinking a cup of Bromide free tea and watching David Jacobs on the TV hosting Juke Box Jury when my Dad dropped a letter onto my lap to read which he said he had received from HMS Ganges the day after I joined. I opened it and read its contents:

Tel: - Shotley 244

H.M.S. Ganges

Ipswich

Suffolk

Dear Sir/Madam

Your Boy has now arrived safely at Shotley. He will be here under training for about one year. In order to get him used to naval routine and give him time to settle down he will spend the first four weeks in a separate part of the establishment known as the Annexe.

While there he will be amongst boys who joined with him; he will be introduced to naval discipline, have a full medical and dental examination, be vaccinated and finally be put in the class for which he is best suited.

When this preliminary period is completed he will join the main establishment. One third of his instructional time will be devoted to ordinary school work, one third to seamanship or technical training and one third to physical and recreational training, religious knowledge, work on his kit and learning about the Royal Navy. He will be able to play games most afternoons and evenings.

During this period many boys suffer from some degree of homesickness which is only natural. They all get over this, with few exceptions, and your encouragement in your letters greatly assists the staff in settling your boy down.

Each term in H.M.S. Ganges lasts fourteen or fifteen weeks and while your boy is serving here he will be granted 21 days long Leave at the end of each term.

Local Leave is granted for 1.15pm to 8.45 pm to a Junior when visited by his relations. Such visits should be confined to Saturday or Sunday, and should not be made for five weeks after your boy has joined as this initial period is a particularly busy and important one for him.

During this period telephone calls cannot be accepted.

You do not need permission to visit your boy after this first five weeks although you must ask his Divisional Officer for any Special Leave, but if you write to me before you visit and require a reply please allow plenty of time for a reply to reach you.

A sheet giving details of Junior rating's pay is enclosed.

Should you find it necessary to write about your boy at any time your letter should be addressed to the Captain and not to me by name.

I would like to add that our aim here is to build up a boy's character and at the same time continue his general education. We cannot do this unless he is keen and happy and in our task we need your co-operation as parents and guardians. I am always happy to discuss a boy's problems either by letter or in person.

The letter was signed by some unrecognisable squiggle of a signature but it was the contents that annoyed me. What a trick I thought, they had scared parents off from making contact with us for the first five weeks at Ganges by which time the Navy had us boys snared and the brain washing process was in full swing. The cunning bastards!

I spent the rest of my Christmas Leave with my old school friends Dave and Les and we enjoyed a couple of evenings at the Wimpy Bar in Seven Sisters Road eating hamburgers and rum babas and then, suddenly, my Leave was over.

The day before I had to return I spent several hours pressing my uniform and polishing my boots and on the morning of departure I decided to get out of Finsbury Park unseen while it was still dark. I scampered down onto the underground along with the city cleaners who were making their early morning journey to clean the offices of London.

CHAPTER NINE

RUM, SODOMY AND THE LASH

I had seriously thought about not going back to the Navy but the punishments I knew I would have incurred made it not seem worthwhile.

Reluctantly, I returned, arriving back at HMS Ganges along with hundreds of other boys who poured out of a fleet of buses that had transported us all from Ipswich Station. We were ushered into Nelson Hall and told to line up and then instructed to place our suitcases on the ground whilst a team of Chiefs and Petty Officer Regulators searched us and our cases.

They said they were looking for alcohol and knives which would be confiscated. The boy next to me had a copy of a magazine called Parade hidden in his pyjamas. Parade was a magazine that was full of pictures of naked women; anything below the waste however was airbrushed out so that no hair or genitalia were seen. People often said that any young man brought up reading Parade magazine would be in for a real shock on his wedding night. I had brought with me the bottle of bay rum which had been given to me by my Aunt for Christmas and my copy of Orwell's "1984". The Chief inspecting my suitcase confiscated the bay rum as he thought I might drink it and looked for a long time through the pages of my book.

He said: "bit of an intellectual are we?"

I didn't know what he was going on about so I just shook my head.

He put the book back into my suitcase and told me to shut the case and return to my mess. As I left Nelson Hall I noticed a big pile of confiscated Parade and Playboy magazines on a table but no knives.

Back in the Green Mansions Petty Officer Stewart told us not to change as we were to have our photographs taken and we were dispatched to Fisk the Photographers for this.

Junior Assistant Cook S Mann

On our return to the mess we changed into our number 8 uniforms and with a cup of tea we began exchanging stories about our Christmas Leave. Some reported that they now had girlfriends, others that they had lost them. Long reports of football games that had seen and on the chances of their teams, Aston Villa, Leeds, Blackburn, Everton, Nottingham Forest or Arsenal winning the First Division title that year were discussed in earnest. Geordie said that his team would win the Second Division but a boy from Northampton disagreed and said the "Cobblers" would. Andy came in and joined us saying that he was sure that his team, Kilmarnock, would win the Scottish First Division and he seemed to be in a good mood.

Towards the end of January I was in my mess getting ready to go to breakfast when Petty Officer Stewart burst in shouting out that Winston Churchill had died.

Andy had only spoken to us once before about Churchill when he told us the story that many years ago when Churchill was First Lord of the Admiralty he had started mothballing a lot of ships which upset people in the Navy. A disgruntled Vice-Admiral complained to Churchill that the tradition of the Navy was being attacked to which Churchill allegedly replied:

"Don't talk to me about naval tradition; it's nothing but "Rum, Sodomy and the Lash."

This was later denied by a Churchill aide but from then on members of the Royal Navy altered this quote and would state that the service now ran on "Rum, Bum and Baccy."

I thought about Churchill's alleged quote that the Navy was run on "Rum, Sodomy and the Lash." I knew that rum was issued daily to sailors once they were twenty years old so that part was correct, I had no idea yet about sodomy in the Navy but as for the lash we were informed at HMS Ganges that if we stepped out of line then we would receive a punishment called "cuts." This meant that we would be caned on our bare buttocks until they bled which I guessed was a modern day version of the lash, so there was some truth in what Churchill said!

I looked around the mess to see the reaction to the news of Churchill's death among my mess-mates but they didn't seem overly concerned so I decided to recall what I remembered about the man. I knew he was a Tory who, my Dad had told me, campaigned and voted against the setting up of the National Health Service. He also said that contrary to the image portrayed by the Tory press, Churchill was not very popular with many ordinary servicemen. My Dad had served throughout the Second World War on tank landing craft and was at a number of landings including D Day. One story he told me related to a time in Italy where following a successful allied landing Churchill had turned up several days later and was being driven through the crowds of sailors and soldiers in a jeep giving his two fingered salute and throwing cigarettes to the troops. According to my Dad the troops picked up the cigarettes and threw them back, giving Churchill a different sort of two fingered salute in return.

Also relatives of mine had related the famous occasion when they had joined a crowd of 20,000 people, many being soldiers, sailors and airmen in uniform, upset by Tory policies, particularly on housing and health, booed and heckled Churchill when he tried to speak in an election rally on the 4th of July 1945 at Walthamstow Dogs Stadium, drowning him out with the constant chant:

"LABOUR, LABOUR, LABOUR!"

CHAPTER TEN

WE SHOOT SOME GERMANS

The next morning following a big fried breakfast and then Divisions we were introduced to the rifle range.

Petty Officer Stewart marched us to the range and handed us over to a Gunnery Instructor whilst he pulled up a chair behind us to observe our shooting skills. The Gunnery Instructor, or GI as they were called, told us his name was Chief Gunnery Instructor Head. We decided within minutes of being in Chief GI Head's company that he should be Christened "Dick Head."

"First of all you will learn to shoot a .22 rifle," said Dick Head.

We were shown how to load a rifle, how to adjust the aim and how to squeeze the trigger properly with the objective of hitting a bulls eye on a target somewhere in the distance

We had to lie on the ground and place our rifles onto sand bags and when we were told it was OK to do so we fired at the targets. We repeated this several times but the boy next to me was having no luck and missed the target completely every time.

"It's not my fault it's this gun," he muttered.

Behind us Dick Head exploded.

"A gun, a fucking gun!" he screamed.

I had noticed that Dick Head was carrying a long, thin metal stick which I presumed was for cleaning the rifle barrel. However, I was wrong.

He stood behind the poor sod next to me and administered a stinging swipe of the stick over the back of the boy's thighs. Dick Head then walked away returning moments later with a rifle in one hand and a plastic toy gun in the other.

"All of you pay attention," he demanded.

Holding up the two weapons he sung us a little ditty:

"This is a rifle this is a gun, this is for killing this is for fun."

After pausing for effect he told us to resume our firing positions and then walked up and down our line singing his little song over and over again and giving us all a whack on the thighs with his metal stick as he did so.

Once we had all shot at the bulls eye for the allotted amount of times we were taken to another part of the rifle range and handed a Lee Enfield .303 rifle and two bullets each. In the distance were cardboard German soldiers that we were to shoot at. It occurred to me that as Germany was now a NATO ally these cardboard cut outs may not be the most appropriate targets to shoot at.

"Right, .22 rifles can kill but they are really for sport but .303 bullets will definitely cause death and today I am going to teach you the best way of killing someone with a Lee Enfield .303 rifle. Is that clear?" asked Dick Head.

He was standing next to me when he said this and looking straight into my eyes so I thought his question demanded an answer. Without thinking through the consequences I said:

"Er, excuse me Sir, I don't think I joined the Navy to kill people, I joined to learn how to cook."

Ho looked at me in disbelief and out of the corner of my eye I saw Andy hurrying over to join us as he too must have heard my reply. I already regretted the answer I had given as Dick Head looked at Andy for an age before turning back to me screaming:

"You stupid bastard don't you think Navy cooking has ever killed anyone? Put the rifle down boy and do forty press ups now!"

As I was doing my press ups I could hear the Gunnery Instructor and Andy singing another little ditty together:

"They say that in the Navy the food is very fine, but a spud rolled off a table and killed a mate of mine."

"Ha Ha Ha!" they rolled around together in wild laughter, " Ha Ha Ha, this little Trog thinks he didn't join the Navy to kill anyone, Ha Ha Ha, why did he become a cook then?"

Their pinks were certainly tickled at my expense.

After my press ups I was handed back the rifle and spent the next half an hour being handed more bullets to shoot the cardboard Germans. All the time I was wondering when I would actually start learning to cook.

**

In fact I didn't have much longer to wait as later that week the cooks of Hawke Division were taken at last to the Cookery School where we were introduced to Chief Cook Browning, a large jolly looking man in his mid forties. He told us that from now on we would spend three mornings a week having cooking lessons and that when we left HMS Ganges we would be sent to the Naval Cookery School at Chatham to learn to cook on a full time course before being let loose on the Royal Navy. He also said not to call him Sir as he was not an Officer but a cook and anyway, unlike an Officer he worked for a living.

"Call me Chief," he said.

We were issued with our working uniforms called cooks' whites which consisted of hat, tee shirt, apron and trousers and our galley boots which were designed to protect our feet from hot liquids if they were spilt. We were also given our own copies of the Manual of Naval Cookery issued by the Victualling Department of the Admiralty containing recipes and guidance on producing substantial meals for sailors at sea. Once changed into our cooks' whites we stood in a line and awaited orders.

"What is the golden rule of cooking?" asked Chief Browning.

"Making tasty food?" someone suggested.

"No," said the Chief.

"It is cleanliness; I want to see a clean cook and a clean galley before I start thinking about cooking. What's the first thing that the TV chef Fanny Cradock does before she starts cooking?" he didn't wait for an answer.

"She scrubs out her kitchen that's what she does and that is what you will do."

"Right then all of you make sure that your finger nails are short and scrubbed and your hands thoroughly washed, make sure all of your hair is covered by your hats and then make up a bucket of soapy hot water and get scrubbing, I will inspect all of you and the galley in one hour."

As we set to work I noticed Chief Browning went outside where he had placed a chair against a wall and proceeded to smoke several cigarettes and read the Daily Mirror while we scrubbed away. Eventually the Chief returned and inspected us and the galley as he promised. One of the boys had a little tuft of hair showing from the front of his cooks' hat and the Chief turned on him:

"You will cover your entire hair lad, we don't want any foreign bodies from your head in our food and if I ever find a hair in a dinner cooked by any of you I will personally shove the entire dinner, plate and all, up your arse!"

The Chief had a point. I remembered back to the cook at Selbys, Edith. She might have blown cigarette ash into the food but she always had her hair covered!

Anyway, duly admonished and at last deemed to be spotlessly clean we started our first lesson on how to cut vegetables with sharp knives without chopping our fingers off. We were shown how to bend our fingers under from the second knuckle down and move the flat side of the knife off our knuckles and away from us as we cut. I imagined what Basher would be like if he had chosen to be a cook and was let loose with knives in a galley. I shuddered at the thought of blood and finger tips all over the chopping board.

After a couple weeks of covering the basics, and lots of mopping the galley and scrubbing ourselves, the pots and pans, chopping boards and knives we were deemed ready to cook a meal when Chief Browning announced:

"Right, we will be cooking a roast dinner for four people. You will notice in your Manual of Naval Cookery that each recipe is for one hundred people. You will divide this amount by twenty five to get the correct amount of ingredients."

"When you make your roast potatoes they will all be the same size and they will be barrel shaped," added the Chief. That sounded like a challenge.

I looked at the recipe for roast potatoes; the Manual of Naval Cookery said I needed 42 pounds of potatoes, 5 ounces of salt and 3 pounds of dripping. I would have to scale that down to make four portions.

"Now, a roast dinner will be no good without decent gravy," explained the Chief.

He turned to me and asked:

"Junior Assistant Cook Second Class Mann, how did your Mother make gravy?"

"She would put Bisto into a jug and add boiling water and stir," I replied.

"That's not the way we make gravy in Her Majesty's Royal Navy," said the Chief.

"I will teach you how to make it as per the instructions in the Royal Navy Cookery Manual and if you ever have to use powdered gravy which will be very rare, we use Pusser's gravy powder not Bisto. Now then, for a start all good cooks will have a stock pot that you will make up each day. This stock will be the basis of your gravies and sauces."

"How do you make stock, Chief?" I asked.

"Right, listen up all of you," said the Chief.

"Open you Cookery Manuals at recipe number 0105, Beef Stock. You will see it tells you how to make stock for beef and a variety of other meats but I'll let Junior Assistant Cook Second Class Mann, who I understand you call Manfred, read out the ingredients."

The Chief was now getting friendly towards me so I obliged and told the assembled cooks that the ingredients were:

22lb of cracked beef bones

10lb of diced beef

64 pints of water

1lb of whole onions

1lb of whole carrots

4oz of salt

3 bay leaves

"How many are you cooking for with that recipe?" the Chief asked one of my fellow cooks.

"Four Chief," came the reply.

"Don't be so bloody stupid," said Chief.

"I told you that the recipes in Her Majesty's Naval Cookery Manual are for one hundred. Now, listen to me, when you roast meat you will have what we call renderings which is the fat and juices from the meat in the pan.

If you have not got sufficient renderings you can add dripping. You will brown the renderings in the pan on top of your stove making sure you do not burn them.

Next you will add flour and mix thoroughly. Then you will add the stock gradually, stirring until smooth. You will cook this until there is no taste of raw flour and remember you will never mix fat and drippings from different kinds of meat as each gravy should have the distinctive flavour of the meat with which it is being served. There you have it, Royal Navy Gravy. Now doesn't sound a lot better than Bisto Manfred?"

I agreed but he went on:

"But what would you do if you didn't have enough gravy made this way?"

"Put Pusser's gravy powder into a jug, add boiling water and stir Chief," I offered by way of a little joke.

"That's correct Manfred," he said, obviously warming to me.

I liked Chief Petty Officer Browning, I liked him a lot.

From that day on we gave Chief Browning the nick name Gravy and every time I saw him I thought of the quote in a Hancock's Half Hour Radio programme I had listened to in which Sid James, surveying the gravy that Tony Hancock had made, comments:

"I thought my mother was a bad cook but at least her gravy used to move about!"

CHAPTER ELEVEN

THE GREAT ESCAPE

School lessons at Ganges had continued on a daily basis over the months and eventually I passed all of my exams in English, Maths and Royal Navy History;

I came top of the class in History, and shortly afterwards I was promoted to Junior Assistant Cook First Class. My wages were increased to £2 a week and I was allowed ashore on Wednesday evenings as well as Saturday afternoons, subject to passing an inspection each time to make sure I was clean and tidy and that my hair was short enough to be let out.

Ipswich on a Wednesday evening did not hold many delights for a 15 year old boy having two pounds in his pocket with short hair and a uniform on. Harwich was even worse and had nothing to offer at all so when I found out there was an HMS Ganges Theatre Club that visited Ipswich Theatre on a Wednesday night I joined.

Not only did this give me something interesting to do in the town, it also meant we stayed out later as we couldn't leave until after the play had finished. Also, we were treated to a small degree of celebrity status. Sitting in the cheap seats in our uniforms, there were about ten of us and each evening before the performance started we would be announced to the audience with the words:

"It is with great pleasure we welcome the boys and Officers of HMS Ganges to our theatre," at which the audience would give us a little clap.

The first time this happened I felt like shouting out something nautical like "shiver me timbers" or "kiss me Hardy" but I thought better of it.

The theatre club was a welcome cultural distraction from the hard and brutal life back at Ganges as we saw a play by Oscar Wilde, a Gilbert and Sullivan Operetta and ironically "Sailor Beware!"

**

The boy from Blackburn, who had been mercilessly scrubbed clean in the Annexe, Tony, or Smelly as some of the other less forgiving members of the mess still called him, also joined the theatre club and we enjoyed several evenings at the Ipswich Theatre together. There was nothing dirty or smelly about Tony but in each mess they wanted a scapegoat and he was theirs. One evening some of my more ferocious and easily led mess-mates were encouraged again to give him a scrubbing with hard brushes in the shower that once more drew blood from his back and chest and that night I could hear him crying himself to sleep.

The next evening after tea when we given various cleaning jobs to do to prepare for the Duty Officer's rounds and inspections I was conscious that I hadn't seen Tony in the mess but someone had mentioned that his raincoat was missing off of his peg.

At lights out Tony had still not appeared but in the middle of the night I was awoken by a noise and could just make out that two Regulating Petty Officers had come into the mess. As it was the middle of the night what could they be doing? Then I noticed that the Petty Officers had Tony with them. He seemed to be covered in mud and was sobbing quietly. One of the Petty Officers took Tony to the showers while another took his pyjamas from his locker. They returned ten minutes later with Tony dressed for bed and they waited while he got into his bunk. When they had gone I crept up to Tony and asked in a whisper what had happened. He told me that he had found a hole in the perimeter fence beyond the sports fields which he had crawled through before tea and had run away. He said he couldn't take the bullying anymore and he was so miserable he had tried to hitch lifts to get home to his Mum and Dad in Blackburn.

He said that it had been pouring with rain so no one took much notice of his clothes and he got two lifts that took him to other side of Ipswich. However, a Navy patrol that had been sent out to look for him had discovered Tony trying to hitch another lift on the A12 so they picked him up and had brought him back.

The next morning he was summoned to Captain's Defaulters and administered with the punishment of "six cuts", which were six strokes of the cane on his bare backside. He was also awarded stoppage of local leave for the rest of the term as punishment. Tony said that immediately after being told what his punishment was a Regulator had taken him into a side room pulled his trousers and underpants down to his ankles and bent him over a table.

"He hit my arse six times as hard as he could with a cane, it bloody well hurt a lot!" said Tony.

Each blow, he confirmed, had cut him and drawn blood, so much so that he was attended to by a sick berth attendant afterwards.

When people in my mess talked about that night they referred to it as "the Great Escape" and instead of calling Tony smelly he now had the nickname Steve McQueen. Also, most people in the mess stopped bullying Tony as he had become a bit of a star and many would whistle the theme tune to the Great Escape as he walked past them. I made a mental note though not to try that means of escape!

**

One day during this term we were introduced to the Assault Course. As if our Instructors had run out of ways of inflicting their sadism on us another means of doing so turned up. We were marched to the assault course dressed in our number 8s and once assembled were told that speed was of the essence in completing the course. If we did not get around it in super fast time we would have to do it again. It goes without saying that we did have to do it several times that day. The assault course consisted of a high wall to be climbed over, rope covered frames that had to be scrambled over or crawled under, poles over deep muddy murky water that had to be swung along, one hand over the other until we got to the other side, ropes that we had to jump out to and swing over even muddier stretches of water. We all fell in at some stage and we were soon covered with thick and dirty mud that smelt disgusting.

Next we were pushed into partially submerged sewer pipes which we had to crawl along, propelling ourselves by our elbows to get through them.

Half way along these pipes our Instructors came up with the bright idea of chucking jumping Chinese fire crackers behind us, huge noisy fireworks that banged and chased us through the pipes. Once introduced to the assault course it became a frequent method of forced "recreation" for us.

Another activity that we were initiated into was self defence classes. At these we were instructed by PTIs on some basic judo moves and also how to poke someone's eyes out with our fingers and then how to disarm an attacker and get them to drop the knife they were about to stab us with and break their arm in the process. Another trick we were taught was how to approach an enemy from behind and kill them by snapping their neck; a bit extreme I thought but something to bear in mind in the future if someone complained about my cooking.

I was still desperately unhappy at HMS Ganges and I wanted to leave this sadistic hell hole so I decided to give it another go and ask to speak to an Officer even though most Officers had only said two words to me since I had come over from the Annexe. I asked Andy if I could see the Officer.

"What for?" he asked.

"I want to ask him if I can leave the Navy" I replied.

"Don't be so bloody stupid, they don't talk to Trogs like you and any way there's no way you will be allowed to leave the Navy," came the response.

It was two weeks later as I was painting the stones outside at the rear of the mess, a ridiculous task that was repeated on a regular basis, when a Lieutenant Commander walked by. I took my chance and putting my paint brush down I smartly saluted and said:

"Sir, can I have a word with you?"

He looked at me as if I was something that had stuck to the sole of his shoe.

"What is it boy? - be quick."

I asked him if I could leave the Navy.

"Haven't you heard of a contract boy?" he barked the words scornfully at me.

"Yes sir," I replied, but I was only fifteen when I signed and I didn't really know what I was letting myself in for."

The Officer was not impressed by my argument as he snapped back:

"You signed in good faith and since then the Navy has invested heavily in training you. We are not going to throw that money away by letting you leave now, so get back to your duties and I will report your insolence."

"Thank you sir," I said and as I saluted him I realised yet again I was stuck with the Navy for the next twelve years and there was no way out.

I was not sure if it was the question I asked or the way I asked it that caused offence but the next day a member of the Regulating Branch came to see me and told me that my punishment for being disrespectful to the Lieutenant Commander was to spend an hour every evening for a week marching around the Parade Ground at the double with a .303 Lee Enfield rifle on my shoulder. At the end of the week my shoulder was bruised and my shoulder bone ached with the bashing it had taken from the rifle that had bounced up and down on it as I saw out my punishment.

CHAPTER TWELVE

PIGS TO THE SLAUGHTER

The misery of being at HMS Ganges continued so it was a welcome relief to be told that as part of our education about all things to do with food the aspiring cooks in my mess were to be taken on a day trip out in Suffolk to an abattoir or slaughterhouse as they are more commonly known.

The reason we were given was that we should know about the food we cook and our learning would include starting at the beginning of the food chain.

Chief Gravy Browning accompanied us in a Royal Navy mini bus which took us to the abattoir early one morning and on arrival we were taken into a small room and given protective clothing which we put on over our uniform. Along with most people who eat roast dinners, steaks, lamb chops, bacon sandwiches and sausages I had never given much thought to where they come from. I knew that these food products started off as animals but never really thought through the process.

Inside the abattoir men in white overalls were busy everywhere, hosing down areas, sharpening knives and ensuring that the animal pens were secure. Then the first Lorries began to arrive and a dozen beef cattle were herded out of them. One by one the animals were led into pens which had a door into the abattoir.

I was asked if I wanted to see what happens so I walked up to a pen where a brown heifer had been led into and the gate behind her closed.

I stroked her head as she turned to look at me. Her hot steamy breath was on my face whilst her big pink tongue licked her lips. As with most cows and heifers she had lovely doleful eyes which looked at me in an inquisitive manner. Abruptly, through the interlinking door from the abattoir a man in a white overall appeared with what looked like a gun, it was in fact a bolt gun.

"Stand well back!" he ordered me.

As I did so the bolt gun was put to the animals head and a long bolt shot into its brain. It took no more than a couple of seconds before the huge beast fell and was lying on the ground twitching madly. I felt ill and I quickly made my way to the yard where the vehicles were parked to get some air. As my fellow trainee cooks witnessed similar acts they followed me outside and some even threw up behind the mini bus. After a short break we were encouraged to go back into the slaughterhouse by Chief Gravy to witness what was happening to the carcasses. As these animals were killed a hook was attached to them and they were hoisted off the ground. A team of meat cutters appeared and using knives and cleavers very quickly cut the animal into recognisable joints of meat.

As I was watching this I was told that the pigs had arrived so we were ushered back out to the reception area for newly arrived animals on death row. From the back of a small truck a family of pigs were shooed off. There was a large boar, a sow and two smaller pigs. I was told that this was Mum and Dad and their two children. I had heard that pigs are social animals that can make friends with their own and other species and that they are very intelligent. Whilst the heifer calmly and unknowingly went to meet her fate these pigs were having none of it. They squealed and fought every inch of the way as if they knew that their demise awaited them and would be administered by the people in white overalls. When the pigs were finally put into their pens a contraption that had two pads on it, one for either side of their head, was applied and a huge electric shock stunned them to death.

As with the heifer a hook was placed into the pigs and they were raised onto a track that took them into the main part of the abattoir. Almost immediately their throats were cut and a bucket was placed under them to capture the blood. This would go into making black puddings and sausages I was told.

Again the meat cutters were on hand to split the pigs open and turn their meat into known joints. Once this was done the fat and what looked like inedible stuff from their spines, some of the less appealing bits of offal and other parts of their carcasses, in fact everything I assumed that couldn't be sold as pork, was trimmed off the pig and placed into a mincer. The minced "pork" was then placed into a large mixer with breadcrumbs, rusks, herbs, salt and pepper and some of the blood. The resulting substance was put through a machine and out of the other end, hey presto! - sausages appeared. On the way back to Ganges we quietly chatted about what we had experienced and agreed we would have preferred to have gone to a farm to see wheat produced or vegetables dug up. Watching so much death in one day had been a harrowing experience for a group of young boys. After our trip to the slaughter house we all became vegetarians for about six months, not that there was a vegetarian option at meal times, we just ate the vegetables. I don't think though that any of us ate a sausage for many years.

CHAPTER THIRTEEN

IN AT THE DEEP END

We were told that as sailors it was imperative that we knew how to swim. After all if your ship sunk you might be obliged to perform a few strokes in the water as a form of life saving.

I had used the pool recreationally since arriving at Ganges as I enjoyed swimming. What I hadn't realised was that some people who joined the Navy couldn't swim so one morning we were marched to the swimming pool to find out who could and who couldn't.

The Ganges swimming pool was a large one and even had diving boards and I noticed that the deep end was eleven feet six inches to the bottom, enough to drown someone I thought. We were told though that only one boy had ever drowned in this swimming pool so we were not to worry.

We were then asked who could swim and who couldn't and were then divided into the two groups. Several PTIs appeared and one I noticed carried a long pole with a hook on the end. That will be to get people out who are experiencing difficulties in the water I presumed. There were nine of us who could swim and three who couldn't. Those who couldn't swim were asked to stand on the edge of the deep end where a PTI pushed them in.

This act surprised me but probably not as much as those who were now splashing and sinking in the water. As they came up for air the PTI with the pole appeared and I assumed that he was going to hook them out.

I was wrong, he used the pole to stop them getting near to the edge of the pool and safety. Surprisingly one of the non-swimmers actually started swimming after a fashion towards the other side of the pool where there were no PTIs. After a few moments of great struggle with the water the other two just sank so the cry came up from the leading PTI:

"All swimmers get into the water and save those two clowns who have just gone under."

This we did and we deposited two choking, spluttering boys onto the side of the pool and they were soon joined by the boy who had managed to swim to the other side.

"You three will report to the pool at 06.30 every day for swimming lessons," he ordered them.

The rest of us had to swim four lengths to prove that we could in fact swim. As I was a good swimmer I was asked if I wanted to try my hand at scuba diving. I jumped at this offer and began regular training sessions in the Ganges pool with a small group of other diving enthusiasts. Once we had achieved the required level of proficiency we were taken several times to Felixstowe harbour and tried out our diving there.

Surprisingly, the harbour was very deep in places and I didn't enjoy it as much as diving in the swimming pool as:

a) The water pressure gave me severe ear ache at deep levels,

b) The harbour was so murky I couldn't see anything and

c) It was full of rubbish and not at all a pleasant place to dive in. Nevertheless, I had developed another skill.

**

Time passed slowly and painfully at HMS Ganges but as promised by Andy our time was divided into one third school work, one third cookery lessons and one third physical and recreational activities. We still had Divisions each morning which involved being inspected and then marching around the Parade Ground and being shouted at but more of our afternoons were now given over to sports and other recreational activities.

For sport I nearly always volunteered to play football which I liked. The other sports: rugby; tennis; hockey; water polo and cricket had not been played at my school so I didn't know too much about them.

One day however, I was told I was needed to make up the numbers in a game of rugby. Although this was my first venture into this sport I started enthusiastically enough and even managed to appear to know what I was doing but the ball didn't come anywhere near me for about twenty minutes so I started just standing around and keeping out of the way of those who knew how to play. Then a loud shout suddenly went up:

"Catch it!"

I looked up and the oval ball was falling from a great height straight towards me and I did as I was told as the ball fell into my arms. I don't remember much else about this apart from lying in a prone position on the ground, face down in a muddy puddle with a dozen voices talking about me. I was told later that as I caught the ball three big guys had jumped on me. I was eventually lifted up and when it was deemed that I was compos mentis I was told to report to the sick quarters.

Arriving for my first visit to the main establishment sick quarters I knocked on the door and went in. A male sick berth attendant told me to sit down on a chair next to several other boys who appeared to be suffering from a range of ailments. I looked like the only sports injury. As I sat there waiting the door opened and in came a sour faced proper sailor with his hand in a bandage. I recognised him as one of the cooks who usually scowled at us juniors over the counter when we were filling up our plates at mealtimes. After five minutes or so I decided to engage him in conversation:

"What happened to your hand?" I politely enquired.

He looked at me and then the rest of the room before addressing no one in particular.

"I hate you bloody Trogs," he said before adding:

"Why the fucking Joss Man should send me to this godforsaken hole I'll never know, what have I done to deserve being sent to this place, have you ever tried to have a decent run ashore in Ipswich?"

All went quiet in the waiting room and the other boys decided to stare at the deck. Maybe it was my knock on the head but I was intrigued by this outburst and I wanted to know what he was talking about.

"What's a Joss Man?" I enquired.

He looked at me for a long time and then said:

"You Trogs really wear your green jackets all the time, you know sod all."

Sour Face might as well have been speaking Albanian as I didn't know what he was talking about. Then, as seemed to be the want of the sailors I had come across, he had a little ditty to explain himself and he burst into song:

"Oh I wonder oh I wonder, if the Joss Man made a blunder, when he made this draft chit out for me. For I've been a Barracks stanchion, and I've lived in Jago's mansion, but I've never ever been to sea."

None of the boys looked up as he wasn't singing in the jolliest of fashions but I must have been concussed as I seemed to have no fear of him:

"I'm really keen to learn these things you are talking about, like Joss Man and Jago's mansion," I said.

He remained silent so I decided to try and butter him up, "I really do like the food you cook, and I think it's very tasty, especially your fried bread."

This seemed to cut no ice with him either and he still said nothing for a while and then I heard him mumbling:

"I hate bloody Officers, they like being posted to Ganges because they have cottages in nice places like Woodbridge and Aldborough while we have to live in this shit hole."

"I hate bloody Trogs too," he added again.

I was wondering what a Trog was but I assumed he was referring to the junior sailors at Ganges.

"I'm training to be a cook too," I said to him after a while.

He thought about this and then he seemed to mellow slightly as he said:

"A Joss Man is a Master at Arms; he decides which ship to draft you to."

He was in full flight now as he continued:

"I did my basic training at HMS Raleigh a bloody stone frigate, a Barracks that is, just across the River Tamar from Plymouth. Then they send me to another Barracks in Chatham, HMS Pembroke to learn to cook then the Joss Man sends me to my first ship and it's another bloody stone frigate, bloody HMS Drake at Devonport in Plymouth. They call that place Jago's Mansion."

He then got very agitated again:

"After 18 months there the Joss Man sends me to HMS Puma, a real ship at last and you know what? All we do is sail around ports in the UK recruiting snotty nosed schoolchildren to join the bloody Navy, just like you lot," he said surveying his audience in the waiting room.

"Then the Joss Man's sense of humour really kicks in, he sends me to bloody Ganges to cook for baby sailors. I joined the Navy to see the world, not stone frigates and bloody Ipswich."

Sour Face certainly seemed to have gone into a bit of a rant so I changed tack and returned to my first question:

"What happened to your hand?"

"I was frying battered fish last Friday and got distracted and put my hand into the hot fat with the fish."

I winced and a cold shiver went through me as it does when someone describes pain to you.

"Then you know what? They bloody put me on a charge and I've been stopped my leave for two weeks."

"That doesn't seem fair." I decided to sympathise with him.

"No, well, when they saw that my hand was burnt in the galley they sent me straight here and the sick berth attendant bandaged me up and gave me some strong pain killers. I then decided to go to back to the mess and have a few cans of beer to relax. Anyway I suppose the beer and the pills had a strange effect on me. I went to my bunk and got my head down but after a while I needed a piss. I was still half asleep but I got up and walked to the heads where I got the old fella out and starting peeing, the trouble was as I was sleepwalking I hadn't gone to the heads at all. I was just standing in the corner of the mess where the TV is and I thought the television was the urinal so I pissed all over it. My mates in the mess weren't too chuffed; they were watching Coronation Street at the time. Anyway a flash comes from the TV and then the valve explodes which blows the fuses and the lights go out just as the Duty Officer is coming into the mess to do evening rounds."

"So just for that they put you on a charge?" I said.

"Yes and my Oppo's won't talk to me as they haven't got a TV to watch anymore."

Luckily, at that point a sick bay attendant came out and loudly called out "NEXT!" We all let Sour Face go ahead of us as we didn't want to incur any more of his wrath so off he trotted to have his dressing changed. Everyone else in the waiting room just stared at me wide eyed but kept quiet. I was examined soon after and found to be OK apart from some bruising and a headache which the sick berth attendant gave me two aspirins for and told me to go back to the mess and rest. I was given a note to give to Andy excusing me any more duties for the rest of the day. I decided to go back to the Green Mansions via the mess decks of Keppel Division. Keppel was deserted as everyone was off at lessons or games but for some reason I decided to look into Basher's mess. I peered through the window and there to my surprise was Basher, sitting on his bed and dressed in his best uniform with a suitcase by his side. I went into the mess smiling at him.

"What's up Basher?" I called out.

Sitting down next to him he explained to me that he was just waiting for someone to take him to Ipswich Train Station. He went on to say that he'd been discharged from the Navy as he was not suitable for further training according to the powers that be.

Then with a wink and a smile he said:

"Basher's not as daft as he seems, is he

"You jammy bastard, you've worked your ticket!" I said, full of jealousy?"

CHAPTER FOURTEEN

YEH YEH

One morning after breakfast my class in Hawke Division were told to get dressed into number 2 uniforms for morning Divisions instead of our number 8s but as usual we were thoroughly inspected.

We were then marched around and around the Parade Ground to perfect our skills of doubling and right and left wheeling, halting, about turning and everything else you do on a Parade Ground. We were given heavy Lee Enfield .303 rifles to march around with which bounced up and down on my already bruised and painful left shoulder. Much time was spent on the art of "dressing" which was a method of extending your arm to the person next to you and shuffling about to get into a straight line with the correct distance between each other.

Today we were told that we were practicing Parade drill to get us ready for the big one, Captains Guard at the Sunday Parade, and in particular we spent a long time using the rifle to present arms. I thought we had completed the session when loud barking noises started emanating from the mouths of numerous Chiefs and Petty Officer Gunnery Instructors. None of which were orders to do anything interesting like "stand easy" or "go back to the mess and have a fag" they were just all trying to outdo each other for insults.

"You weren't marching in a straight line you looked like a dogs hind legs" said one and "your present arms wasn't done together you were all over the bloody place, it sounded like the ripple of rain on a fucking tin roof" said another and "you wasn't even bad, you were bloody awful."

After listening to this tirade of nonsense for a few moments I let Diana Ross and the Supremes *"Baby Love"* enter my head.

For the next couple of minutes I watched but didn't pay any real attention to a surreal display by this gang of uniformed bullies as they strutted around me with their mouths opening and closing but with the help of Diana Ross I had cut out their noise. After a while I suddenly focussed again on the Gunnery Instructors who I realised reminded me of a group of pigeons I had once seen in Trafalgar Square scampering around the pavement occasionally pecking at a discarded piece of bread or the dog end of a cigarette, their necks popping forward and backwards as they did so. The Instructors did this pigeon neck movement as if to emphasise each insult:

"You!" (Pigeon head forward)

"Fucking!" (Pigeon head back)

"Horrible!" (Pigeon head forward)

"Pile!" (Pigeon head back)

"Of!" (Pigeon head forward)

"Shite!" (Pigeon head back) - And so on.

I wondered what job would suit the skills of these Instructors when they left the Navy but I couldn't. Maybe they stayed in their job until they died, like the Pope, well like most Popes anyway.

After several months of intense Parade Ground Drill we were considered good enough to be the Captain's Guard at Sunday Parade and come the day we were made to wear our very best number one uniforms and shiny boots and have white gaiters on instead of the normal green ones. The Parade was a very formal affair and a Royal Marine band appeared playing jolly sailors' melodies. We were marched around the Parade Ground and past a platform where the Captain and other dignitaries were assembled.

We had to keep straight lines and perform a smart "EYES RIGHT!" when we got in line with the Captain. The Marine Band played on with nautical songs such as *"A Life on the Ocean Wave"* and *"Hearts of Oak"* while our marching in time with the music continued.

When the marching finished we had to stand to attention and present arms with our rifles held in front of our noses to impress the Captain.

As the formal inspection of the Guard commenced the Royal Marine band struck up "*Yeh Yeh*" a recent hit for Georgie Fame and the Blue Flames.

Very hip I thought and I started singing the words of the song to myself.

The Captain walked up and down our ranks very slowly and made the odd comment to the following entourage of Officers, Chiefs and Petty Officers. The Captain of HMS Ganges at this time was Captain, later to become Rear Admiral, Basil Charles Godfrey Place VC, CB, CVO, DSC. He was in fact a real wartime hero. This being my first Captains Parade as a member of his Guard it was the first time I had come close to him. I was still quietly singing the words of "*Yeh Yeh*" when suddenly he stopped in front of me and started to speak.

"How are you enjoying the Navy lad?" he asked me.

For a second I was going to tell him the truth but the thought of unimaginable retribution from the Chief Petty Officer standing next to him encouraged me to say something else.

"I am enjoying it very much Sir, thank you Sir," I lied.

I looked at his medals and was impressed to see the Victoria Cross on his chest which is the highest award for gallantry in the face of the enemy that can be awarded.

I later read in my Royal Navy History lessons how he got the VC. I found out that during the Second World War when my skipper was 22 years old he was commanding a Midget Submarine. On 22 September 1943 at Kåfjord, North Norway, he and another Lieutenant, Donald Cameron who was commanding another Midget Submarine, carried out a successful attack on the German Battleship Tirpitz. The two submarines had travelled 1,000 miles, negotiated a mine-field, dodged nets, gun defences and enemy listening posts. Having eluded all these hazards they finally placed the charges underneath the ship where they went off an hour later, doing so much damage that Tirpitz was out of action for months.

Since I had joined the Royal Navy not a single person in uniform had inspired any respect from me, only fear and loathing but I was quite taken aback to see a holder of the Victoria Cross in person although I only saw him up close once more in my stay at the Ganges, on Parents day.

**

A few days later we were taken back to the mast after breakfast and told we could have a go at reaching the button, a disc measuring one foot in diameter 143 feet in the sky. If we managed to do this and stood upright on it and saluted we would be considered for the role of Button Boy at official mast manning ceremonies and would be paid a silver crown for doing so. It was compulsory to have to climb 130 feet up the mast to the Half Moon. The top 13 feet was voluntary and in order to climb this last part of the mast there was no more rope or wires, you had to shin up a pole and climb onto the button.

"They can stuff that!" or similar words were said collectively by my class and none of us ever went above the 130 feet mark.

Having done my first climb of the day, up to the top yard arm and sliding quickly back to the bottom via a rope I stood at the foot of the mast, still shaking and recovering from the ordeal. I was spitting onto the burn marks on my hand which were made by sliding down the ropes to descend and wondering what the trick was to stop the blistering that always occurred. I looked up and saw the gates to the main establishment open and in marched a new intake from the Annexe.

"Poor bastards," I thought as they marched through the gates. I could see them all giving the mast a sideways glance and I caught the look of fear on their faces as they did so. Fanny and Psycho were with them barking out marching orders, "left, right, left right left right, left, class HALT!" and they stopped about ten feet away from us where Fanny went through his well rehearsed talk about the history of the mast. As I looked at these new sailors I was amazed to see Sparky, my friend from sea cadet days among their number. I would keep an eye out for him over the next few days so that we could catch up on old times.

In fact I didn't see Sparky again over the coming weeks and then our next period of leave arrived.

It was the same routine as for our Christmas Leave and we were dispatched in the early hours to Ipswich Station to catch our trains. I entered a compartment on the London bound train and there was Sparky glaring at me.

"You bastard, why didn't you warn me not to join up?" were his first words.

"I would have warned you if I had known that you were as stupid as me."

Sparky calmed down and told me about his experiences in the Annexe and they were identical to mine. He had been sworn and screamed at, he had asked to leave the Navy and been told he couldn't. He had been kicked and made to run around the Parade Ground at night naked with a mattress on his back, a "smelly" boy in his mess had been mercilessly scrubbed in the showers, he had been made to hold a dustbin over his head several times, he had been made to do press ups numerous times and his head had been held under freezing cold water in the bath at the laundry. He had also been battered by someone in a boxing match. I told him my view was that the people who run the place must work off a script and dish out the same sadistic punishment to everyone who passes through. We spent some time comparing notes on our life in the Royal Navy so far and we concluded this discussion by both of us committing ourselves to getting out as soon as we could. I thought I would then change the subject to better times in our lives.

"Is there any news on our sea cadet friends?" I asked.

"I heard that Anchor joined the Army instead of the Navy as he found out he got sea sick and that a life on the ocean wave was not for him." Sparky informed me.

"How did he find out that he suffered from sea sickness?" I asked.

"I bumped into a mate of his and he told me that Anchor went on a school trip to France on a cross channel ferry, the sea was rough and he spent the entire time calling out for Hughie" replied Sparky.

"Hughie?" I enquired, intrigued by this news.

Sparky imitated someone leaning over the side of a ship throwing up and I had to admit it did sound as if they were crying out the name Hughie.

As I took this information in it occurred to me that I'd never been on a ship in my life, would sea sickness afflict me? Bloody hell I'd not thought out this navy lark at all.

I used my period of leave to catch up with my friends and to get myself up to date with world affairs. A friend from school informed me that there was a visit planned from Tollington Park School to HMS Ganges in the coming months and he would tip me off when the date was known. I made a mental note to ask Andy if I could spend some time with them when they came. I also went to see a great show at the Finsbury Park Astoria with the Supremes who sang *"Baby Love"* and Georgie Fame who sang *"Yeh Yeh"*. I decided to buy two more George Orwell books to take back with me: *"The Road to Wigan Pier"* and *"Homage to Catalonia."*

Returning to Ganges I read the Daily Mirror on the train and in particular an article informing readers of the worrying news that the USA had started bombing North Vietnam.

CHAPTER FIFTEEN

A VISIT FROM TOLLINGTON PARK SCHOOL

A letter arrived from a school friend informing me of the date that Tollington Park Comprehensive would be visiting HMS Ganges.

It was to be a Saturday so I asked Andy if I could be allowed some time with them. On Saturday mornings we were normally given cleaning jobs to do and in the afternoon, if we passed an inspection, we were allowed to go ashore to Ipswich or Harwich as long as we were back by 20.45. I had visions of having tea and sticky buns with my old school pals in the morning and then wandering around Ipswich with them in the afternoon before they returned to London. Andy said he would get me assigned to a job in the Central Messing Galley which is where they took the school parties that visited HMS Ganges for a cup of tea and a bun. The dining hall in the CMG also served the purpose of being a good setting for a talk by an Officer who would try to recruit them into the Navy.

I was told that their itinerary meant they would be arriving mid morning, have their snack in the CMG, have a lecture from the Officer and be shown round Ganges, leaving for London in the afternoon via a trip to Ipswich. He said twenty five pupils and a teacher had volunteered for the trip.

Two days before my school chums arrived I was pulled up by a Regulating Petty Officer whilst coming out of the NAAFI where I had just purchased my weekly tin of Nestles condensed milk that I was addicted to at the time.

"Is your hair hurting you son?" he screamed.

"Here we go again; you're not very original in your observations." I mumbled under my breath.

Next you will say: "Well it should be because I'm standing on it."

"What's that son? - speak up."

"I was just saying that I didn't think it was Sir," I said a bit louder.

"Well it should be because I'm standing on it," was his predictable reply.

He then personally double marched me to the barbers shop and ordered that they give me a special. A special it transpired was not just very short but very badly cut too. I was left with the worst haircut of my life. Even the haircuts I had when I was ten years old at Arthur's Barber shop in Lennox Road were not this bad. Arthur was a self taught barber who had practised his trade in the North African desert with the Army in World War Two and he still used the same scissors. He had a sign above the door saying: "don't do your nut, let Arthur do it" and his method was to put a pudding basin on your head and cut off everything left poking out, sometimes this also included cutting bits off your ears! He always had a fag clenched between his teeth and when he breathed out he sent a cloud of hot ash onto the back of your newly shaven neck. Even Arthur's haircuts now appeared stylish against this latest naval butchering.

The day of the visit arrived and I was really excited about my school coming here. I was very worried about my hair but I thought I might put my cap on when I spoke to my friends to cover up the damage. I reported to the CMG for work and a Petty Officer Cook, known to me ever after as "Shit Brains," as he had the intelligence and charm of a turd, put me to work in a room behind the serving hatch. The room was huge with industrial dishwashers and large sinks. There were metal crates full of stained tea cups that had to be cleaned. I was told there were a thousand cups and I would need to fill up a sink full of soapy water and clean each run thoroughly with wire wool and teepol liquid.

This task seemed never ending and as I cleaned the cups the gravel voiced Petty Officer would come in and inspect them and bark at me to start again. As I pressed on it felt like the labour of Sisyphus was upon me.

My hands soon became red and raw from using the wire wool but I carried on and was eventually almost finished. One positive thing that day was a radio situated in the sink room which was thankfully tuned to Radio Caroline. A recording by a group called the Byrds of *"Mr. Tambourine Man"* came on the radio and I sang along to the lyrics as I cleaned the cups.

The good feelings I got from singing along to the record faded as I took stock of my situation. There I was standing in front of a sink and my duty for the morning had been to clean out and then rinse one thousand white china cups with wire wool. There was even a mirror in front of me so I could admire my horrible new haircut as I worked away at this task! I was wallowing in self pity when I heard a chatter of obviously non HMS Ganges voices in the CMG. I knew they were non Ganges as firstly they were enjoying themselves and secondly some were female. I peered through a hole in the serving hatch and saw a group of boys and girls from my old school and my heart was lifted. There they all were along with one of my favourite teachers, Mr. Fraser.

My school chums were all dressed in civvies rather that school uniform with the girls in the fashion of Sandie Shaw or Dusty Springfield and most of the boys looked like they could audition for the Beatles or the Dave Clark Five. There I was in my number 8 uniform, with an apron on and wearing galley boots and I had hair that made me look like a sheep that had been sheared in the dark. I was also aware that whilst the boys out there must be wearing designer boxer shorts under their trendy jeans, underneath my uniform I was sporting my yellowy off white Pusser's passion killers that flapped about my knees and had my name stamped on them. I felt miserable again but I was steeling myself to go out and greet them. Then things got even worse. Although I had now completed the cleaning of one thousand cups, and they were very clean indeed, Petty Officer Shit Brains came back and inspected my work. He pretended to see a miniscule mark on the handle of one of the cups. He put his face an inch away from mine and shouted:

"THIS IS NOT GOOD ENOUGH BOY, DO THEM ALL AGAIN!"

"But I was going to see my friends........" I tried to say but he would not allow me to explain.

"But you are going to do nothing, do as you are bloody well told and I'll come back in an hour to make sure you have cleaned those cups, don't you dare leave this room until I return."

There was certainly no place I was going to in the near future and the shame was too much; I could not even go and speak to my school friends.

Some of the school party knew I would be around somewhere so they asked one of the cooks who advised them to look in the sink room. One of them came in and said hello and I begged him not to tell the others of my plight. He took pity on me and said he wouldn't but he knew there were a few of my mates who had said they wanted to see me as well.

"Damn the consequences!" I said to myself as I decided to ignore the Petty Officer's orders and I went up to the first table where I could see half a dozen of my old pals and chatted with them for five minutes before I saw Shit Brains returning. I scuttled back into the sink room and made myself busy as my old school friends from Tolly Park were given a short talk on what a wonderful career the Royal Navy was before they were taken off on a tour of HMS Ganges after which I didn't see them again as they were soon ushered back onto their coach to set off back to London via a look around Ipswich.

It was later told to me that on the coach back someone mentioned to my old teacher that several of the pupils had spoken to me and that Mr. Fraser had exploded in anger that I hadn't come over to say hello to him as well. By all accounts Mr. Fraser was in a bad mood for the entire journey back to London but he wasn't to know that Shit Brains had scuppered my plans to talk to everyone and enjoy a nice day with them.

Feeling humiliated I completed my task of cleaning the cups again and when eventually I left the CMG I passed the cook, Sour Face.

"I hate this bloody place," I complained to him.

"Join the club matey!" was his reply.

CHAPTER SIXTEEN

HELP!

The biggest public relations exercise of the year at HMS Ganges was Parents Day which took place on a warm Saturday in June.

Some of my best moments had been in June and I recalled that almost exactly a year ago I had stood outside Holloway Prison waiting for Christine Keeler to be released. How ironic I thought, that at that time as she had obtained her freedom I was about to give mine up!

For Parents Day we were drilled for weeks beforehand on what we had to do and say when our parents came to view the establishment I was incarcerated in. At 12.30 on the big day the main gates opened and in streamed the Mums, Dads and friends. I was really pleased that arriving with my parents was Dave Charie, my best mate from school who had come along too. The events of the day were against a backdrop of nautical and pop tunes played by a Royal Marine band as various Divisions showed off their skills in rhythmic physical training, cutlass swinging, dancing the hornpipe, field gun competitions with a one ton gun, marching and counter marching by the bugle bands and my very own diving display where I had to give endless demonstrations of my skills as a diver with the full breathing apparatus on.

Unfortunately, between displays I was tempted to eat a bar of chocolate and an ice cream.

This led to me becoming the first diver in the history of the establishment to vomit into his diving mask in front of several hundred astonished parents.

There was a formal "Manning the Mast" display before the final act of the day which was the ceremonial parade where Captain Place appeared once more to be marched past and saluted.

My parents had hired a caravan at a holiday park in Dovercourt for a few days and I was given permission to stay with them overnight as long as I was back on the Sunday morning. As Dave left on a bus to Ipswich to get the train home to London we boarded the ferry across the river to Harwich. Arriving at the quay I looked up to see a big sign that proclaimed "Harwich for the Continent!" I mentioned to my Mum and Dad that they should have booked a caravan in Frinton instead of Dovercourt but I think the joke was lost on them.

I really enjoyed the night of normality in the caravan with my parents and especially having my Dad cook egg and bacon for breakfast next morning. When the time came to return to Ganges my Dad came with me to the Ferry. Looking across the River Stour I could see the HMS Ganges mast in the distance and I felt so wretched having to leave my Mum and Dad that I made a momentous decision.

"I'm not going back, I'm coming home to London with you," I said.

My Dad was not one for creating trouble and he insisted that I did go back but I refused. Several ferries came and went whilst I stubbornly held out for my position but eventually I gave in as I could see that not returning would only lead to me receiving punishments including the dreaded "cuts." Reluctantly, I boarded a ferry but by the time I re-entered Ganges I was deemed to be late returning and therefore I was "awarded" the punishment of seven days stoppage of local leave plus I had to spend an hour every evening during that week marching at the double around the Parade Ground with a rifle on my shoulder.

One evening I was again given the task of cleaning the windows so I armed myself as usual with a bucket of soapy water and a cloth and got to work.

Whilst doing this the Ganges Chaplain came by to chat to us boys in Hawke Division. After talking to some others he came and stood next to me as I cleaned and said he knew a better way of washing windows. He took me to the store in the mess where all the cleaning materials were kept and picked up a large bottle of vinegar and some sheets of old newspapers.

"Right, make up a bucket of warm water and put some vinegar in it. Get the newspaper damp and start rubbing, if there are any difficult smudges then use more vinegar and more newspaper," he told me.

We worked together for almost an hour during which time we had a normal conversation and at the end we stood back to admire our handiwork, the windows were sparkling. As he was being kind to me I decided to make a plea to him.

"Before you go Sir, can I ask you a question?"

"What's that? He enquired.

"Can I leave the Navy and go home?"

He replied quietly: "I'm sorry lad the Law of this Country allows the Royal Navy to keep you in its service even if you wish to leave, there's nothing I can do. Chin up though, I'm sure that you'll start liking the life soon enough."

Before leaving me he added:

"Just make sure you keep your nose clean and you will be alright."

Apart from the routine of school lessons, cookery classes, gym and Parade Ground drill we were told that we would experience a week at sea as part of our training. When the day arrived we packed our kit bags and put on our best uniforms and were taken by bus to the naval dockyards at Portsmouth on the south coast of England where we joined a rusty old ship called HMS Wakefield. After we were shown around the ship we were all encouraged to have an early night onboard. The next day we sailed into the Solent and did nothing more adventurous than circumnavigate the Isle of Wight before dropping anchor near Cowes, a routine we did each day for the rest of the week. I was initiated into the confined living area of a ship's mess and as I was training to be a cook I was given duties in the galley.

These duties consisted almost entirely of having to scrape congealed fat from the cooker hood, peeling potatoes and serving the food at meal times. I wondered how such a grimy galley ever passed an inspection but was told that no one ever bothered to inspect the galley properly since the Wakefield became a training ship.

The trainee seamen who were with us spent a lot of time learning how to rub down the iron decks and bulkheads of the ship with sandpaper and then apply coats of grey paint and were also taken to the ships bridge and operations room to be told what various instruments were used for and how to look through binoculars.

One night onboard the Wakefield I went onto the upper deck on my own to get some fresh air and also to look at the Isle of Wight. After a matter of seconds a Petty Officer Seaman came up to me and handed me a pair of binoculars and said that as I seemed to have nothing to do I should make myself useful and scan the sea for enemy attackers. I thought that an attack was unlikely so I watched the twinkling lights of Cowes instead and wondered what teenagers there were doing. Whatever it was it would most likely be better than what was happening to me. On a radio playing in a nearby mess one of the big hits of the year by the Beatles, "Help!" was playing so I sang along to no one in particular with my voice carrying out across a lonely sea.

No one came to help me so after a while I trained my binoculars on the dark waters that were lapping against the ships side. The lights from the Wakefield made it just about possible to see if there was anything in the water and to my surprise and horror I did see something. At first I thought it might be a large bag or even a seal or a dolphin. Then I realised that the object had arms that were floating in front of a human head which was face down in the water. My God, it was a dead body! I quickly went and found the Petty Officer who had given me the binoculars and told him and within minutes a boat was launched with four seamen onboard it. With the beam from my torch lighting up a section of the sea I could just make out the actions of the seamen who managed to get a net under the body and haul it into the boat.

They then returned to the ship where the boat was winched onboard and the body was covered in tarpaulin where it was left for the night before being handed over to the authorities in Portsmouth the next morning.

The seamen from the boat, who were ashen faced after handling a dead and decomposing body, went into the galley for a hot bowl of soup and I joined them. Something I had never heard of then happened and the Duty Officer announced that he would "splice the mainbrace." This meant that an extra ration of Pussers rum was given to the boats crew to revive them after their ordeal. I was too young to be given any rum but in recognition of my sighting the body I was given a couple of sips of his tot by one of the seaman. My goodness it was strong, but very tasty and as I watched the seamen drink theirs I could see the colour being restored to their faces. I stood and listened to the sailors chatting to each other and they said that finding dead bodies in the Solent wasn't uncommon. Apparently, after a good night out in the pubs of Portsmouth people would see the lights of the Isle of Wight in the near distance and try to swim over to the island, something that no rational person would do but the effects of alcohol gave people a false sense of what they could achieve. Unfortunately, when their strength failed half way across the Solent they would drown.

After a week at sea I returned to HMS Ganges with three new pieces of knowledge to add to my CV. I knew how to clean congealed fat from a cooker hood; I was taught the recipe for what was known throughout the Navy as "shit on a raft" which actually was a delicious dish of kidneys in gravy on crispy deep fried bread and I also found out that the Isle of Wight was very close to Portsmouth, but sadly not close enough for some.

**

My year at Ganges was coming to an end. I had tried to make the best of it but I had hated it. I couldn't understand how I was being kept in the Navy against my will and how a fifteen year old boy could be allowed to make a binding decision to give twelve years of his life to any job, especially one where they butchered your hair and shouted and swore at you and concocted a range of terrible punishments to hurt and humiliate you and also allowed sadistic Junior Instructors to kick you.

Every now and again during my stay at HMS Ganges I had experienced the tingle of excitement I first felt when I set off on my great adventure to become a member of the Queen's Navy but this was always quelled by the actions and words of my Instructors who soon reminded me of my real situation in this hell-hole.

I didn't resent the hard work or having to get up early every morning, or cleaning and scrubbing the mess and the heads to keep them clean, or having to climb the mast, or the endless physical training. I did resent the haircuts though and the humiliation, the verbal and physical violence, the bullying and the perpetuation of the class system where those who ran the place treated us minions as sub human idiots. I was in an institution where I had no one to complain to and no trade union to protect me, I was on my own.

I had been placed at the mercy of the people put in charge of training me and I resented this year of my life at HMS Ganges beyond mere words; Ganges had been a real shock. I had been a trusting naive boy who had unwittingly entered a sadistic and bullying institution that I did not know how to extricate myself from. As my year at Ganges came to an end I was handed a letter by Petty Officer Stewart jointly signed by the Captain and a Lieutenant Commander. I recognised the signature of Captain Place but as always with a squiggle, I couldn't decipher the name of the Lieutenant Commander. As Andy shook my hand and wished me good luck I asked him again if there was a way of getting out of the Navy.

"You don't bloody well give up do you? Just put in a written request when you get to HMS Pembroke, but don't hold out any hope and don't forget that wherever you go, keep your nose clean," was his advice.

I thanked him and read the letter he had just given me.

Junior Assistant Cook 1 Mann
HMS GANGES
15TH October 1965
You have now successfully finished your training at GANGES and will soon, I hope, be at sea doing the job for which you joined the Navy, and in which all of us at GANGES wish you a happy and successful career.

Remember always, that you belong to the finest Service in the world and in most ships and stations there will be opportunities for sport and recreation of all kinds; take advantage of these whenever you can. You will also have plenty of spare time onboard; try and cultivate a hobby to interest you during these periods and so avoid boredom.

The Royal Navy offers great opportunities for advancement and you can certainly get up the ladder if you try. Remember that you will not be chased or persuaded to pass for higher rate. It is up to you. You will have to work on your own and often have to do so when it is much easier to sit back and take things quietly. Neither will you be nursed domestically; again, it is up to you to pay constant attention to your kit and keep yourself clean and tidy, to the standards we have taught you here.

Keep out of trouble. The most important thing of all that you should have learnt at GANGES is instant and cheerful obedience. The Navy depends on it.

Always remember this. When you are unfairly picked on, when you are very tired, perhaps when you have had a little too much to drink, those are the times – remember –and do what you are told, and if there is good reason complain afterwards. Another important point for keeping out of trouble is to return from Leave on time. In this and other things you will come across ship mates who set bad examples, who will probably try to persuade you that there is no point in getting on in the Service; you must use your will power and refrain from being led astray. Don't forget that it is fairly easy to do your job when things are going right; it takes a man to produce results when life appears black. Do not marry young. Although you will find that you have plenty of spending money as a young bachelor, the financial responsibilities, separations, difficulties caused by moving house, to name but a few drawbacks to early marriage in the Service make it necessary for you to think particularly carefully before you decide to marry. Remember the principles of your religion and the vows you have taken here, and try to live up to them. The very best of luck to you in your career, wherever you may go.

Signed: Lieutenant Commander Squiggle   Signed: Captain Place

So, today I was really leaving this terrible place, I was to get on a Royal Navy bus along with my mess-mates and set off from HMS Ganges and head towards Ipswich Station for the last time.

Waiting to board the bus by the main gate of Ganges another unfortunate group of new entrants were being marched past us from the Annexe into their next eleven months of misery in the main establishment. To my delight Psycho was marching alongside them shouting out orders.

"Left, Right, Left Right, Left Right Left!" he sang out as he instructed their feet to move in a synchronised way. As he marched past me my moment had come. I stuck out a foot which he tripped over and flew onto the Parade Ground, face first.

"Sorry mate an accident," I said.

As he got up I could see blood coming from his scraped nose.

"Don't call me mate, call me Sir!" he bellowed back.

"Got you Sir, you Bastard!" I chuckled under my breath as I turned and hurried onto the bus to be taken away from Ganges forever.

As we went through the gates, manned by two stony faced members of the Regulating Branch and into the village of Shotley Gate I didn't look back and I never returned.

CHAPTER SEVENTEEN

RABBIT PIE AND SINKING SHIPS

The next stop in my Royal Navy career was another stone frigate, HMS Pembroke, the Royal Navy Barracks at Chatham dockyard in Kent.

It was here that my full time job for the next couple of months or so would be to complete my training as a cook. When I arrived at Liverpool Street Station en route for HMS Pembroke I met up with my Dad who I had arranged to see there so that we could have a cup of tea and a chat in the station café. Saying goodbye to him I bought a copy of the Daily Mirror which I read on the train from Charing Cross to Chatham. The paper reported anti Vietnam War rallies had taken place in forty American cities and also in London and Rome. I wondered why a country like the USA wanted to get involved in a war thousands of miles away from their shores. I also worried that Great Britain might be drawn into supporting their main ally in this war.

Arriving at Chatham I was picked up by a mini bus at the train station and driven to my new ship. Entering HMS Pembroke I was taken past a number of accommodation blocks before being deposited at the doors of one of them. I was surprised to see people chatting with each other and walking along the pavements in ones and twos instead of marching at the double in groups. This place seemed more relaxed that Ganges.

I was also surprised to see Wrens, women members of the Royal Navy, although I was to discover that men and women were well segregated at HMS Pembroke, the Wrens had their own accommodation block which male sailors were not allowed to go near and the jobs they did never brought them into contact with me so I didn't have the opportunity to actually speak to a Wren during my time in Chatham. Once inside my new mess I discovered that I was to sleep in bunk beds and I was allocated a top bunk. I unpacked and stowed my kit in a locker, went to tea in the dining hall and prepared myself for my first full day of training to be a cook before tucking myself up in bed to read my latest George Orwell book.

The first thing I did on entering the cookery school next day was to request yet again an early discharge from the Royal Navy but unsurprisingly, a week later I was told that my request had been rejected.

HMS Pembroke was the home of the Royal Navy Supply School and I discovered that the cookery lessons here were similar to the ones at Ganges in as much that we had to use recipes from the Manual of Naval Cookery which were designed for a hundred people so we again divided the amounts by twenty five so that we cooked for four. We made soups, gravies, sauces, meat dishes, vegetables and cheese and egg dishes and desserts. We were even taught how to cook entrées which were a starter course that was only provided for Officers. My favourite was Devils on Horseback, prunes wrapped in bacon.

During my cookery training I was allowed to go ashore in the evenings twice a week and at weekends. All of us trainee cooks, or chefs as other sailors now called us, were under age for drinking alcohol and as we looked very young and therefore wouldn't be served in pubs we would go to the cinema or hang out at the coffee shops for entertainment. However, given the proximity of Chatham to London I found that I had the opportunity to spend the occasional evening along with a couple of weekends at home as the journey only took about two and a half hours door to door.

In my first week at HMS Pembroke I practised my cookery skills Monday to Fridays but on Saturday I was free after 14.00. When I had finished lessons at the cookery school I went back to the mess for a shower and changed into my best uniform before walking to the main gate of the Barracks to get a bus to Chatham Station to take a train home for the rest of the weekend. Before I got through the gates I heard the scream of a Regulating Petty Officer:

"Where do you think you are going son with fucking hair like that?" came the shrill noise behind me.

"Go and change into your number 8s, have your hair cut and report back here!"

I did as I was told and when I reported back to him I was given a bucket and scrubbing brush and told to report to the nearby toilet block where I had to spend the next three hours cleaning the heads. Not for the first time the Royal Navy had scuppered my plans to be an ordinary human being. I discovered though that if I kept my hair extra short and my clothes, shoes and nose clean, I could get past the Duty Regulating Petty Officer without too much trouble and my next attempt at getting home for the weekend succeeded. I was glad to be met at Finsbury Park Station by Dave Charie who accompanied me home and waited for me to change before we went off to a party in a friend's flat in Haden Court where we had a thoroughly enjoyable time.

With Dave Charie in Finsbury Park Underground Station

Returning from a lovely day and a half spent at home I was to discover that one of the trainee cooks on my course, Bunny Warren, was heading for trouble in his attempts to try and get home for the next weekend. He told me that his brother was getting married and Bunny had asked for time off to attend so he needed to leave on Friday afternoon to get to Newcastle in time for the wedding on Saturday morning. He was grumbling angrily to me that the leave had been refused. On Saturday morning when I went to the cookery school Bunny was nowhere to be seen. It was a couple of weeks later that he appeared.

"I went on the trot and managed to get to the wedding which was great and we all got pissed on Saturday night," he told me.

"The police picked me up on the Sunday though and brought me back and I've spent the past ten days in cells as a punishment."

**

Whenever I did go to London for the evening I had to get up very early the next morning to get back to the Barracks. I noticed that a man stood outside of Chatham Station in the mornings selling a newspaper called the "Daily Worker" and I stopped off one day to buy a copy. The articles and editorial struck a chord with me and I felt that the newspapers point of view was similar to my own concerning the war in Vietnam and also injustices in the world and in the workplace. I became an avid reader of the paper and reading their reports about the war in Vietnam I was increasingly concerned over the escalation of fighting and the number of American troops arriving. I read reports of an increase in the number of bombs the United States were dropping on the North and areas of the South where the National Liberation Front, or Viet Cong as the US called them, was strong.

I liked the Daily Worker a lot. Even the racing tipster in the sports column was often right in his predictions, not that I had any spare money to bet with although my Dad had a small flutter every Saturday so I used to give him some tips from the sports pages of the newspaper. I noticed that the Daily Worker pronounced itself the newspaper of the Communist Party of Great Britain and when I had the time I chatted with the paper seller about politics. When I told him that I was a keen reader of George Orwell he accused Orwell of being a leftist socialist and too anti communist for his liking.

I was a bit confused by these finer points of left wing politics so I said I would keep an open mind. He recommended a book for me to read which I bought the next time I was in Foyle's in the Charing Cross Road. It had a profound influence on my thinking and was called *"The Ragged Trousered Philanthropist"* by Robert Tressell. The book advocates a socialist society in which work is performed to satisfy the needs of all rather than to generate profits for a few and it helped me to confirm my belief that I was becoming a socialist.

**

Towards the end of the cookery training each of us was told to cook a meal for four hundred people. We were taken to the main galley to prepare and cook our dishes which all contributed to a dinner for the one thousand plus sailors at HMS Pembroke. I was given a small area of the galley and told to make rabbit pies.

"In France they call this dish Tarte au Lapin," said my apparently classically educated Petty Officer Cookery Instructor.

I had never seen so many dead animals in my life. One hundred whole and skinned rabbits had been delivered and I had to bone them and cut the meat up into bite size pieces. The area I worked in, cutting my way through this huge number of Lapins, resembled a war zone with rabbit blood everywhere. I made a stock from the bones and some vegetables in a huge pot and then I placed the rabbit pieces into dishes. These I covered with the stock and added a sack of peeled and chopped onions and lots of diced bacon with parsley, thyme, salt and pepper. I covered the dishes of rabbit with greaseproof paper and cooked them in an oven. Whilst these were cooking, with the aid of a giant mixing machine, I made up enough short crust pastry or clacker as they called it in the Navy, to cover the pies. When the meat was cooked I drained off the liquid and thickened this with flour and then simmered the gravy for ten minutes before pouring it back over the rabbit. I covered the dishes with the clacker and egg washed the pie tops before finally baking the pies in a hot oven for twenty minutes. Watching me take the cooked pies from the oven my Petty Officer Instructor said:

"Right, if these pies are any good we'll put them in the serving cabinet ready to dish them up to the hungry Matelots. If they are a disaster we will slide them into a well greased dustbin and open up some tins of steak and kidney puddings."

I was pleased that the pies turned out fine and I enjoyed watching the sailors eating them at dinner time. This was my first venture into cooking for the masses, my first of many.

Before we were allowed to leave HMS Pembroke and let loose to work on a proper ship as qualified and competent chefs we first had to pass our exams which we all took at the end of our course and then anxiously awaited the results. Whilst waiting to see if we had passed or whether we would have to retake the exams we were given some safety lessons. Firstly, we were instructed in the art of saving ourselves at sea if our ship was to be attacked or start sinking. We were taught how to survive by means of blocking up holes to stop water getting in. Secondly, we were shown how to wear gas masks to stop ourselves being gassed to death in the event of attack. Not far from the cookery school at Pembroke was a substantial brick built building that we were taken into to begin our lessons in survival. Inside it was constructed to look like the compartment of a ship. In the ships sides were several holes which we were informed could have been made by enemy torpedoes or shells or even icebergs. As I surveyed these holes in the "ship's" side my mind went back to a film I had seen some years ago called "A Night to Remember" about the sinking of the Titanic starring Kenneth More. I recalled a scene as the ship was sinking where hundreds of poor souls were thrashing about in the freezing cold seas awaiting their imminent deaths; I shivered and started to concentrate on what the Instructor was telling us.

"You are onboard a ship that has been torpedoed and there are holes in the bulkheads. You will find around this room the types of things you would normally find in a ships mess. Use whatever materials you think will shore up these holes to stop water coming in and your ship sinking."

Around the room were bits of wood, blankets, old kitbags, mattresses, chairs and tables so we would have to use our imagination to see how we could block up the holes.

The Instructor had forgotten to mention one thing to us though, there would actually be water pouring into the compartment we were in! As he exited the "ship" he locked tight the hatch to the outside world and water started coming in through the holes. Our group of suddenly terrified chefs got to work.

We helped each other to put mattresses and tables over the holes and shored these up with bits of wood. Our lack of expertise in this type of activity soon became apparent and the water still poured in despite our best efforts to block the holes. It was getting frightening and our attempts to keep out the water became more urgent. Despite considerable effort and manpower being expended erecting our shoring on the bulkheads, the room was flooding and the water had reached my chin. When it started to trickle into my mouth I decided to start climbing on anything I could to get above the water and I noticed my fellow distressed chefs were doing all they could to avoid drowning too. We were now past trying to stop the water coming in, we were just trying to keep our faces above the water level and we were failing. Luckily, at this point the water was turned off and started to be drained out by pumps that our Instructor must have had turned on from somewhere outside of what had nearly become our watery tomb. When the water had disappeared completely he opened the hatch door and came back in.

"You're all fucking dead!" he informed us. "Now go and get changed into some clean number 8s and we will try this again after you've had some Kye."

Following our change into dry clothes and the warming mug of Pusser's cocoa or Kye as it was called we were taken into a classroom and shown a film of sailors shoring bulkheads before we returned to the mock ship's compartment where a couple of experienced seamen came in to show us some useful tips on how to plug up holes in the ship's side. When the seamen left us we started the same exercise and the compartment we were in began to flood again. However, with our newly acquired skills we managed to more or less stem the flow of water this time. I wondered for a moment though how we would fare in a real situation if a torpedo or iceberg had holed our ship.

How would we really cope on a ship in the middle of the Atlantic a thousand miles away from the nearest land with icy water pouring in and no lights on? I put these thoughts out of my head as we returned to our mess to have a welcome rest.

The next day, after nearly drowning us, the Royal Navy decided to gas us as well.

We were each given a gas mask and shown how to wear it. It was heavy, old fashion and claustrophobic to wear. One at a time we were led into a big brick shed and told to make sure that our gas masks fitted properly. A Petty Officer then let off a gas canister in the room and hastily retreated, locking the door behind him. Through a window I could see faces watching me. Within seconds of the canister beginning to emit a yellow cloud of some sort of gas I was getting into a distressed state. Gas was somehow finding its way into my mask and my eyes, nose, throat and chest were stinging. I banged on the door and after what seemed an eternity but was probably five seconds or so I was let out. I ripped the mask off and was sick over the feet of the Petty Officer who was standing in front of me. After swearing at me for a while he went off to supervise the others going into the gas room. Following a short rest period I was again shown how to adjust my mask and sent back into the room to repeat the test. This time it worked better and I had to stay in the room for several minutes before being let out. My eyes though were red and stung for the next couple of days.

It was soon after that I was called into a room by the Petty Officer Cookery Instructor who told me that I had passed my exams with a score of 76%. I also learnt that all of my fellow trainee cooks apart from Bunny had passed their exams. Bunny was informed that he had to do the whole thing again. That evening our Petty Officer Instructor took everyone from the class who had passed the examinations ashore to a restaurant in Chatham called the Jade Garden and I had my second ever Chinese meal in a Cantonese restaurant. My first had been at the White House in Finsbury Park with Dave Charie and some other mates. We had tried to persuade Dave that lychees were a slug found in paddy fields but I don't think he was convinced. The following day after my meal in Chatham I packed my kit bag and left Pembroke for my Christmas leave after which I was to join my new ship.

A mini bus took us newly trained cooks from HMS Pembroke to Chatham Station. As we passed through the main gate of the Barracks I stuck my tongue out and gave a two fingered salute to the Regulating Petty Officer on duty. "Put your foot down!" I urged the mini bus driver as I realised that the Regulator had seen me

CHAPTER EIGHTEEN

DOWN AND OUT IN PARIS AND GOSPORT

On the 28th December 1965 following my Christmas Leave I left home and got a morning train from Waterloo Station in London to Portsmouth to report to my very first ship as a trained cook.

My posting was to be HMS Dolphin, another bloody stone frigate. It was a Navy shore establishment sited at Fort Blockhouse in Gosport just across the water from Portsmouth. This was the home of the Royal Navy Submarine Service and the location of the Royal Navy Submarine School. My paperwork stated that I was to be employed there in the Chiefs and Petty Officers galley.

A cold wind blew into my face as I got out of the train at Portsmouth Harbour Station and as I looked around I could see this was very much a naval town. Behind me was the harbour, to my left was HMS Victory and to my right HMS Vernon, both naval shore establishments. My instructions were to go through the grounds of HMS Vernon to the water's edge where a Royal Navy motor launch would pick me up and ferry me across the harbour to HMS Dolphin in Gosport. I reported to the main gate at Vernon and was directed to the motor launch where I threw my kit bag onto the deck, climbed onboard and looked around at the scene as I was transported across the water. I could see dozens of Royal Navy ships of every size, from an aircraft carrier to a mine sweeper tied up alongside the docks and they were all painted battleship grey.

A radio on my launch was playing *California Dreamin'* by the Mamas and Papas telling me that the sky was grey.

Never mind the sky being grey I thought, I was surrounded by grey ships, and the Navy had lots of them in Portsmouth! I sang the words of the Mamas and Papas song quietly to myself so as not to alarm the boats coxswain as I wondered if one of those big grey ships would one day take me to somewhere warm; but then my overriding thought returned to me which was I still really wanted to get out of the Navy. I was shaken out of my day dreams as the motor launch's fenders bounced off the jetty to signal that I had arrived at HMS Dolphin where I was met by a member of the Regulating Branch who asked for my paper work. Once this was scrutinised I was directed to the chefs mess (I like being called a chef by my fellow sailors!) where one of my new mess-mates pointed out a spare bunk bed I could use. I then stowed my kit into a locker, changed into my cooks' whites and was directed to the Chiefs and Petty Officers galley to take orders. It was now late in afternoon when I was shown around the reasonably sized galley by a Leading Cook and was then told to help out with cooking the evening meal, tea. Unsurprisingly, I was given potatoes to peel. I was also asked to help with breakfast next day which meant that I was awoken at 04.30 in order that I could get to the galley by 05.00 to start work. Once there I helped open some tins of tomatoes and tins of beans and put them into deep dishes which were then placed into a steamer to heat and keep warm until our first customers arrived at 07.00. As the Chiefs and Petty Officers turned up for their breakfast I was placed on egg frying duties for over an hour. The routine in the galley at Dolphin was such that the cooks who had prepared breakfast would then help get dinner ready and at 08.00 all the other cooks appeared and the preparations began for dinner. I was allowed to finish at 13.00 and as I had worked on the previous day's tea and then breakfast I was off duty until 08.00 the next morning. This was called a "make and mend" which went back to the days when sailors would sow and repair their clothing and bedding on an afternoon off.

On my way back to my mess I decided to briefly inspect my new ship. The first thing that intrigued me was a tall concrete tower with windows, or portholes in it. I noticed a sign next to it that said it was the Submarine Escape Training Tank.

A real submariner came and stood next to me as I gawped at the tank and seeing that I was interested he started to tell me all about it. He said it was a thirty metre deep container of water used to instruct Royal Navy submariners to conduct a pressurised escape.

"Put your name down to have a go," he urged me.

"I certainly will," I replied.

The rest of HMS Dolphin was pretty standard Royal Navy Barracks but I did notice a few submarines in the harbour which was something a bit different for me to look at. I found the NAAFI and bought myself some sweets, a tin of nestles condensed milk and a packet of twenty Players Number 6 cigarettes. Back at the mess I showered and changed into my number 8s, made myself a cup of tea and looked out of the window. The mess was at the end of a peninsula and through the window I saw boats, ferries, ships and then a hovercraft going by. I could see the faces of the passengers, most of who were heading for the Isle of Wight. I wrapped myself up with jumpers and scarves and took my latest George Orwell book, "*Down and out in Paris and London*" and my cup of tea with me as I climbed out of the window and sat on some rocks to be even closer to the boats where I spent the afternoon in the winter sunshine reading. As the hovercraft went by I waved at people peering out at me and some waved back.

That evening I discovered that anyone who had not gone ashore had to clean the mess to get it ready for evening rounds by the Duty Officer. I was told that although these inspections or rounds were not as demanding as those at HMS Ganges if dust was found on a window ledge or a dustbin was not shining to the correct degree this would result in a lot of shouting and further cleaning having to take place. I was given the job that evening of applying polish to the deck and buffing it until it was shining. When the Duty Officer arrived I stood to attention and saluted him and announced:

"Chefs' mess ready for inspection Sir!"

"You're not a fucking chef you're a cook," he answered me dismissively.

Despite the bullshit of being in a Royal Navy shore establishment I enjoyed my afternoons off at Dolphin spending time on my own on the rocks and it became a routine on those days for me to climb out of the mess window to read my book and wave at the boats going by.

One day I looked up as a ferry sailed by and I started my usual smiling and waving when I noticed one of the passengers was not waving back. In fact this particular passenger was as an angry looking Regulating Chief Petty Officer from HMS Dolphin endearingly named "Bum Face" for reasons unknown but I guessed that he was not very popular. He glared daggers back at me as I waved.

"Oh Dear!" I said and it was no surprise that the next morning he came into the mess and picked me out as the sailor on the rocks.

That morning I was placed on what was called Captains Defaulters where everyone who had done something wrong was marched in front of the Duty Officer and a charge was read out and punishments duly administered. When my turn came I was marched in front of a bored looking Duty Officer and loudly ordered to stand to "ATTEN - SHUN," and then "OFF CAPS!" by the Master at Arms. My charge was read out to me as something like being in uniform in an unauthorised place and bringing the Royal Navy into disrepute, but I wasn't really listening as it all seemed so petty. Unfortunately for me as my cap was off my head it was also revealed that I had committed another abominable offence, I had let my hair grow a fraction of an inch too long according to the Master at Arms so I was told to get it cut that day. For the crime of being out on the rocks and waving at people I was awarded two weeks stoppage of local leave and fourteen days extra cleaning duties which I had to do each evening and at weekends on top of my normal job.

One of my more humiliating punishments during the two weeks was to pick up litter on the public road outside of the back gate of HMS Dolphin. A small group of defaulters were given the patch that stretched from the gate to a hundred yards further along the road. We had to clear all the litter that was in the road, on the pavements or in the shrubs that lined the road. We had Regulating Chief Petty Officer Bum Face in charge of us who would shout out if we had missed picking up a piece of litter or if there was a dog end of a cigarette that had been overlooked. One day he boomed at me:

"Cleaning the road means picking up dog shit too!"

I had just carefully avoided stepping in a pile of dog excrement and didn't think I would be called upon to clean that up as well but Regulating Chief Petty Officer Bum Face had other ideas.

Using a bit of cardboard I had found I was instructed to scoop this into my rubbish sack and as I did so I looked up to see two civilians who were walking by looking at me as if I was some sort of criminal or low life. They must have wondered why a member of her Majesty's Senior Service had to pick up rubbish and dog excrement on the public highway when surely the local council employed people to do that. I went into my mental escape mode as I allowed the Mamas and the Papas into my head with *"California Dreamin'."*

So for the next two weeks when I was not working in the galley I spent my time cleaning the heads, washing windows and polishing brass door knobs and handrails and picking up litter along the road leading to the back gate of HMS Dolphin.

**

At Tollington Park School I was held back academically due to my early morning rising. Basically, I did not get enough sleep as I got up at 05.00 from the age of eleven to do a paper round and from the age of thirteen I had risen at 04.30 to deliver milk. I was streamed into a high enough class at school as I had shown potential but the early mornings had taken their toll and I would often fall asleep in lessons. Also, my mind was made up to become a chef so I had decided that I didn't need GCE O Levels. However, at Ganges I had done well in English, History and Maths which led me to make the decision to start taking correspondence classes in these subjects and in French too, I certainly had time in the evenings to study. I was only occasionally distracted from my studies by an interesting character, a mess-mate named Harry who wanted to play me, well beat me really, at Monopoly. During my first month or so at Dolphin I found that my other new mess-mates and fellow chefs were the usual mixture of individuals. Some were friendly, others distant and not wanting to engage in conversation, there were a few bullies, a couple of loud mouths but thankfully there was Harry who had two loves in life: playing Monopoly and sex. I was to spend many a happy hour playing Monopoly and chatting to Harry. He loved winning and no one, including me, ever managed to beat him at Monopoly during the six months I was at Dolphin.

As for sex I was still only sixteen years old and not very wise in the way of the world but Harry was twenty and he would constantly brag about his conquests with women.

It seemed that after every run ashore in Portsmouth or Gosport he would come back and describe what sexual acts he had been up to that night. According to Harry the young women he met all seemed to end up having sex with him. However, as everyone of them lived at home with their parents and would not take him back with them and as he was not allowed to bring women back to the ship, his love making all took place behind bushes in Parks, on dark streets behind a wall or on the beach at Southsea. To the uninitiated youngsters in the mess such as me this didn't seem like a very romantic way to woo young women. I also wondered if Harry had ever been shown the American film about the dangers of going off with girls and catching venereal diseases that we had been shown at HMS Ganges. I worked out from his stories that he must have had relationships with over a dozen women whilst I was at Dolphin but I have to say though that I think he was stretching his and his messmate's imaginations with some of his tales.

Harry one day invited me to go ashore with him in Gosport and as we sat in a coffee shop sipping a frothy coffee he told me that he had met a girl who was "the one." When I asked him what he meant he told me that he was in love with a young girl who lived in Southsea who he said really loved him too.

"You know that look in a woman's eyes when she really wants your body?" he asked me.

I shook my head as I didn't

So, on my first run ashore with Harry he told me he wasn't looking to meet any more young women as he was now in love.

After walking around the streets of Gosport and getting fed up sitting in coffee shops we bizarrely ended up going into a Spiritualist Church to get out of the cold rain but in no time at all we were invited to take part in a séance. I was asked by a young man if there was anyone on the other side who I wanted to talk to so after a few moments thought I said: "Oscar Wilde." Then, amazingly, after some locals who were in the Church had spoken to their deceased loved ones, Oscar turned up through the voice of the medium, to have a chat with me.

As we became friendly with some of the Church goers we started making a weekly outing, every Wednesday evening, to a Spiritualist's home in Gosport.

There we would have a cup of tea and some digestive biscuits and then sit in the front room holding hands and taking part in a séance, talking to the dead with the lights turned off. Oscar Wilde managed to show up every week through the voice of the medium. I found that I had to start reading more of Oscar Wilde's books and plays in order to keep up with the conversation. I read *"The Ballad of Reading Gaol"* and *"The Importance of being Earnest."*

At these séances the medium and I regularly acted out parts from The Importance of being Earnest which was the play we most enjoyed, particularly the revelation where Jack tells Lady Bracknell that as a baby he was found at a London railway station in a handbag. In my best upper class voice I would imitate Lady Bracknell and say:

"And where did this charitable gentleman with the first class ticket to the seaside resort find you?"

The medium, i.e. Oscar Wilde would say: "In a handbag."

Again imitating Lady Bracknell's voice I would say:

"A handbag?" and Oscar and I would have a jolly good laugh.

Well the séance was free and we didn't have much else to keep us amused in Gosport! I must admit that I did wonder why someone of Oscar Wilde's eminence would choose to spend his Wednesday evenings in damp, cold Gosport and I didn't believe for a moment that I was really talking to him but it was good fun. If, however, when my time comes to pass over to the other side and Oscar is waiting for me with a joke about a handbag I shall be pleasantly surprised.

I have to say that the people we met at the séances were decent ordinary folk, very nice people in fact and I don't doubt that some actually did manage to talk to people on the other side and many of them told me that they certainly got peace by doing so. Also, on one occasion, in the gloom of the darkened room, I actually did see the ghostly form of an elderly lady with a hat on sitting on a Chaise Longue staring at me. I closed my eyes and rubbed them and when I opened them again she was gone; was she a spirit we had summoned up or was it a trick of the light?

**

At HMS Dolphin I was starting to be given more responsibility in the galley despite of still being rated as a Junior Assistant Cook.

I was also still on £2 per week wages but I was soon to be surprised by a perk that was added to my remuneration. On pay day, as I marched up to receive my wages a box of three hundred blue liner Royal Navy cigarettes was handed to me, gratis! All sailors were given three hundred cigarettes a month for free I was told, I thought this was amazing. On lighting up my first blue liner though I could see the catch in this, they were the worst cigarettes I had known and appeared to be made of very tiny tobacco leaves with a lot of dust. Never mind I thought one shouldn't look a gift horse in the mouth, so along with everyone else we smoked our blue liners. An alternative I found out was to have tobacco instead of the cigarettes but this was the same tobacco dust which made hand rolled cigarettes difficult to make as the dust fell out from the end of the cigarette paper.

The first weekend at Dolphin when I was neither on duty or under punishment I decided to spend a weekend at home in London. When I told Harry about going to London he said that he too was spending the weekend in the Smoke as sailors called London. He had been invited to stay with his Aunt in Greenford. On Friday afternoon we set off for Portsmouth Harbour Station together and on the train we got a seat in a sparsely occupied carriage. The first stop was at a place called Fratton which is on the outskirts of Portsmouth. Harry started to tell me that there was an expression that naval folk used called "Getting out at Fratton". As most of Harry's conversations were about sex I guessed that this saying would have some sort of sexual connotation too.

Before Harry had time to enlighten me though a young women struggled into the carriage with a large case. Harry lost no time; he stopped talking to me as he sprung up out of his seat to take the case off the girl and place it into the string luggage rack.

She looked like she was a teenager; probably about eighteen and Harry immediately used his charms to get to know her. Harry used his best chat up lines as we proceeded to London and when he told her we were going to have a drink at Waterloo before setting off to our respective destinations she agreed to join us in a nearby pub.

Out of her hearing I asked Harry about the love of his life, the girl from Southsea and he informed me that she had gone off with a Stoker from HMS London so he was a free agent again.

After one drink I set off to get the number 4A Bus to Finsbury Park and I left Harry and his new friend, who told us her name was Gloria, to have another drink together.

I spent Saturday wandering in and out of record and book shops along Holloway Road and I bought a copy of the Daily Worker outside Finsbury Park Station. In the evening I tagged along with my brother's friend Geoff and his mate Joe, who was on leave from the Army. They took me to a Cantonese Restaurant, my first experience of Chinese food in London's West End. I ordered sweet and sour chicken which I had never eaten before and boiled rice while Joe ordered his meal to be accompanied with fried rice. Even though I was still under age to drink we had been in a pub earlier where they thought I was eighteen so I had several pints of beer. We ordered another beer to have with our meal and as I eagerly awaited my new eating experience I was conscious of the room beginning to sway a little and our conversation begin to slur. The food was brought to us on a trolley and as the waiter placed the rice on the table Joe exploded and he shouted at the waiter:

"Listen, I've spent two years in the Far East and I know what fried rice should look like, take it back and get the chef to fry it properly this time."

The rice looked fine to me but the waiter bowed and duly took the rice away.

"I'll keep mine," I said.

I didn't know much about eating in restaurants but I guessed that if the food was sent back as not cooked properly the chef would do something horrible to it before it was returned. I was reading *"Down and out in Paris and London"* by George Orwell and he told many tales of the nastier side of kitchens he had worked in. Based on my reading of the book I was going to tell Joe that the chef would no doubt spit into his rice or worse before giving it a bit of a stir fry but Joe didn't look like he was in the mood to listen.

Soon a much greasier looking bowl of rice was returned and this seemed to placate Joe but I tried not to think about any added ingredients as I didn't want to be put off my own food.

While we ate our meals Joe told us about his adventures in the Far East and then we ordered some more beers to be followed by some fried bananas and ice cream.

Whilst awaiting our dessert course something strange and unexpected happened. With no warning to me my two fellow diners got up and ran out of the door without paying. I looked down the restaurant to the kitchen and saw a couple of waiters and a chef coming towards me. I noted that the chef had a large cleaver in his hand which he had been using to chop up ducks. Even in my semi drunk state I sensed danger so I got up very quickly and threw down onto the table what money was in my pockets and ran out of the door too. I could not see which way my friends had gone but the following posse must have thought I would lead them to the "runners." I set off at a fast pace and I hardly remember my feet touching the ground as I ran between buses and cars, over a building site, down alleys, all the time hearing wild shouts from the chasing pack who were literally breathing down my neck. Eventually, I managed to get to Leicester Square Underground Station where I threw myself down the escalator and onto a tube train that was bound for Finsbury Park. I watched nervously as the doors shut and with my heart and head pounding and my lungs fighting for breath I placed my head between my knees. I waited for the train to start moving before I dare look up again. I was half expecting to see the angry face of the Chinese Chef with a meat cleaver in his hand pressed up against the window but to my relief there was no one there. As the train picked up speed I was sure I could hear the shouts of the chef and waiters in the distance as I entered the tunnel and safety.

"What did you do that for?" I asked my eating companions when I saw them next day.

"We thought it would be a laugh to see what you would do," they explained.

"Ha bloody Ha!" I made the decision never to eat out with them again.

**

I met up with Harry again at Waterloo Station on Sunday evening to get the late train back to Portsmouth and to my surprise he had a black eye and evidence of some recent cuts on his face.

"What happened to you?" I enquired.

"I'll tell you on the train," he whispered back to me.

It transpired that Harry and Gloria had set off, after a few drinks in the bar, to a flat in Camden Town as Harry had kindly offered to carry her heavy case for her. At the flat they had some more drinks when Gloria suggested that Harry undress himself and get into bed. When he was in bed waiting with anticipation there was a knock at the door and Gloria excitedly told Harry to hide in the toilet. A man entered the flat and Harry heard Gloria shouting:

"Don't hurt him, he hasn't done anything!"

The man opened the toilet door which annoyingly for Harry did not have a lock and proceeded to beat Harry up.

"He was like a bloody Gorilla, I didn't stand a chance," explained Harry.

After punching and kicking him for a while the Gorilla told Harry to get dressed and get out warning him not to go to the police as he would say he found Harry and Gloria, who he said was only fifteen, having sex in his flat. Harry dressed and ran for his life; he was at Mornington Crescent before he stopped to get his breath back. Leaning on a wall panting he took his wallet out of his trousers pocket and discovered his money was missing; he had been robbed.

"That was a bloody scam, I was set up, and that's bloody London for you!" he complained.

Luckily, Harry still had his ticket to get to his Aunt's house so he made his way there and managed to borrow some money from her for the weekend.

"I'll be more careful the next time I'm invited back to someone's flat," he sighed.

"We both had an eventful weekend then," I said.

**

Back at HMS Dolphin I decided to read again the section in George Orwell's book *"Down and out in Paris and London"* [1] that related to working in kitchens. In the book Orwell recounts his experience that French cooks will spit in the soup, if they are not going to drink it themselves and he also observes that for food to look smart it needs dirty treatment.

To explain Orwell says that when a steak for instance is brought up for the head cook's inspection he picks it up in his fingers and slaps it down, runs his thumb round the dish and licks it to taste the gravy, runs it round and licks it again, then steps back and contemplates the piece of meat like an artist judging a picture, then presses it lovingly into place with his fat, pink fingers, every one of which he has licked a hundred times that morning. Orwell also says that whenever one pays more than, say, ten francs for a dish of meat in Paris, one may be certain that it has been fingered in this manner. In very cheap restaurants it is different; there, the same trouble is not taken over the food, and it is just forked out of the pan and flung onto a plate, without handling. Roughly speaking, says Orwell, the more one pays for food, the more sweat and spittle one is obliged to eat with it.

One day, helping to prepare dinner for the Chiefs and Petty Officers at HMS Dolphin I witnessed my first "'Down and out in Paris and London" moment in a Royal Navy galley. A chef who for some reason was named Chopper was cooking the vegetables for the meal. He scooped his cooked cabbage out of a large cooking copper into a colander. Placing the colander over a scupper that ran the length of the galley he pressed the sole of his right boot onto the cabbage and trod it down to squeeze the water out. He then tipped the cabbage into a large serving dish, put a knob of margarine on top and placed the dish into a steam cabinet to keep warm until dinner was served up. Chopper had a reputation as a bullying loud mouth who hated the Navy and just about everyone in it and anyone he came across ashore as well, there were even stories about drunken fights in Pubs in Portsmouth that he had started. Putting this knowledge to one side I decided to confront Chopper about what I had witnessed. His first reaction to my complaints about his unhygienic method of straining cabbage was to grab my tee shirt and lift me into the air with threats of various painful things he would do to me but after a while he lowered me to the ground and just said:

"You've a lot to learn about being a chef in the Navy Laddie."

An old but impressive looking submarine had recently appeared and was anchored in the harbour at HMS Dolphin a lot closer than the other ones I had seen. I had stood and admired it on a number of occasions when one day to my amazement the Chief Petty Officer Cook called me into an office and told me that I was to spend a day on this submarine as a part of my development as a cook. He also said that submariners were volunteers and as they were short of submarine cooks I might want to volunteer to become a cook in the submarine service of the Navy. I said that I doubted that very much but I was willing to spend a day onboard. The next day I was dispatched to the thirty metre deep Submarine Escape Training Tank so that I could be trained on how to get out of a submarine in an emergency.

As a trainee my escape kit consisted of an oxygen bag hung around my neck and strapped to the front of my chest, a pair of goggles, a mouthpiece and a nose clip. I had to get into a compartment at the base of the tower which was then sealed with a watertight door. The Instructors opened a valve to flood the compartment and once the compartment was full the lid was opened. I was observed through the glass ports in the tower where Instructors watched me and the other trainees escaping and I was told that there were rescuers at the top of the tank ready to dive in if anyone got into difficulties. I successfully performed an escape from the tank and was adjudged competent to go on a submarine so not many days later I climbed onto a motor launch that took me out to the submarine.

Climbing onboard and then down inside the submarine the first thing that struck me was the space, or rather, the lack of it. Inside I was led along a narrow aisle where a curtain was pulled aside to reveal a dozen miniature looking bunk beds which is where the submariners slept I was informed.

I walked along looking at various small rooms and compartments unable to locate the galley so I asked a sailor with a beard and a big woolly jumper if he could help. He pointed to one of the small rooms I had already passed that I thought was a storeroom but to my surprise was a proper ships galley, but in miniature.

A Petty Officer Cook came in and welcomed me onboard the submarine. He informed me that one of the dishes on the menu for dinner would be mushroom omelettes so he asked me to be in charge of that. Looking around I found a box of mushrooms but unable to locate them I enquired where I could find the eggs.

"In number one torpedo tube," said the Petty Officer.

Incredulously, and with some degree of trepidation I made my way forward to the torpedo tubes. The reason for my concern was that in my short naval career I had already been the subject for a number of practical jokes. At Dolphin I had been sent to the store for a jar of elbow grease and once was given a form to apply for a muff diving course that I presented to the Master at Arms to much hilarity from my fellow chefs.

I wondered if this was this another wind up? Would alarms go off as I opened the doors to the torpedo tube and would I be dragged off and clapped in irons for breaking the rules? Then a shout came from the galley:

"Once you've closed the torpedo hatch don't press that big red button otherwise you'll launch the rest of the eggs and if they hit a foreign ship that would be an act of war!"

"Ha Ha!" I said.

I opened a torpedo tube with the label, number one torpedo on the door. Inside the tube there was not a torpedo to be seen. Instead what I found were indeed trays of eggs! Hopefully, we would not be called upon to fire at an enemy ship whilst I was at sea otherwise five hundred eggs would be dispatched at speed and scrambled against the ships side. I took a tray of eggs back to the galley and made omelettes as we sailed from Portsmouth Harbour into the Solent and beyond. When my short training session on the submarine was over I decided that it was not the life for me but from the moment I gratefully placed my feet on dry land again I was forever in awe of people who were part of the submarine service, I could not imagine ever getting used to living and working in such a confined space.

Towards the end of May I was informed that I was to be drafted from HMS Dolphin to another ship.

"Where to now?" was the question I asked myself.

CHAPTER NINETEEN

LA MER

On Friday 3rd June 1966 I left HMS Dolphin to join my first proper sea going ship, HMS Hecate, which was currently tied up in Devonport Dockyard at Plymouth.

Having cleared my locker and packed my kit bag I said goodbye to my mess-mates and set off in my best uniform leaving HMS Dolphin the way I had entered her six months earlier as a motor launch took me across the water to HMS Vernon from where I made my way to Portsmouth Harbour Station. I boarded a train for Plymouth and settled down for the journey in an empty carriage, just me and my thoughts about what my next adventure was to be.

The journey took five hours and I had to change a couple of times. Changing trains at Exeter I was amused by the station announcer who shouted out in a very strong West Country accent:

"Eggseggeter! This is Eggseggeter!"

Eventually arriving at Plymouth Station my instruction was to get a cab to the ship. However, I was feeling hungry after such a long journey so I asked the cab driver if there was a decent café anywhere en route to the dockyard. My cab driver had already informed me that he was ex Royal Navy so he made a suggestion which I agreed to and so it was that he deposited me outside the establishment he recommended which was called "Aggie Weston's." He said he would return in thirty minutes which should give me time to eat a meal.

"Get out of Aggie's as soon as you have finished your meal and before an Amen Wallah sits down next to you otherwise you will never get away," he advised.

Aggie's was a place where sailors and their families could get a room for the night and be well fed at reasonable prices. I didn't need a room, just food and I ordered steak, egg and chips with tomatoes and mushrooms and set about clearing my plate in the thirty minutes the cab driver had allowed me. The food was good, cheap and the welcome at Aggie's a warm one. I made a vow to frequent Aggie Weston's regularly in the future. I finished my meal and made my excuses as a man with a bible sat down next to me. I was outside well before the thirty minutes were up and while I waited for the cab to return a strange thing happened. A woman came up to me and asked if she could stroke my Dickie. I was taken aback and blushed but when she saw my confusion she explained that to stroke a sailor's Dickie meant to touch my naval collar. She told me that stroking a sailors Dickie brought good luck, it was an old custom. After she had touched my collar the cab turned up and when I related my story to the driver he had a good chuckle.

"You had better watch out, there'll be plenty of women in Plymouth wanting to stroke your Dickie!" he laughed.

We stopped at the Devonport Dockyard gates where my papers were checked before the cab weaved its way around the docks to where HMS Hecate was tied up. Getting out of the cab I stood back to admire my new home and was very impressed that the ship was painted white and not grey and that also she had no guns. I walked up the gangway and went onboard where I was taken below to my mess which I was told I would share with sixty other souls for the next couple of years. The only spare bunk bed was a bottom one near to the ladder and there were two occupied bunks immediately above me. There was more room here than in submarines and even HMS Wakefield but the living space was still very tight but I was told that my bunk was the least popular on board as sailors returning drunk from shore would sometimes stop at the bottom of the ladder and vomit over the inhabitant of that bunk. Unhappily for me I was to discover that this was true so as soon as I could, some months later I vacated it for a bunk at a higher level.

For now, having stowed my kit in a locker, I was given a tour around the ship and told something about it by one of the duty seamen, a Welsh lad who said he was called Taffy. (Sometimes the nicknames given to sailors were not very original.) Taffy was a talkative and likable person and he informed me that HMS Hecate was an almost brand new Hecla Class Ocean Survey Ship, built in Yarrow's Shipyard at Scotstoun near Glasgow and commissioned the previous year, in December 1965. He said he was present when it was commissioned in the shipyard and he told me that the ship had been launched by Lady Yarrow herself. He was reading out some facts and figures from a sheet of paper and he told me that as a survey ship she had been built for hydrographical and oceanographic operations and had a strengthened hull made to repel ice. He also said that the ship had a top speed of 14 knots which at times seemed to make her quite slow and she weighed 2,800 tons. The Ships' Company was made up of 12 Officers and 104 ratings a handful of scientists and there was another civilian, an engineer employed by the firm Decca to look after the ships Navigator equipment. Taffy took me onto the flight deck and opened the helicopter hanger to reveal a Westland Wasp light helicopter. He also pointed out the two 31 foot Survey Motor Boats hanging on the sides of the ship. He said that we were to set sail on Monday for a six week stint at surveying the sea along the Spanish coast. Receiving that information gave me butterflies in my stomach at the thought of going to a foreign country, I was excited! After tea I showered and had an early night taking my Manual of Naval Cookery to bed with me to catch up on the recipes for the meals I was told we would be cooking next day.

In the morning I joined two other chefs in the galley, one a Cornish Petty Officer the other was Geordie and we cooked meals throughout the day for a skeleton crew. The following day was Sunday which started quietly but the number of people onboard grew as the day wore on and by evening the entire ships' company were back onboard which meant we also had a full complement of five chefs in the galley.

The next day was hectic onboard, orders were being shouted and the dockside was full of dockyard mateys preparing to untie ropes and wires to free the ship ready for sailing.

In the galley we were working at full speed to prepare a three course dinner with three main meat options for 120 sailors. As well as soup to start with, the main choices were Braised Ox Hearts, American Hash which was made from corn beef and potatoes and also Babies Heads, Naval slang for individual steak and kidney puddings. We also cooked roast, mashed and chipped potatoes, cabbage, (strained properly!) carrots, peas and baked beans and a choice of Eve's Pudding, Spotted Dick or tinned fruit and custard for dessert. I was given the job of preparing vegetables and making soup. When I was taught to make soup at the cookery school we would use fresh vegetables or real meat or chicken but here it was much easier. I had to half fill a cooking copper with water and stir in soup powder and heat until it was cooked at which stage it thickened and resembled quite reasonable soup. By the time dinner was over we had set sail and a pilot boat escorted us as we slowly made our way out of the harbour. I was given a short break before I had to return to the galley to help wash up and also prepare the food for tea.

Disappointingly, during my break I was not allowed on the upper deck until the ship was clear of land. It was a rule; I was told that only those who had a job to do on the upper deck were allowed there until we were out at sea. I went down to the mess and looked out of a port hole as land became more and more distant until it had disappeared completely.

Once the tea had been cooked and served I had the job of washing up the dishes and then, with Plymouth, the Cornish Lizard and the Eddystone Lighthouse well behind us I sneaked up on deck to see what being at sea was like. A soft warm breeze blew and caressed my face as I watched a large number of noisy seagulls follow in our wake, waiting for the rubbish or 'gash' as they called it in the navy, to be thrown overboard.

I climbed up a couple of decks and made my way up to the highest point on the ship where I had a clear view of the sea and the horizon. I slowly turned my body a full 360 degrees and surveyed the first completely circular horizon I had ever witnessed. I stood in amazement and wonder contemplating the beauty of it all.

A huge red sun was setting in a clear sky and the sea was as calm as Finsbury Park's boating lake. All the sadism and bullying I had been subjected to in training almost seemed worthwhile if this tranquil and beautiful world at sea was my future. Had my time at HMS Ganges really been worth it? I reflected on all of this as a life on the ocean wave beckoned. I concluded to myself that it certainly had not been worth it but things might now be on the up. This was at last true excitement for me as a life at sea and visiting foreign countries seemed to be my immediate future.

Apart from studying domestic science, the other lesson I loved at school was French. I used to attend extra lessons after school where my teacher used to play records and get me to learn the words of songs and translate them. As well as the Edith Piaf classics I loved a song written and sung by Charles Trenet called *"La Mer"*. Apparently he wrote it on a train in 1943 while travelling along the French Mediterranean coast, returning from Paris to Narbonne. My image of the sea was very much coloured by this charming song. I now sang the words I remembered from Mr. Howell's French class at Tollington Park Comprehensive School to the glorious calm and twinkling sea before me.

In a good mood I went down below still singing *"La Mer"* as I entered the galley where I had a cup of tea with the duty cook, Ginge who proceeded to tell me jokes before we listened to the news on the radio and chatted about world events and before going back to the mess I listened to the shipping forecast. A man with a clipped BBC accent was saying:

"Biscay, Cyclonic five to seven, becoming west gale eight to storm ten, rough or very rough, becoming high later."

I didn't know what that meant really although it didn't sound too good and I certainly didn't know that overnight we would be entering the sea area the weather man had called "Biscay." As I was about to set off for bed Ginge came out with another joke.

"Why are Pirates called Pirates?" he asked

I shook my head.

"Because they Arrghhhh!" said Ginge, chuckling away to himself.

I smiled at the daft joke and I was at peace with the world as I got into my bunk bed that night where I felt only the slightest rolling motion as the ship calmly made its way south to survey the Spanish coast.

My awakening the next morning was violent, never in my life had I felt so ill and the forces making me ill were unrelenting. The ship was caught in a storm and as I tried to sit up my head struck the bunk above me. The ship was taken forty feet or more into the air by giant waves and as the waves disappeared I could hear the ships propeller spinning noisily in thin air as the ship felt and sounded like a giant pneumatic drill. The entire ship was left aloft by the waves that had whipped us up there and were now gone. We then crashed into the next rising wave and the one after that and then another as if we were rolling down a hill and bumping off each boulder as we descended. We then proceeded to pitch and roll violently at the same time until another enormous wave lifted us again out of the water only to come down what this time seemed to be a staircase of waves which plunged the ship into the deep angry sea again.

This process was repeated again and again and my head was spinning, it felt as if my brain was being tossed around and hitting the side of my skull, like a dried walnut in its shell. With a great amount of effort I somehow managed to get out of bed and put some clothes on. I made it to the heads where I was sick. I must have had my head in the toilet bowl for at least an hour until only yellow bile was coming up. After splashing my mouth and face with cold water I eventually managed to wash as best I could and made my way unsteadily to the galley to report for duty, bouncing off the ships bulkheads as I did. I lasted no longer than ten minutes in my workplace before I again ran to the heads. I lay prostrate with my head in the bowl and discovered that my body had even exhausted its supply of bile.

Blood spotted phlegm was all I had left in my system as I retched and my head pounded as well. After a long while I got to my feet and looked in a mirror. My face was ghostly white and the side of my neck under my ears looked decidedly green. I lurched and fell and somehow crawled back to the mess and collapsed into my bunk. I had found a bucket that I held onto in case there was any more vomit to come up.

I was now conscious of a nauseous mixture of smells, diesel from the engine, food from the galley, socks, stale cigarette smoke, sweat and the body odour of my sixty mess-mates. Despite this I soon fell asleep only to be woken by a kick in my side from a fellow chef, Robbo, who said I was needed in the galley. I opened my eyes but my head was spinning and I couldn't move so I ignored his request and again fell into a dizzy sleep. It must have been an hour later that I awoke as the ship's doctor shook my arm. He had a glass of water and some pills for me to take and he said I should stay in bed for the rest of the day but I would have to get up for work in the morning.

It was Thursday morning in fact before I came round properly and I had lost two days. In that time I had been kicked some more, pulled out of bed a few times but I had always crawled back in and fallen back into my stupor. The storm had now abated and although there was a significant swell that caused the ship to roll along in a figure of eight movement I felt I was able to cope with that. I had a shower and changed into my cooks' whites and made my way to the galley. I was met with a mixture of cheers, applause and derision as I entered but I was up to doing some work at last. As I started preparing some cabbage for dinner I imagined myself in a warm and cosy Kings Bakers in Stroud Green making crusty bread and having a nice cup of tea to admire my handiwork when I had taken the bread out of the oven. I should have gone for that job I thought to myself as I was now more convinced than ever that I had made the wrong decision about my career by joining the Navy. During the morning the ship's Chaplain came around the galley to chat to people. He had heard about my sea sickness and asked me how I was. He told me that about a dozen others onboard had been in a similar position as me although I seemed to be the worst affected. He described sea sickness as having three phases, first you feel very ill, secondly you think you are going to die and thirdly you wish you were dead.

"Not to worry," he said, "worse things happen at sea."

"We are at sea!" I replied.

"Oh, yes you're right about that, never mind, chin up!

CHAPTER TWENTY

ABROAD

It was only a couple of days after my violent bout of sea sickness when I was feeling a bit better that I visited the NAAFI shop we had onboard to buy some treats for myself.

I found a new invention on sale there, biological washing powder that revolutionised my washing as it did two things, firstly it removed stains that up to now had stubbornly refused to go from my laundry and secondly, it gave me the worse dhoby rash I had ever had, oh well for every positive you have to have a negative I told myself. The NAAFI also sold cigarettes which, although they were cheap, were of good quality. I decided to buy myself two hundred Piccadilly filter tips but as I inhaled the smoke from my first cigarette for some days it made me feel ill. I became nauseous just inhaling once so in a fit of pique I went on to the upper deck and threw the remaining one hundred and ninety nine cigarettes into the sea before vomiting over the side. It was not just cigarettes that made me ill, I also found that sugar in my tea made me queasy so I stopped taking sugar and I could no longer bear condensed milk as this too made me feel ill. Being at sea was changing me as my body and mind had to start getting used to life on a small overcrowded house that made random and sometimes violent movements and was forcing me to give up some of the things I had previously enjoyed.

With this thought in my mind I returned to the galley to work. As I was rolling out some pastry to put onto an apple pie I was distracted by a hissing noise from the door. Looking up I saw a conspiratorial looking Taffy giving shifty glances left and right as he whispered to me:

"Have you any scraps for the ship's cat?"

"What ship's cat?" I replied. This was news to me.

"I sort of found it wandering around the dockyard in Plymouth and it wanted to come onboard," explained Taffy, rather unconvincingly I thought. He had probably just stolen it on the way back from a drunken run ashore.

Anyway I was concerned that the cat shouldn't starve so I rustled up enough bits of cooked meat to give it a decent meal. I gave this to Taffy who grinned and made off to feed his new pet. I have to say that the cat soon became an acceptable feature of life onboard, seeking cuddles and food from sailors as they went about their work and generally cheering people up. I thought it was comical observing so many grown men talking to the cat as if it was someone who was interested in their conversation.

Not many days after leaving Plymouth and with the sea still heavy but no longer as rough as it had been I was aware of the fact that we were sailing close to Spain but too far out at sea to have sight of land. Onboard ship I was beginning to find people I liked and people I didn't like. One of my fellow chefs, Ginge, was a lovely man, with his soft Devon accent he called everyone "my lover" and every night as we were falling asleep in bed his voice could be heard as he told us corny jokes in the darkness of the mess. I remember him saying:

"I got lost last time we were in Vigo, so I decided to ask a man in uniform for directions and I said to him are you a policeman?"

"No," he said, "I'm an undercover detective."

"So I asked to him why he was in uniform."

"He says to me it's because today is my day off! Ha Ha Ha!"

Ginge always laughed at the jokes he told, often he was the only one laughing.

I joined those people onboard that I got on with to make up teams to play our most popular entertainment outside of working hours which was the game of Ludo or Uckers as it is known in the Navy.

This was played in the dining mess with a giant board and large green, yellow, red and blue counters and the sessions were normally led by Taffy. Card games were avidly played too and an Able Seaman called Legs taught me how to play cribbage. Legs was called by that name because he had real sailors bow legs and when he stood to attention with his feet touching together his knees were so far apart you could kick a football between them. Crib and another card game called Sergeant Major were very popular but a small group of enthusiasts played poker with matchsticks instead of money as gambling for cash was banned. I also played draughts and chess and I became a member of the ships chess club that had tournaments played around the various messes including the Chiefs and Petty Officers Mess. I was getting a fairly wide group of friends but my usual card partners were a Seaman named Pat, Geordie and Ginge who were fellow Cooks and Legs. The quality of my work in the galley was improving and I was becoming competent in most aspects of cooking three meals a day for a hundred and twenty sailors. As was becoming the usual part of my job as the Junior Assistant Cook though I was sent up onto the upper deck each morning after breakfast to throw the gash over the side, these were the leftovers from breakfast, tins, packaging, bottles and vegetable peelings. A huge army of seagulls would descend onto the sea squawking and fighting over every morsel. One morning as I was watching this battle for bits of bacon rind and bread crusts I happened to look up and I saw, for the very first time in my life, another country, Spain!

It was someway in the distance and it appeared light brown, mountainous, dusty and hot. I was suddenly aware that I had never felt such heat on my skin before as I stood in bright sunshine with my mouth open and my heart beating fast at what I was seeing and feeling. As I gawped a trawler went by bobbing up and down on the waves with its crew of Spanish fishermen casting nets that spread out behind it. I waved at them and they waved back. HMS Hecate had a good reputation with the local fishermen because on a previous visit the ship's Helicopter had hoisted to safety the crew of a distressed and burning fishing boat.

Having now made my first personal contact with people from Spain, albeit just a wave, I was excited and this sudden spectacle of foreignness almost overwhelmed me.

I would have stayed out there forever allowing my senses to be thrilled by all of this if it wasn't for the urgent calling of Petty Officer Tiddy Oggy demanding my presence back in the galley. (We called our Petty Officer Cook Tiddy Oggy because he was Cornish).

Over the coming days, although I managed to control my sea sickness to a certain degree this did not stop me from time to time succumbing to the dreadful nauseous feeling brought on by pitching into a heavy sea. At such times I took to leaning over the ships side or putting my head down the bowl and crying out for Hughie! I discovered that if I was being sick over the side of the ship I should never do so into the wind, I did it once and that was a good lesson to me. After throwing up over the ships side one day I was recovering and just staring at nothing in particular and stroking the cat who had come up to see me when Ginge stood next to me. As we looked into the empty sea Ginge suddenly said:

"I see no ships! Only hardships! Ha Ha Ha."

We continued to sail up and down the coast and I took every opportunity to gaze on the hot dusty mountains and rugged brown coastline of Spain and tried to imagine what lay in wait for me when I eventually stepped out onto foreign soil. I was so excited at the thought of what might be awaiting me.

Now I was sufficiently recovered from sea sickness to work in the galley I was being taught some of the tricks of the trade of a sea going chef. In cookery school we had to manage our time precisely to get each dish cooked at the last minute so that it was served fresh. At sea we had to find as many ways of getting our dishes prepared in advance with freshness being retained. Food we cooked was covered with greaseproof paper and placed in steam cabinets until required.

Chips were great and made our job easier as these were served with two meals every day of the week and could be prepared hours in advance. I was taught the best way of doing this. I peeled the potatoes and then put them though the chipping machine, the raw chips were then soaked in water for thirty minutes to wash off excess starch.

Once drained and dried the chips would be fried in medium heated oil until cooked but not coloured which we were told was called blanching.

Ten minutes before they needed to be served the chips were deep fried for a second time in very hot fat and it took only a couple of minutes to turn them a lovely golden colour. Once cooked the chips were then transferred to a tray and put into a hot cabinet ready for serving. I was indebted to Tiddy Oggy for three cooking skills that he taught me; the first was how to crack open an egg using one hand; secondly how to make a decent omelette and thirdly, after much begging by me, he gave me his secret recipe for traditional Cornish Pasties which with a slight modification, adding a dash of Worcester sauce, I improved. Tiddy Oggy wouldn't let me write the recipe down on paper so I placed it into my memory and recalled it every time I made pasties.

I was discovering that cooking at sea was very hard work and my duties included feeding the Officers, Chief and Petty Officers and the junior ratings, everyone onboard in fact. The Officers ate after the ratings but mostly the same food. The food for the junior rates was put into large serving dishes from which it was ladled onto their plates. I had to take out some portions from the serving dishes for the Officers which I arranged into silver salvers. These I covered with greaseproof paper and placed into a steamer to keep warm. When it came to serving their food a steward would take these salvers from me and serve the food onto each Officers plate. If there was something on the menu such as steak or omelettes these would have be cooked to order which meant hanging around for quite a while after the junior ratings food had been served up. Also, Officers had to have their entrées. This would often just be a slice of melon with a cherry on top or devils on horseback but sometimes I would cook quails or some such delicacy for them. One evening as I was cooking a steak for a particularly unpopular Officer an Able Seaman came into the galley. The Officer had upset this man during the day for some reason so the seaman pushed me out of the way and forked the hot steak from the frying pan onto the deck before he proceeded to kick it around the galley for a few minutes before jumping up and down on it a several times.

"Run that under the tap to wash off the dirt and heat it up for him," demanded the Seaman.

I tried to protest but was threatened with violence if I didn't do as I was told.

The effect of kicking the steak around seemed to have tenderised the meat and after the meal the steward came into the galley to pass on the complements of the Officer to me for the best steak he had ever tasted!

**

My working days in the galley were very long and I started to reflect on how many hours I actually worked. I had read in the newspapers that trade unions in the UK were campaigning for a five day, forty hour working week so as a way to pass the time I worked out how many hours a week I was working. Of course I was incarcerated on the ship twenty four hours a day, seven days a week but the actual hours I was obliged to be working in the galley came to a seven day seventy hour week! I decided that I would see someone about this when I was next on leave in the UK.

As I grafted away in the hot galley it appeared to me that time almost stood still as our survey of the Spanish coast continued and each week seemed like a month. Then one day I suddenly realised that it would not be long before we actually docked in the Port of Vigo to replenish our stores, take on water and have a run ashore.

Finally, that day arrived and I was actually going to be abroad! For the first time ever I saw a foreign country close up as we gracefully sailed into the harbour at Vigo, a city situated in north-west Spain where we were to spend three whole days in port before returning to our survey duties. When HMS Hecate tied up in Vigo docks I looked around taking in all of the new sights, sounds and smells. I noticed that we appeared to be the only foreign ship in the docks so I assumed we would not bump into any other British people while we were here and in fact we didn't.

As it was my afternoon off I was one of the first to be allowed ashore. After a detailed inspection of our hair and uniforms to make sure that we didn't disgrace Her Majesty's Navy by not being smart enough, a group of four of us, I had Geordie, Pat and Legs with me, were walking down the gangway onto foreign soil! We were two chefs and two seamen and we decided to explore the town together.

The first thing I noticed about Vigo was the smell. I could smell Spain as soon as I stepped off the ship

. It was a mixture of sardines and wine, of oranges, olive oil, roasted coffee, strong Spanish cigarettes and warm dust from the streets mixed with a strong whiff of drains, it was an alien but heady concoction.

As soon as we left the dockyard gates behind us we were besieged by young children begging. Many were barefoot and most held out their hands for money while others tried to put their hands into our pockets. They followed us for about a hundred yards before Legs had the idea of throwing some money on the ground to divert their attention while we got away. Between the four of us we scattered our small change, British pennies and Spanish pesetas and as the children scuttled around picking them up we made a run for it. In the town we wandered down narrow streets and through squares with ornate Churches. Men with berets passed by and stared at us and we saw young women with their chaperones being led along into dress shops and the smarter looking restaurants. We found wide boulevards with orange and lemon trees growing along them and I reached up and plucked an orange and sucked at the warm sweetness of the freshly picked fruit. I felt that I needed more senses than I had to take in this strange new world I was experiencing.

We looked into the windows of cafés and restaurants and saw demonstration plates of food that they were using to entice us in. There was a plate of what looked like fried battered onion rings in one café so we went inside to try them. We didn't speak Spanish and the locals didn't speak English but after a lot of pointing and hand gestures on all sides we discovered that the battered onion rings were called Calamar.

We ordered a plate each with some salad that was dripping in olive oil which we ate and enjoyed very much. Later I was told that I had in fact eaten squid, not onion rings, which was another first for me. We found bars in back streets that we surmised foreigners had probably never ventured into before and we discovered wine for the first time.

Back home in the United Kingdom beer or sometimes cider were the drinks of choice but here it was red wine. I was still underage for drinking but this did not seem to matter to the waiters in these bars.

They probably thought that if I was old enough to wear the uniform of the Queen's Navy and therefore be old enough to go to war and be killed then I must be old enough to drink alcohol as well. With no experience of drinking wine of any sort behind us we did not know if the stuff we was drinking was good or bad but it certainly had an acceptable taste to me and with the exchange rate being 200 pesetas to the pound and a glass of wine costing two pesetas we got drunk for the cost of a florin.

In one of the bars I had my first encounter with Spanish toilets. Being directed to the far end of the bar there was a small area, not particularly segregated from the main part of the establishment, with two cubicles. Neither cubicle had a door but each had a dirty looking small hole in the ground with marks where to put your feet either side of the hole. The toilets were for the use of both male and female customers and were referred to as squat toilets. No one had warned me about this and I was shocked and embarrassed to use one in case I was observed carrying out my bodily functions. I seriously thought about not bothering to use the inodoro but my full bladder was telling me otherwise and all of the time I was in there I was nervously looking and listening to see if anyone was going to appear. I hadn't realised that much of Europe had yet to catch up with Britain in terms of WCs.

As evening came upon us we walked, or rather staggered, to the edge of the docks where we sat on a sea wall and watched the twinkling lights from the ships and boats reflected in the water. One by one we vomited and I began to feel the same symptoms from being drunk as I had felt being sea sick. I did not like this sensation at all and I decided that if I was to drink ashore I would moderate my consumption. We eventually walked back to the ship trying, not very successfully, to keep ourselves as steady as we could and appear to be sober. After stumbling down the ladder into my mess, drinking a pint of water and taking two aspirins, I went to my bunk and fell into a drunken sleep.

**

Most ships had a problem with cockroaches. I didn't know where they came from but they were there. The next day as we all nursed our hangovers Geordie was lying asleep in his top bunk with his mouth open wide and he was snoring loudly.

Someone pointed out that a cockroach was crawling in a haphazard fashion upside down along the asbestos lagged hot water pipe that was situated eighteen inches above his bunk. This event grabbed the attention of everyone else in the mess. Every now and then the cockroach would miss a step as it made its way along the pipe and would almost fall but each time just managed to hold on. This was great entertainment and we even stopped playing crib to watch as the cockroach got within range of his open mouth. What if it fell! We discussed waking Geordie up or try to divert the cockroach but concluded that either action would not be wise. Whoever woke Geordie up would incur his wrath as he was likely to lash out and ask questions later. Then real drama, the cockroach stopped above his open mouth and Legs made the rash decision to take a swipe at it before it fell. Using an old folded up copy of the Daily Mirror he flicked the cockroach with the intention of knocking it onto the deck and away from Geordie. Unfortunately, instead of flying off to safety the cockroach fell straight into the open mouth of Geordie who smacked his lips with his tongue, closed his mouth and made a munching sound for a while then continued snoring. We all withdrew to a safe distance in case he woke up but after a few moments he hadn't so we carried on with our card games. No one ever had the nerve to tell Geordie that he had consumed a cockroach!

Following another three weeks at sea sailing up and down the Spanish coast we were told we were going back to Gus, as Plymouth was known to sailors, in order to allow the bulk of the ships' company to take some Summer Leave. I welcomed the news that we would be on dry land again.

We arrived back into Devonport Dockyard in the afternoon of Thursday 28th July 1966 to find the country gripped by football mania. The Football World Cup was reaching its conclusion and England had made it to the Final.

The match was contested between England and West Germany on Saturday 30th July 1966 at Wembley Stadium in London where a crowd of 98,000 people watched the game. In Devonport Dockyard twenty sailors onboard HMS Hecate were watching the match on a 17 inch black and white television screen at the back of the dining mess and I was one of those sailors.

With a mug of tea in my hand I sat next to a seaman called Smiler, I deduced that he had got this nickname as he was such a miserable person, anyway we all cheered England on to a 4–2 victory, won after extra time and I watched with pride as the team was presented with the Jules Rimet Trophy, the World Cup. The game proved to be a very evenly fought match with the fourth goal almost the last kick of the game. Geoff Hurst who scored a hat trick that day, had run up the pitch to wallop the ball into the German net as the television commentator pointed out that there were already England fans running onto the pitch to celebrate victory.

"They think it's all over!" he was shouting.

As the ball flew into the back of the net for Geoff Hurst's third goal the commentator's voice went up a few decibels as he exclaimed to his and our delight: "Well it is now!"

England's third goal had been hotly disputed by the West German team who claimed the ball had not crossed the line and we had a few anxious moments while the Swiss referee and Soviet linesman conferred before the referee pointed up field and announced it was a goal. Of course, on our black and white seventeen inch TV screen we could clearly see that the ball had crossed the line.

To celebrate winning the World Cup someone vigorously shook and then opened a large tin of beer, Watney's Red Barrel in fact, spraying it over the assembled cheering fans. The next programme on TV after the football was Gus Honeybun. Gus was a puppet rabbit and the station mascot for Television South West and the star of Gus Honeybun's Magic Birthdays. Smiler told me that Gus Honeybun attained a cult status among the sailors onboard the ships coming and going at Devonport Dockyard. If you had a birthday while your ship was in Plymouth someone would send your name into the television station asking for it to be announced. Whatever your age Gus Honeybun would perform that number of bunny hops. As twelve was the official age limit for having a birthday read out on air members of the Navy who were twenty years old were presented as being two and so on! When the programme started the entire audience of grown men around the TV would shout out "GUS HONEYBUN!" If you did not join in this ritual you were frowned upon by your ship mates.

"Daft," I thought, but it did have a certain charm about it.

CHAPTER TWENTY ONE

SPARKY ARRIVES

Summer Leave on dry land was welcomed by all of the ships' company with the chance of getting home to our families.

In the Navy we were issued with a limited number of travel warrants each year and therefore excess train journeys had to be purchased out of our own pocket. To save money I was talked into hitch hiking my way back to London by Smiler who said that he regularly did it and had no problem getting lifts. We started off by getting a bus from Plymouth out to a roundabout on the A38 where we spent over an hour thumbing in the bright sunshine before a van eventually pulled up. It was going to Honiton to pick up some pottery to take back to a gift shop in Cornwall. Smiler got into the passenger seat while I settled myself among the straw and packaging in the back. As we were driven through the countryside of South West England I reflected that as lovely as hot and rugged Spain had been it was good to see the green rolling hills and the rich red soil of Devon again. We were dropped off on a roundabout on the A30 where we decided to sit down on the grass and open our packed lunches which I had prepared in the galley that morning out of the leftovers from breakfast.

When our next lift arrived, a lorry taking farm equipment to Marlborough, we got into the not very clean and seriously oily cab of the vehicle which had two passenger seats.

We spent the journey chatting away about our adventures in Spain to the driver and when we arrived in the town we asked him to drop us off so that we could get something to drink. Smiler was all for going into a pub that was just opening but I really wanted a mug of tea. My argument won the day when I said that if we went to a café we could get a bacon sandwich as well as a drink so we found an all day diner that was open and had several mugs of tea to slake our thirst after which Smiler decided to discuss politics with me, in particular he launched into one of his tirades against the Labour Party.

"Of course if you vote Labour you're really voting for Communism," he stated.

"Take the NHS, all those people getting free treatment when they've hardly paid anything in. We should have the same system as the USA, if you can't pay for it you shouldn't get the treatment," he concluded his argument

I had learnt from my discussions with Smiler onboard ship that he had a peculiarly right wing view of the world and he also loved to wind me up.

"You stupid Tory bastard, I hope you don't ever end up being refused an operation to save your life just because you can't afford it," I told him before buying a bottle of Tizer.

Suitably refreshed and with the bottle of fizzy drink in my hand we put our thumbs to work again. Once more hundreds of vehicles passed us before a van driver going to Swindon was kind enough to stop but by the time we were dropped off just outside the town centre it was beginning to get dark. In Swindon that night was a demonstration by the Campaign for Nuclear Disarmament and we spent some time listening to speeches and reading the literature given to us.

"I certainly agree with what they are saying," I said to Smiler.

Amazingly he concurred with me.

"One nuclear war and you can whistle goodbye to the human race," he said.

Smiler suggested we get a bus to where his Mum lived and said I had better stay the night and make my way up to London the next day.

Reluctantly I agreed and I spent an uncomfortable night on hard wooden floorboards in Smiler's front room. In the morning, after being given a cup of tea and some cornflakes to eat for my breakfast, I decided I had done enough hitch hiking for one lifetime so I got the bus to Swindon Train Station and a train back to London. Arriving home I realised that by economising on not taking the train from Plymouth I had lost a whole day of my leave, I had got sunburn on my face and the skin on my nose was peeling, I had torn my trousers and scuffed my shoes getting in and out of vans and lorries and I had oil and clay from the seats and backs of the vehicles I had travelled in stuck to my clothes. "I'll take the train next time," I promised myself.

Whilst on leave in Finsbury Park I decided to talk to someone about my long hours of work onboard ship. The Transport and General Workers Union were prominent in the campaign to reduce the working week to forty hours and I found out that they had offices in Green Lanes near Manor House, walking distance from where I lived. I visited the building and asked to see someone about working hours and I was ushered into a room where a small glum looking man who I deduced was suffering from stomach ulcers asked me to sit down. I explained that the hours I was obliged to work came to a seven day seventy hour week and although where I worked nobody was in a union I was keen to join one.

"Do those hours include overtime?" he asked.

I told him that there was no overtime where I worked, these were the normal hours and this news suddenly perked him up.

"This is a case of real exploitation!" he cried out, like a man ready to go into battle on my behalf.

"I'm in the Royal Navy," I explained.

He looked a little perplexed and scratched his head before asking me to wait why he checked something out with a colleague. He re-entered the room ten minutes later with a glass of milk in his hand that he was taking sips from so I guessed that my assumption that he was suffering from stomach ulcers was correct, indeed his expression had changed back to one of a person suffering from this affliction as he said:

"Trade Unions are not allowed to recruit in the Armed Forces, I'm sorry there's nothing I can do for you." I was beginning to think that I had no one on my side.

Whilst on leave I was introduced to Folk Music and was taken to a pub near Mount Pleasant Post Office where various acts performed in a hall at the back. I was delighted to listen to Peggy Seeger singing there and when she sang a song by her brother Pete I was charmed. *"Where have all the flowers gone"* was a song that summed up the futility of war, in particular for me, the war in Vietnam. I loved the fact that Peggy taught us the chorus and encouraged the entire audience to join in the singing, which we did. I was hooked on folk music after this and spent as many evenings as I could visiting venues where folk music was performed and singing along with the songs.

**

When I returned to the ship I was still singing *"Where have all the flowers gone"* to myself as I went down to the mess to have a cup of tea where I imparted my hitch hiking adventure to some others who had thumbed lifts home. It was during this conversation that the secret of how to hitch hike successfully was revealed. I knew that we were not allowed to hitch hike in uniform but the trick I was told was to carry a Navy cap with the ship's cap tally on display tied to the outside of your bag so that it could be seen by motorists who would then know that you were an upright member of the Queen's Navy and safe to give a lift to. When I found this information out I went searching for Smiler! The lesson I learnt from this was not to embark on anything new or risky until I had done some research into the matter. If only I had applied this logic to joining the Navy would I have joined? No I wouldn't, I would have first investigated if I got sea sick on ships and I would have asked how long I could have had let my hair grow and importantly, could I leave if I didn't like it! Hindsight is a wonderful thing I thought to myself.

We had a week before we had to go to sea again and after a couple of days in Devonport Dockyard I couldn't believe my eyes as I was standing on deck getting some fresh air when Sparky came walking up the gangway carrying his kit bag on his shoulder.

I shook his hand and welcomed him onboard and then took him to see the Master at Arms, I couldn't believe he had been drafted to the same ship as me.

After he had reported onboard, Sparky and I went down to the mess where he told me his story. After leaving Ganges Sparky said he had been sent to HMS Collingwood where he had become an electrical artificer and just a few days ago he had received his draft chit sending him to Hecate. Sparky told me that he had made a number of requests to leave the Navy but all had been rejected, he was very unhappy as he wanted to emigrate but he wasn't able to. He told me he had a plan he was working on to get out. Once settled in and shown around the ship Sparky was told he was free until 08.00 the next morning and as I was off too we decided to go ashore that evening and have a drink and catch up on gossip.

We put our civvies on and made our way to a pub I knew in Plymouth which was a nice venue as it was never too crowded and it had a juke box with good songs. As we sat in the pub a customer who was dressed in flowery clothes and clearly wasn't a member of the Navy put on the Lee Dorsey song, *"Holy Cow"* and then began to sing the words loudly in a very demonstrative and altogether camp fashion, waving his arms and feigning crying at the appropriate places. There were about a dozen people in the pub, mainly Royal Navy and we all stopped talking when he started singing. I have to say that one thing about members of the Royal Navy that never ceased to surprise me was their lack of inhibitions in public places and very soon they all joined in singing *"Holy Cow"*. Seeing that he had our full attention the man bemoaned his situation to us all:

"My eiderdown has sailed off in the Ark Royal," he cried.

He then introduced himself to us all as Larry and everyone in the pub listened to him as he explained what he meant about his eiderdown sailing. His boy friend who had apparently kept him warm at night, just like an eiderdown, was a sailor onboard the aircraft carrier HMS Ark Royal. I had noticed the Ark Royal leaving the harbour the day before and was told it was off for a long cruise.

"He's away for a year so I'm on the lookout for a new bed cover to keep me warm at night," declared Larry.

I hadn't really thought about people having different sexuality until then but the more I thought about it I was aware of a number of sailors on the ship who I assumed were more than just good friends.

Although they tried not to bring this fact to the attention of others. I thought it was a shame that people had to hide their feelings for each other but I was told that being homosexual was against the Law in the United Kingdom.

CHAPTER TWENTY TWO

A FASCIST DICTATOR

I sat in the dining mess with Ginge and Sparky the next evening and listened to the shipping forecast. We were to sail in the morning and I felt for Sparky as this would be his first time at sea.

"Here is the shipping forecast for sea area Plymouth, wind southerly, six to gale eight, veering northwest five or six later, moderate or rough, rain, visibility good, occasionally poor," reported the BBC man on the radio.

"We are in for a bit of roughers," warned Ginge.

"Go and see the Doc in the morning before we sail and ask him for some sea sickness pills," I advised Sparky.

I could see Sparky turning pale at the thought of being sea sick and I didn't have the heart to tell him that the pills wouldn't work anyway. As it happened, next morning, not long after we had set sail for the open sea again I joined Sparky for a half hour session of calling for Hughie in the heads.

"Those bloody sea sickness pills didn't work" Sparky complained to me as he gargled cold water to clean his mouth out before setting off to his workplace.

Back in the Mess I decided to keep an eye on Legs. The bunk the other side of the partition from me was where he slept and at night I heard him crying into his pillow

. One morning as I was getting dressed I saw that on the inside door of his locker Legs had a big sign that simply said: "ROMFT."

I couldn't resist asking him what this meant.

"Roll on My Fucking Time!" he explained before confiding to me the reason for his recent state of unhappiness.

"My wife had a baby when I was on Leave in Plymouth, a little girl and it just breaks my heart that I have to be at sea on this bloody ship rather than being at home with her."

"ROMFT!" I agreed.

When I had been on Summer Leave I knew that we were to spend the next three months or so continuing our survey of the Spanish coast so I had stocked up on books in London to bring back to the ship with me. I had brought back *"The Ragged Trousered Philanthropists"* by Robert Tressell and my copy of George Orwell's *"Homage to Catalonia"* to read again and as I sat on the upper deck in the sun, reading my Orwell the realisation dawned on me that Spain, the first foreign country I had visited, still had the Fascist regime that George Orwell had fought against in the thirties. How was it, I thought, that Hitler and Mussolini had been defeated but their ally, Franco was still in power over twenty years after the end of the Second World War?

**

A peculiar but amusing interlude to our daily routine then took place onboard ship when it was discovered that one of the seamen in my Mess had contracted pubic lice, or as they are more commonly known, crabs, whilst on Leave. In order to stop an infestation the ship's doctor arranged for a huge tub of DDT powder to be placed in the Mess and one by one we were made to strip off naked and jump into the powder. We had to stay unclothed for thirty minutes while the DDT did its work so it was decided that tea would be made while we all sat and waited for the time to pass before we could get dressed. The sight of sixty naked sailors covered in white dust sitting around drinking tea whilst rubbing DDT powder into their pubic hair was a strange one indeed and I wish I had remembered to bring my camera with me, I could have sold the pictures to all sorts of magazines I am sure.

Anyway, after several weeks of more sailing up and down the coast we docked in a different place this time, in El Ferrol which like Vigo was also a city in the Province of La Coruña in Galicia in north western Spain.

It was only about thirty miles north of Vigo and it was a Spanish naval town with shipbuilding yards. El Ferrol was also the birthplace of Spain's Dictator, General Francisco Franco and was officially known as El Ferrol del Caudillo. Ironically, it was also the birthplace of the founder of the Spanish Socialist Workers' Party, Pablo Iglesias.

My first run ashore in El Ferrol consisted of five of us, Myself, Pat, whose birthday it was, Geordie, Sparky and Legs, who we had decided to try and cheer up. In the Mess we were putting on our best uniforms and generally getting ourselves ready to go ashore when Pat burst into a little ditty that I was to hear hundreds of times being sung by sailors preparing to leave ship for a run ashore:

"Oh I don't give a fuck for the Killick of the Mess or the Killick of the working Party, I'm off ashore at half past four and Jack's my fucking hearty."

I knew that a Leading Hand was referred to as the Killick but I'd not heard this song before.

It was Sparky's first trip abroad and as we walked down the gangway he told me he was so excited he had goose pimples. Geordie had been to El Ferrol before and he suggested a nice bar he knew that specialised in a drink called Cuba Libra which is made up of Bacardi rum, Coca Cola and lime juice. There were five of us so to avoid having to keep going back to the bar for refills Geordie ordered five bottles of Bacardi, five limes and a crate of Coca Cola.

My eyes almost popped at the sight of so much drink so I decided to take it easy. The bar was elevated over a very pleasant looking street that was lined with orange trees and the bar's large doors had been removed so that we had a nice view as a gentle warm breeze blew onto us.

On a television set perched on a shelf in the bar an episode of Bonanza dubbed into Spanish was playing so as we drank our exotic drinks, we tried to make out what Hoss Cartwright was saying to Little Joe and we chatted the day away and got drunk.

Sparky and I drank a lot more Coke than rum but the others made up for that. Several hours later when we had finished our drink and had partaken in some Tapas snacks from the bar we thought we would go for a walk around the town.

Unfortunately for Pat, every time he stood up his legs would give way and he crashed to the ground. We decided to order pots of black coffee to sober us up, or at least Pat as the rest of us could actually stand up. After a long time of trying to get Pat into an upright position that he could maintain, to no avail, we decided the only option left was to carry Pat back to the ship.

We received instructions from Geordie.

"Two of you will take his legs and the other two can have an arm each, altogether now, on the order two six lift him - TWO SIX - LIFT!" and we had Pat up in the air and ready to carry off in no time. Pat was a very likeable and funny man and as we held onto his limbs and started to carry him off he started laughing and continued to laugh all the way back to the ship. As we carried Pat along the streets his white front lifted up to reveal a large tattoo of Popeye the Sailor Man on his belly, it was the best tattoo I'd ever seen and when he realised we had all noticed it he asked us to lay him down on a bench. We did what he asked and he said:

"Watch this."

As Pat breathed in Popeye's legs were sucked into his belly button. When he breathed out Popeye appeared again in full. This was very amusing and as Popeye disappeared and appeared a few times a small crowd of locals had gathered. Some were giggling as this clearly amused them as it did us but other more conservative individuals looked disdainfully at this group of drunken British sailors who they clearly thought were disgracing their uniform and their country. What they could not have comprehended was the hardships and deprivations these sailors had suffered during weeks at sea and that letting their hair down by getting drunk was a release for their pent up frustrations.

It became heavy going carrying Pat but we eventually made it back to the ship and amazingly as we carried him noisily over the gangway we somehow escaped being spotted by the Master at Arms so none of us were taken down to the cells and put on a charge of drunken behaviour.

On our next run ashore it was the turn of Geordie to get so legless that we had to carry him back to the ship. This time we were seen by the Master at Arms and Geordie was taken to the cells and also put on a charge of drunken behaviour.

It happened that during that particular night when Geordie was snoring away in the cells and dreaming of Newcastle winning the F.A. Cup and also of what punishment he would get for being drunk, a very common occurrence onboard HMS Hecate took place. One of the ship's Officers came into the mess when we were all asleep and stood next to my bunk, I awoke and opened my eyes and through the darkness I could see that he was staring at me. This particular individual would often wander around the ship during the night going into various messes and he would just stand there and stare at people. Waking up in the darkened mess to see him standing next to you always made you jump. The main reason for this creepy behaviour was that he was drunk. He was drunk most nights as Officers had no restrictions on their alcohol intake. His favourite tipple was pink gin which he drunk a lot of. The other odd thing about this Officer was that he always had a violin with him when he went wandering around the ship.

The attitude to the drinking too much alcohol was just another example of the class system at work. When an Officer got drunk, which some frequently did, they were deemed to be "tired and emotional" and would be helped back to their cabins. If an ordinary sailor from the lower decks drunk too much he was deemed to be "drunk and disorderly" and would be thrown into the cells. The class system was indeed alive and well in the Royal Navy.

**

On future runs ashore in El Ferrol, Sparky and I decided against drunken nights out and instead we would wander the town looking to see what the place was really like, this time armed with a Spanish phrasebook and dictionary. We stopped off at cafés and bars for an occasional drink but never more than a few glasses of wine in an evening. We noticed that there was a lot of political graffiti on the walls, Communist Party hammer and sickles were stencilled everywhere and the flags of the anarchists and socialists painted here and there too.

We also noticed that leaflets and posters issued by an organisation named the Union of Democratic Forces which called for peaceful action to end the Franco dictatorship appeared regularly on walls, trees and billboards but were quickly removed.

We met some locals one day in a café and luckily one of them could speak good English which enabled us to have a good chat. In the conversation I told him of my socialist views and he in turn told us very quietly that he was a communist. He informed us that under Franco workers rights were non-existent and strikes were illegal. Political parties including the Communist Party were banned and anyone calling for action to end the dictatorship would be in trouble, possibly imprisoned. The police were armed and kept an intrusive presence on the streets and political opposition was kept underground. My own observations were that under the Franco regime Spain was a deeply conservative country run by a Fascist state and El Ferrol was an enigma that summed up the contradictions of Spanish political and social life. In El Ferrol you would never see a young woman alone, she would always have a chaperone with her, yet in the streets around the docks, even though it was against the law, prostitutes freely walked and plied their trade and were welcome in all the bars.

Respectable looking Spanish men in business suits would be approached as they slowly walked along the streets by the docks, clearly they were there seeking sex and you could see them entering one of the many seedy looking hotels together. In the bars Spanish sailors, dockyard workers and even armed policemen would be led upstairs to part with a handful of money in exchange for the services offered.

My observations were that most sailors ashore from HMS Hecate seemed more interested in getting as drunk as possible in order to blot out the knowledge that for the foreseeable future they would be at sea with no further opportunity to have a good drink and get legless; and being drunk they were of course not capable of anything else anyway.

One evening I went ashore in El Ferrol with Sparky and Ginge. After a walk around the streets and a couple of drinks we decided to round off our run ashore with a meal in a restaurant. We ordered the classic dish that British sailors ashore eat whenever they get a chance to, steak, egg and chips

All of our eggs were double yoked which seemed to be common in Spain.

We were discussing this gastronomic quandary when we heard a commotion going on outside in the street. Looking out of the window two sailors from our ship ran past with their uniforms in disarray so we went outside to see what was going on. Looking in the direction of where they had come from we could see Spanish police and when they saw us they took out their pistols and fired several shots above our heads. In a confrontational situation the human body will go into one of two modes: fight or flight.

Without too much thought the three of us decided flight was the better option so we ran down a side street as fast as we could and we managed to get back to our ship and safety.

I'm not exactly sure what the sailors from our ship had done to draw such an angry response from the Spanish police but later that night they were identified, probably to do with their uniforms looking worse for wear, as having been involved in a fight with some local people with a bit of criminal damage thrown in for good measure. The end result was that a couple of days later the ships' company was called up on to the flight deck in our best uniforms while officials from the British Consulate and some local Spanish Government representatives stood next to the Captain who read out the charges against the two sailors who had been apprehended. As well as a number of Royal Naval punishments being dished out to them they were also officially deported from Spanish soil, so there would be no more runs ashore for them in El Ferrol and Vigo.

Back at sea I continued my reading and I got stuck into George Orwell's "Homage to Catalonia" [2]. I was particularly moved by Chapter Seven where Orwell shares his memories of the days he spent on the war front and its influence on his political ideas. When he described his time in Aragon where in theory it was perfect equality and even in practice it was not far from it, Orwell says that there was a sense in which it would be true to say that one was experiencing a foretaste of socialism, by which he meant that the prevailing mental atmosphere was that of socialism. Many of the normal motives of civilised life – snobbishness, money grabbing, fear of the boss, etc. had simply ceased to exist. The ordinary class divisions of society had disappeared to an extent that is almost unthinkable in the money tainted air of England. I said to myself:

"Wouldn't it be wonderful to have a society built on equality?"

CHAPTER TWENTY THREE

WHY PEOPLE WHO WORK STAY POOR

Another book I read again whilst we were at sea was *"The Ragged Trousered Philanthropists"* [3] a story which advocates a socialist society in which work is performed to satisfy the needs of all rather than to generate profits for a few.

The book is set in a seaside town on the south coast of England where a group of painters and decorators are about to have dinner. The men are renovating a big, ramshackle Victorian house called the Cave and the socialist in this group of workers, Frank Owen, demonstrates for his workmates the "Great Money Trick."

In the book, as the workers have a break and unpack their cheese sandwiches Frank Owen organises a mock-up of capitalism with them, using slices of bread as raw materials and knives as machinery. Owen 'employs' his workmates cutting up the bread to illustrate that the employer generates personal wealth whilst the workers remain no better off than when they began. I sat three of my mess-mates, Ginge, Geoff and Robbo at a table with me and I asked anyone interested to observe what was going on. I pretended to be the socialist in the book, Frank Owen, and paraphrasing the story I said to them:

"Money is the cause of poverty because it is the device by which those who are too lazy to work are enabled to rob the workers of the fruits of their labour and I will prove it."

I had taken several slices of bread left over from tea and three knives from the galley and I told my three seated mess-mates:

"These pieces of bread represent the raw materials which exist naturally in and on the earth for the use of mankind; they were not made by any human being, but were created for the benefit and sustenance of all, the same as were the air and the light of the sun."

I continued:

"I am a capitalist; or rather I represent the landlord and capitalist class. That is to say, all these raw materials belong to me. It does not matter for our present argument how I obtained possession of them, the only thing that matters now is the admitted fact that all the raw materials which are necessary for the production of the necessaries of life are now the property of the landlord and capitalist class. I am that class; all these raw materials belong to me."

"Now you three represent the working class. You have nothing, and, for my part, although I have these raw materials, they are of no use to me. What I need is the things that can be made out of these raw materials by work; but first I must explain that I possess something else beside the raw materials. These three knives represent all the machinery of production; the factories, tools, railways, and so forth, without which the necessaries of life cannot be produced in abundance. And these three coins" - taking three pennies from my pocket - "represent my money, capital."

I then proceeded to cut up one of the slices of bread into little square blocks and I told the working class that these represent the things which are produced by labour, aided by machinery, from the raw materials.

"We will suppose that three of these blocks represent a week's work. We will suppose that a week's work is worth one pound," I said to the working class, and then went on:

"You say that you are all in need of employment and as I am the kind hearted capitalist class I am going to invest all my money in various industries, so as to give you plenty of work. I shall pay each of you one pound per week, and a week's work from you will mean you must each produce three of these square blocks for me.

For doing this work you will each receive your wages; and that money I pay you will be your own, to do as you like with and the things you produce will of course be mine to do as I like with. You will each take one of these machines and as soon as you have done a week's work, you shall have your money."

My three mess-mates, the working classes, set to work, and the capitalist class, me, sat down and watched them. As soon as they had finished, they passed the nine little blocks to me and I put them by my side and paid the workers their week's wages, one pound each. I then told them that:

"These blocks represent the necessaries of life. You can't live without some of these things, but as they belong to me, you will have to buy them from me: and my price for these blocks is one pound each."

I explained that as the working classes were in need of the necessaries of life and as they could not eat, drink or wear the useless money, they were compelled to agree to the capitalist's terms. They would each have to buy back, and over the next week consume, one-third of the produce of their labour. As the capitalist class I was able to devour two of the square blocks, and so the net result of the week's work was that me, the kind capitalist had consumed two pounds worth of things produced by the labour of others, and reckoning the squares at their market value of one pound each, I had more than doubled my capital, for I still possessed the three pounds in money and in addition four pounds worth of goods. As for the working classes, having each consumed the pound's worth of necessaries they had bought with their wages, they were again in precisely the same condition as when they had started work - they had nothing. I repeated the process several times; for each week's work the producers were paid their wages. They kept on working and spending all their earnings. As the kind-hearted capitalist I consumed twice as much as any one of them and I demonstrated to my mess-mates that my pool of wealth continually increased. In a little while, reckoning the little squares at their market value of one pound each, I was worth about one hundred pounds, and the working classes were still in the same condition as when they began, and were still tearing into their work as if their lives depended on it.

"Well, what do you think of that?" I said to my assembled congregation of hopefully embryonic socialists.

"What you said is true enough" said Ginge "but anyone can become a capitalist if they want."

As I was about to argue this point with him I noticed that Robbo was spreading jam on my squares of bread and eating them.

"You can't do that" I protested.

"You've stolen the property of the capitalist class and what's more you have contaminated the machinery of production, they're covered in strawberry jam. I was going to take them abroad to get cheaper labour to do your work but now they're ruined." The crowd I had gathered round laughed and broke up and then started getting out their packs of cards. Also, Taffy had come in and set up a game of Uckers so that was my lesson on socialism for the day abruptly finished. I think I did Robert Tressell's book some justice and it passed an hour at sea and Sparky even asked me if he could borrow the book to read!

CHAPTER TWENTY FOUR

AMERICAN HASH

We had finished our Spanish adventure and HMS Hecate was back in Devonport Dockyard for a short break while we re-stocked our provisions and the sailors who had wives and families in Plymouth were allowed to spend some time at home with them.

The bad news for me was that after a few days in Plymouth the ship was to return to the Atlantic where we were to take part in manouvers with some of our NATO partners. I never understood why these games always took place midway between the USA and the UK, in other words a round trip of three thousand miles in nothing less than choppy waters which of course meant lots of bouts of sea sickness. One day however the sea was unusually still and calm and I had been sent to the upper deck to throw the gash overboard. I stopped to look at the sea and I worked out that the nearest land must be over a thousand miles away but everywhere I looked I could see bits of rubbish. There were bottles and tins and plastic bags and pieces of broken wooded boxes everywhere. Having just tipped the ships gash into the sea I had added my contribution to polluting the environment and I thought that there must be a better way of dealing with rubbish from ships and hoped that someone was working on that project.

A few days into the NATO exercises the true value of our ship being part of the manouvers became apparent when we were told that an American sailor on one of their frigates had suffered a heart attack. As his ship didn't have a Doctor onboard and ours did he would be flown onboard to be looked after by us as we did have a Doctor. This incident was for real; it was not part of the games so our helicopter flew off to pick the American up. About an hour later the ship's Doctor appeared in the galley and spoke to me.

"The sick Yank's not too bad," he said.

"I think he would like something to eat, what's on the menu?"

It was Monday and on Monday we invariably had the same menu.

"Braised Heart or American Hash," I answered warily.

The Doc gave me a withering look so after a few moments of thought I suggested:

"Maybe I could knock him up an omelette?"

We returned to Plymouth where our American patient was transferred to hospital and the news I heard was that several weeks later he had recovered sufficiently enough to be flown back home.

Our next port of call would be Birkenhead and then we were off on a survey mission to North America and Bermuda but before that the delights of Plymouth awaited us.

In Plymouth we had discovered Union Street and in particular the Majestic Ballroom known to all as the Magic Stick. The Ballroom was a dance hall with a live band and a female vocalist who would belt out the latest tunes for people to dance to or just stand around listening. The ballroom was always hot and sweaty but it had great character and was always a good venue to spend the evening.

I had managed so far to get through my time in the Royal Navy without ever having a tattoo. This was despite the fact that all ports in the UK had their fair share of tattoo parlours but the trick was not to get so drunk that you were dragged into one as you would wake up the next morning with an anchor on your thigh or a heart on your arm with some girls name in it. I had been pulled into a couple of these establishments but luckily sobered up in time before the tattooist got to work. Any trip to Union Street had to take this into consideration so my alcohol intake was always kept in check when I was there, just in case.

Union Street though had a lot more going for it than a dance hall and tattoo parlours and it was here that Sparky and I found the John Collier clothes shop where we put down thirty bob as our deposit for our first made to measure suits. Mine was a light grey woollen mohair suit and it would cost six pounds and ten shillings, I was to pay the rest when I was back in Plymouth sometime in late December when we returned for Christmas Leave.

It was now October 1966 and I had been in the Navy for almost two years. We were told that we were to sail to Liverpool for a few days and were to dock in the Birkenhead shipyard to make some minor repairs before setting off to North America. The weather report the day we left Plymouth was not good. Although I was curious to know what the places I was to visit were going to be like I was not looking forward to a rough journey up to Liverpool even if it would be a short voyage. I took some sea sickness pills and prepared for the worse. My fears were well founded as the ship pitched and rolled and we were tossed about violently on our journey around the Lizard and up the Welsh coast. Surprisingly, when we arrived in the Irish Sea the storm abated and the sea became calm and almost smooth. I had gone onto the upper deck to get some fresh air as I was feeling queasy and to my amazement, between our ship and the coast of the Isle of Man I saw what looked to me like a sharks fin slicing its way through the water. The ships Decca Engineer was standing near me so I asked for his opinion.

"That looks like a Basking Shark to me, it's harmless," he said.

The shark looked large and mean to me and I thought that I would make a point of not swimming in this particular sea in the future in case I bumped into one.

Liverpool was a great run ashore. One of the ships Stokers, a young Asian lad who they nicknamed Taj told me that his Mum and Dad came from India and now lived in an area called Toxteth. He invited me to stay at his family home while the ship was in Birkenhead Docks saying we could get a bus and train back to the Dockyard in the morning. I stayed at his parents flat for a couple of nights and was treated to some pretty good curries that they made. I also made a note of the recipes they used and was introduced to the names of spices I had never heard of before but which I decided I would buy if they were cheap enough in order to try a proper curry out on a few of my mates onboard ship.

The ships stores contained only the ubiquitous curry powder but I now had a list of spices that I went off in search for: Chilli; Ginger; Garlic; Jeera; Garam Masala; Dhanya; Haldi and Hing. I found them all in a shop in Toxteth so I bought a small quantity of each and prepared a pot of fish curry for half a dozen mates onboard ship including Taj who said that it was almost as good as his Mum's!

Obviously, Liverpool was the home of the Beatles so we visited the Cavern and a number of other clubs where local pop groups were playing and hoping that they could also be as successful as their idols. Liverpool was a vibrant musical city and one day, standing on the quarter deck of HMS Hecate in the dockyard at Birkenhead reflecting on this together with Sparky we started singing the latest Beatles hit, *"Yellow Submarine."*

I pointed out to him that lots of Royal Navy ships had been built in the Yarrows Ship Yards in Scotstoun, Glasgow and HMS Hecate was one of them. Therefore we lived in a Yarrow Ship not a yellow one. At this point Sparky thought it would be quite jolly to change the words of the song to fit in with our own current position in Her Majesty's Navy. Although we didn't live in a submarine but a survey ship he allowed himself plenty of poetic licence and changed the lyrics. So there we were, standing on the dockside in Birkenhead singing about living in a Yarrow submarine.

Silly really but it was lots of fun at the time even though we did get some strange looks from a dockyard matey who was walking by.

CHAPTER TWENTY FIVE

ABERFAN

As I knew we were going to be at sea for a long time I made sure that I had all the books and papers for my correspondence courses with me.

Also one of the Officers onboard had started a French Conversation class which I was looking forward to, I just hoped that the weather was good enough for me to be able to study and read over the coming weeks.

Leaving Liverpool was smooth enough as a Pilot boat led us out of the River Mersey and we set off to the Atlantic Ocean around the north of Ireland. Our job was to survey a straight line across the Atlantic and in particular to measure the depth of the Atlantic Ridge. We would then go on to Newfoundland and survey the coast of Canada and the United States before making our way to Bermuda where it was planned to spend a month. I went up onto the upper deck a couple of hours after we had left the coast of Ireland behind us to throw some bits of food to the sea gulls or shite hawks as they were called by the sailors of the Royal Navy.

Sea Gulls would always follow us a long way out to sea, diving in and out of our wake to find any bits of food that had been discarded.

What I didn't anticipate though was the ship being joined by other creatures.

Swimming alongside the ship and diving across the bow as if playing a game with us were a dozen dolphins that stayed with us for several days until the weather turned for the worse. Seeing the dolphins at play was a truly wonderful sight but our good mood was soon to disappear.

We were finishing dinner on 21st October 1966 when Taffy burst into the dining mess in tears. He had just heard news of a disaster that had struck the Welsh village of Aberfan near Merthyr Tydfil. He said that a slag heap from the colliery had collapsed and killed 116 children and 28 adults. We later heard that it was caused by a build-up of water in the accumulated rock and shale, which started to slide downhill as slurry. The slide destroyed a farm and twenty houses along Moy Road before hitting into the northern side of the Pantglas Junior School and part of the separate Senior School demolishing most of the structures and filling the classrooms with thick mud and rubble up to 33 feet deep. The pupils of Pantglas Junior School had arrived only minutes earlier for the last day before the half term holiday. They had just left the assembly hall, where they had been singing "All Things Bright and Beautiful" when a great noise was heard outside. They hurried to their classrooms where minutes later they died. Taffy organised a collection to send to the relief fund and I don't think anyone gave less than a week's wages to the collection.

We continued our journey across the Atlantic in a sombre mood and the weather changed. We had been told that it would take us eight days to get to a place in Newfoundland, Canada where we were to take on fresh water. In fact due to the horrendous weather, it took sixteen days and nearly every one of those days we were pitching into a force eight gale that was blowing straight at us.

It became too difficult and dangerous to cook food in the galley during this storm apart from making soup in the large cooking coppers. As well as soup we survived by making endless sandwiches which were mainly corned beef, spam, cheese or fish paste. As well as soup and sandwiches being the only food we could prepare in the galley it was also the only food most people could keep down.

The sea conditions were even worse than those I had experienced in the Bay of Biscay and at night it was sometimes impossible for people to get into and stay in their bunks and those that could get into a bunk had to strap themselves in. Some strapped themselves to the bulkheads and slept standing up.

When we arrived in the waters off Newfoundland there was a sudden and dramatic transformation as a sea fog came down and the water became almost like a mill pond. If we had been a ship that relied on sails we would have been becalmed, there was not an ounce of wind to be found anywhere.

That night I went up onto the upper deck to have a look around at the calm seas but as I strained my eyes I could see nothing other than an impenetrable sea mist that was as severe as any London fog and it occurred to me if another ship or a boat came along we would not be able to see it and it could collide with us. Up on the Bridge there were more seaman than usual with binoculars trying to make out any shapes in the sea around us and I guessed they had that idea too. The ship had reduced speed and we were going along at no more than one or two knots when through the eerie stillness I heard the beautiful and magical sound of whales singing to each other.

The next morning I awoke early as I felt the ship bump into something so I quickly went up onto the upper deck to see what was going on. The fog had cleared completely and it was a clear bright and not too chilly day with blue skies overhead. The bump I had heard were the ship's fenders touching against the side of the jetty and we were now tying up on the Newfoundland shore. I had been told that we were to stop somewhere for water but I had not realised that it would be somewhere so remote. Looking at the jetty I could see a small hut with a tap next to it where a hose had already been connected to take water onboard. Standing next to the tap was a man in a Davy Crockett hat and a rifle in his hand and behind him was nothing but forest stretching as far as the eye could see. At the entrance to the forest was a handwritten sign that simply said: "Beware of the Grizzly Bears!" so when the tannoy announced that anyone not on duty could go ashore to stretch their legs and take photographs I thought about staying onboard just in case the bears were going to take an interest in me.

However, after cleaning up the galley after dinner I couldn't resist the temptation to put my feet on the soil of yet another country and thus add Newfoundland, Canada to the list of places I had visited.

It was autumn and the colours of the leaves on the trees were nothing short of magnificent.

A group of us strolled up and down the jetty and ventured a little way into the forest and I spoke to Davy Crockett and asked him how he got to work.

"They just drop me off by boat with a few weeks supply of provisions and then I look after the water supply for passing ships and boats," he told me. What a job!

When we sailed away it was late into the afternoon and everyone on the ship tried to get as high a viewing position as possible on the upper deck to witness an array of colours in a forest that must have stretched for a thousand miles. If an artist painted this landscape as we saw it they would be accused of exaggeration, you had to see it to believe it. One of the ships Officers was a nature buff and he had a book about trees that he flicked through to try and identify the trees we could see as we slowly hugged the Newfoundland coast heading south. Pointing away like a mad thing he said:

"Look, those are russet coloured oaks and there's some golden ginkgo and that purple is sumac and over there that crimson colour must be dogwood and those rich scarlet leaves just there are maples, the bright yellow must be hickory and look at that yellow birch!"

He went on ecstatically like this for over an hour. I stood next to Tiddy Oggy who was as taken in with the autumnal sights as I was as he took photographs and kept repeating the phrase:

"I've never seen anything so beautiful in my life."

The words to the song *"All things Bright and Beautiful"* came to mind and immediately it reminded me of the poor children of Aberfan and I felt sad that they would never be able to witness beautiful things again.

**

Onboard ship our mission now was to survey the sea off the east coast of Canada and then the USA. After a couple days of surveying the Canadian waters we stopped off for a proper run ashore in a place called Halifax in Nova Scotia.

Arriving into the harbour at Halifax there was no space available for us to berth alongside on a dock so our berth was up against a Destroyer belonging to the Royal Canadian Navy which I soon Christened HMCS Maple Syrup.

The Canadian sailors were very hospitable and they would invite us onboard to play cards and generally chat to them but my favourite pass time was when the Canadian Navy chef made me pancakes, or flap jacks as they called them, covered in maple syrup. This delicious syrup was unknown back in the UK but here it was a natural and bountiful product and I couldn't get enough of it. When I went ashore I purchased a couple of jars in a shop to take home with me. Halifax though was a cold place to be at that time of the year and we couldn't find too much to do apart from going to the cinema. I was intrigued that in the cinemas half of the seats were reserved for non-smokers. They wouldn't get away with that in the UK I thought to myself but as I was now, for the moment at least, a non-smoker I sat in the side of the cinema which was smoke free and was delighted to be able to see the screen without thick smoke swirling around in front of me. The pubs were called Taverns but they were no go areas for me as no one under the age of twenty was allowed in them and ID was checked at the door.

One good run ashore I had was when we were invited to play a local team at football, or soccer as they called it as part of the good will aspect of our trip and were told that the ground was about two miles from the dock yard so we decided to walk there. It was an interesting walk as most of the houses were constructed of wood rather than bricks; they were also completely detached and surrounded by gardens which were so unlike the terraced houses I was used to back in the UK.

Arriving at the sports ground I was surprised to see the size of the pitch. Whereas a good size football pitch in the UK is about 110 by 75 yards this pitch appeared half as long again and a good bit wider and I was told it was not designed as a soccer pitch. My two favourite positions on the football field were either in goal, where I modelled myself on Jack Kelsey or on the wing where I imagined I was Joe Haverty who had played for Ireland and Arsenal and was known for his tricky wing play and expert crosses and was nicknamed Little Joe after the character in Bonanza.

In this game they put Legs in goal and I played on the wing where for ninety minutes I ran up and down this huge pitch until I literally dropped. The tackling by the Canadian team was pretty tough and at the end of the game we were all completely exhausted and nursing cuts and bruises but the important thing was that we won by a single goal headed in from my cross.

Walking back to the ship some local residents we passed gave us a wide berth as we must have looked a motley and potentially threatening crew with our mud caked and bloodied legs, arms, faces and sports kit.

I enjoyed being in Halifax and all of the people I met were friendly, even the bouncers at the taverns who wouldn't let me in did so with a smile but having been told that the temperatures in Bermuda were in the mid seventies Fahrenheit I was happy enough when we set sail. Once at sea the Supply Officer, my boss really, came to see me to inform me that I had been promoted. I was now a fully fledged Assistant Cook and my pay was increased to £4 per week!

The next day I was on duty in the galley and the radio was on and tuned to the BBC World Service. When the announcer said that they were now going to Highbury for the second half commentary of the Arsenal versus Everton game I stopped in my tracks. As the commentator set the scene with Everton kicking into the Clock End and Arsenal attacking the North Bank I was transported to Islington.

"Thank you, thank you, thank you BBC!" I shouted out as I pictured myself being at the match with all my mates, at that magical place, Highbury. North London was three thousand miles away but for me, at that moment in time, I was there behind the goal on the North Bank, cheering my beloved Arsenal to victory. The Highbury roar could be heard coming out of the radio and I closed my eyes and imagined that I was really one of the crowd as I chanted along:

"*Ars-e-nal! Ars-e-nal! Ars-e-nal!*" I sang, loud enough I thought for the players to hear me.

What the fuck's got into you?" enquired Petty Officer Tiddy Oggy coming into the galley.

CHAPTER TWENTY SIX

THE BERMUDA TRIANGLE

When I had last been home I knew that I would be visiting Bermuda later that year so I decided to go to the reference section of my local library in Manor Gardens, opposite the side entrance to the Royal Northern Hospital, to do some research.

I was pleasantly surprised to see the Arsenal centre half Terry Neill sitting in the library studying with a pile of text books next to him, not the normal image of how the press portrayed what footballers got up to in their spare time. Researching my subject, Bermuda, I found out that it was not one island but a group of low lying islands located in the Atlantic Ocean, on the edge of the Sargasso Sea. The islands were divided into nine parishes but there were two main areas of interest to me in Bermuda which were the City of Hamilton where we were to pay a good will visit and St George's where the ship would be based while the motor launches carried out a survey of the waters in and around Bermuda. As I read a couple of books about the islands what kept coming up were stories about the Sargasso Sea and other areas around Bermuda and the phenomenon called the "Bermuda Triangle" also known as the Devil's Triangle where ships and aircraft had disappeared under mysterious circumstances.

I read about this vast triangular area of ocean with imaginary points in Bermuda, Florida and Puerto Rico with tales of missing maritime vessels and of drifting crewless ships.

Some of the stories went back centuries and in 1909 someone called Crittenden Marriott wrote a novel which takes place in the Sargasso Sea called The Isle of Dead Ships. In 1923 the book was made into a film called "The Isle of Lost Ships." As I read on through my books more and more references, both fictional and factual about the strange nature of the seas around Bermuda appeared.

"Should I be scared?" I thought as I left the library with a tiny wave of my hand to acknowledge Terry Neill.

**

HMS Hecate was now heading down the east coast of America en route to Bermuda and the sea, although not exactly rough, was heavy and coming straight at us. This caused the ship's bow to plunge into waves and then be knocked upwards which on occasion caused the stern to be submerged under water. I found out about this the hard way. I was standing on the quarter deck aft of the ship as I had been feeling queasy due to this pitching movement. The quarter deck was a good place to be sick as more often than not the vomit did not get blown back into your face. As I stood there the ship's cat was showing an interest in me and started rubbing itself against my leg. He probably thought that my cries for Hughie were a part of a conversation I was having with him which might involve me giving him some food. I was luckily holding tightly onto the handrails when the ship violently decided to pitch forward. As the bow went down the quarter deck, with me and the cat it's only inhabitants at that moment, was lifted skyward but then as the ship's bow sprung up out of the water the quarter deck went under the sea taking me with it. I was completely submerged and as the quarter deck came up again I ran inside for safety, soaked to the skin, and went down to the mess to dry off. As the realisation came to me of how serious the incident was I said out loud:

"I could've bloody well drowned."

Ginge was watching me in amusement as he said:

"We would have had to shout out Mann overboard! Ha Ha Ha Ha!"

"Do you get it? MANN overboard!"

As I changed into dry clothes I suddenly remembered the cat and went in search of him but sadly he was never seen again and was presumed to now be a resident in Davy Jones's locker.

The next day we sighted Bermuda. The sea was quite choppy but the water was of a colour that I had never seen before, it was almost the same colour as the suit my parents had bought me for my interview with the Navy, turquoise blue. As we got closer to land I could see that the Islands were low and green with pretty pastel coloured bungalows spotted about here and there. We tied up against the dock at St George's and as soon as the gangway was lowered some local officials came onboard. They were dressed in smart suits but were wearing shorts instead of trousers and they also wore long socks and smartly polished shoes and panama hats. I was told that the type of shorts they were wearing were actually called Bermuda shorts and in days to come I would see lots of smartly dressed people, including policemen, walking about in this form of clothing.

On our first night in Bermuda the ships' company, apart from those on duty were invited to a reception at the Governor's Mansion, a large detached residency surrounded by fine gardens. We were led into a large hall within the building that consisted of a long table and some chairs. The Governor gave a short speech welcoming us to Bermuda and before he left us he told us to enjoy the hospitality that had been laid on for us. All around the room were crates of beer that we were told to help ourselves to and before long the most boisterous of the crew were standing on the table singing rude and bawdy Naval songs about Zulu Warriors and another one about going to Trinidad and drinking rum and coca cola and playing tombola. One song that did amuse me was sung to the tune of the Hornpipe ditty Jack's The Lad:

"Do your balls hang low; can you swing 'em to and fro?
Can you tie 'em in a knot; can you tie 'em in a bow?
Do you get a funny feeling when you bang them on the ceiling?
Oh you'll never make a sailor if your balls hang low."

Several hours after we started drinking, when all the free alcohol was consumed, most of us trudged back to the ship for some sleep whilst others went off in search of more drink and excitement.

Much of my leisure time in Bermuda though was spent doing things I had never done before. The air temperatures were about 75 degrees Fahrenheit and the sea was similarly warm.

I discovered little bays where the water was clear and would snorkel among fish that I had only seen in a tropical fish tank before. I was put off swimming too far out to sea though when I noticed a boat that was advertising to take tourists out shark fishing.

Although Bermuda is a British Overseas Territory most people there had an American accent and tourists from the USA were everywhere. This made the cost of goods; particularly for us alcohol, very expensive and it discouraged us from drinking in bars in most parts of the island. In St George's I had noticed a sweet and unfamiliar smell coming from the small gardens of the locals, the black Bermudans, which I discovered was cannabis that was smoked as a cheap alternative to alcohol to get people high. I have to say that I was given a joint to smoke but drugs of any sort, including cannabis never appealed to me and after a couple of puffs and a short coughing fit I handed the joint back to the person who gave it to me. As a bottle of beer in many bars cost 7s 6d I could understand why people with not too much money would go for smoking the local weed though. We soon found out that buying bottles of rum from a shop was much cheaper than drinking in bars so we used to take our rum and coke, our Cuba Libre, onto the beach to drink. One small bay that became a favourite with a group of us, Sparky, Ginge, Geordie, Legs and me was called by the locals Mango Tree Bay as it had real Mango trees growing on the beach. The group of us discussed mangoes and we all agreed that none of us had ever seen one before but we all knew the lyrics of the song made famous in the James Bond film Dr No. We recalled the scene where a bikini clad Ursula Andress climbs out of the sea examining the shells she has just collected whilst singing the lyrics of the song *"Underneath the Mango Tree"* where she is joined in the singing by Sean Connery. After a few Cuba Libras on the beach my small group of sailor friends collectively remembered the lyrics of the song and on the fine white sands of Mango Tree Bay, in the shade of the Mango Trees and much to the amusement of the local people; we collected some shells and acted out the scene from the film whilst singing the song in the style of Sean Connery.

Bermuda has nine parishes: Devonshire, Hamilton, Paget, Pembroke, St George's, Sandys, Smith's, Southampton and Warwick and has two municipalities: the City of Hamilton and the town of St George's. Something that all of us did on our time off was to hire a bicycle with a small motor on it called a moped which would get us cheaply around the nine parishes of the island. I easily rode from St George's at one end of Bermuda to Sandys at the other and back again one afternoon even though the speed limit on the island was 20 mph. To be honest, the mopeds had difficulty reaching that limit but it did not stop one or two sailors from the ship having horrific accidents on them. One unfortunate shipmate, who came off his bike on gravel, breaking bones and taking the skin off of his face, spent weeks in hospital recovering and had nasty scars, probably for the rest of his life. Our hired mopeds however did give us access to some wonderful places on Bermuda; in particular, Horseshoe Bay became a favourite for our gang of five. It was a long walk down to the beach which was made easier by using the moped. The beach was often almost empty of other people but for those who got there it was worth making the effort as it was a long stretch of pure white sand and it had huge waves pounding it. If you've never done it before, find a beach like Horseshoe Bay with ridiculously huge waves and just dive into them. We did this non-stop and each time I threw myself at a wave I was knocked back thirty or forty feet onto the beach. We just kept repeating the exercise until we were so exhausted we just dropped onto the sand with a twenty minute fit of the giggles. It was exhilarating and enormous fun and left me with an immense feeling of well-being. Lying on the beach with my senses gradually returning I began to notice though that the big toe on my right foot was aching. Looking down I saw the toenail flapping in the wind. It was joined to my toe by the smallest piece of skin and I assumed a wave must have got under the nail and just forced it away from my toe. I mentioned this to Sparky who, to my amazement, produced a small first aid box he had attached to the back of his moped and he took from it a plaster that he applied to the nail to fix it back to the toe.

"Best to let it come off naturally otherwise if you pulled it off now it might bleed," he said.

"Cheers Sparky," I said, very much taken with this act of kindness but as I looked at his hands as he applied the plaster I was shocked to see how red and raw they looked.

"What's up with your hands?" I asked.

Sparky looked shiftily around at the others before replying:

"I'll tell you later."

**

The USA had a big presence on Bermuda and the largest construction on the islands was the Kindley United States Air Force Base which was effectively a small town in which you had to take a bus to get around it. The base proved to be a cheap and very enjoyable place to relax and as members of the Royal Navy we were made honorary members of the various bars, shops and night clubs on the base. The place immediately reminded me of Fort Baxter that appears in the Phil Silvers show and I kept imagining that Sergeant Ernest G. Bilko would suddenly appear out of a hut shuffling a pack of cards in his hands and asking me if I wanted to play a game of poker.

One evening Sparky and I decided to take advantage of the invitation to see a band play at a night club at the air base. We took a bus for the short ride from the ship to Kindley and were met at the gate by some military police who gave us badges to wear that allowed us in. We then went to the USA version of a NAAFI shop, a PX store and bought ourselves some Hershey chocolate bars before being guided to the night club.

Going through the doors of the club a small group of American servicemen befriended us and took us to a cabaret style table. The seating was comfortable and everywhere you walked your feet sunk into deep pile carpets.

The only really odd thing I noticed about the place was when I visited the heads I discovered there were no doors on the cubicles. Just like the Annexe at Ganges I thought to myself. This did make me feel a little self conscious though when I visited the "John" as the Americans called it and had the eyes of dozens of American servicemen on me as I sat there.

Back at our cabaret style tables I saw that the band that was entertaining us from the stage was a sort of Drifters tribute act and as we listened to all the classics, *"Save the last dance for me"* and *"Under the Boardwalk,"* the drinks were flowing.

Our guests were very good to us and strange looking cocktails and cold beers appeared without being asked for. The cigarettes that most of the people on the base smoked were Camel but we were asked if we could bring some British cigarettes with us the next time as they were considered superior to the American brands available. I thought better of turning up with a box of Royal Navy blue liners though.

On the bus back to our ship Sparky spoke to me in almost a whisper about his plans to get out of the Navy. He again showed me his hands and I observed that they were as red and raw looking as they had been down on the beach.

"I've got a bad case of dermatitis," he told me.

"I was sent to see a specialist when we were in Plymouth and he gave me some cream to rub in."

"Isn't it helping?" I asked.

"I don't want it to help," said Sparky

"Instead of the cream I rub diesel and oil and any crap I can find into my hands to make the dermatitis worse, it's my ticket out of the Navy."

I was shocked that Sparky had to go to such lengths to get out of the Navy but I wished him well and I only hoped that it worked and that his hands wouldn't be ruined for life.

**

Before leaving the UK I had taken the cuttings of a number of articles from the Daily Mirror and the Morning Star, (which was the new name for the Daily Worker). I read with horror about the escalation in the Vietnam War and in particular the involvement of Australia. The articles told me that during 1966 the Vietnam War had really increased in its intensity.

There had been joint US and Australian military actions during the year against the Vietnamese National Liberation Front or Viet Cong as they called them. Operation Rolling Thunder, which was widespread bombing of Vietnam, had resumed at the beginning of the year and throughout 1966 the number of American troops in Vietnam advanced to over 360,000 men.

More than 5,500 Americans were killed but that was nothing compared to Vietnamese casualties and increasingly people throughout the World were questioning why the war was taking place.

In the USA growing numbers of young people were challenging the draft or they just disappeared into Canada or Europe to avoid it. Thousands of people were becoming Conscientious Objectors as they did not see Vietnam as a just war.

On my next trip to the US Air Base in Bermuda I took a thousand Piccadilly King Size filter tipped cigarettes with me which I exchanged for a very nice and almost brand new American sailor's coat and two Zippo lighters. The coat was very warm and stylish. I took the opportunity also to engage a number of American servicemen in conversation about the Vietnam War. Many told me that they were glad to be in Bermuda rather than South East Asia but some had fought there and they didn't want to go back. A lot more told me that they expected to be drafted there and whilst there was a degree of patriotism in some of the statements that came from those I spoke to the feeling was that there was no reason they could think of why the USA should be involved in the war in Vietnam. I spoke to one young serviceman who told me that he was actively filing papers to become a Conscientious Objector. I told him that in my view he was doing the right thing and that if Britain joined the war I would have to consider what I would do. I have to say that the American servicemen I met were decent and generous people and I decided that I liked Americans a lot. I was deeply unhappy that many of those I met would at sometime be drafted to Vietnam and some would inevitably die there.

As Sparky and I chatted to our American friends and intermittently listened to a band playing on stage the lights suddenly went on and two of our ships Petty Officers appeared. Stopping the band from playing and grabbing hold of the microphone they ordered all HMS Hecate sailors to muster outside the night club immediately. Putting down our drinks we went outside where a mini bus was awaiting to take us back to our ship.

We were told that there had been a hurricane warning and the ship would have to sail straight away to avoid being smashed against the jetty in St. George's. From around the island most of the ships' company had been rounded up and we were at sea within minutes of getting back onboard.

Many of us had been out for a drink or two so as the ship fought its way against the growing storm at sea there was much sickness onboard.

After a day at sea the hurricane had passed over and we returned to Bermuda where we spent our last week anchored in the harbour at Hamilton, the island's Capital. There was a radio station in Hamilton that we received on our ships radios. It was a good station playing pop music and requests and whilst working in the galley one day enjoying the songs the radio station's DJ read out a request from two sailors onboard HMS Hecate for the Animal's single, "*We gotta get out of this place.*"

"I hope they don't mean Bermuda," said the DJ.

Listening to the radio the next day the DJ said that he had received over twenty calls to the station saying that none of the sailors onboard HMS Hecate wanted to leave Bermuda; it was the Royal Navy they were referring to! The DJ also imparted to us the information that the Animal's song was especially popular among United States Armed Forces serving in Vietnam.

Sparky, Ginge, Legs, Geordie and I decided we would make the most of our trip to Bermuda and we had time for one more visit to Mango Tree Bay. Enjoying ourselves no end after a few drinks the five of us decided to carry on the Dr. No theme as we lined up behind each other, holding onto the waist of the one in front and to a calypso beat we shuffled around the beach singing "*Three blind mice*" and laughing our heads off we threw ourselves into the waves at Mango Tree Bay for the last time.

The morning that we sailed out of the harbour at Hamilton and left Bermuda to head back to Plymouth was fine, warm and sunny with clear blue skies. I was told by one of the scientists onboard that the ship would be conducting a survey on the way back and because of this the speed and course the ship took had to be maintained until we were off the Lizard in Cornwall.

It was December and we knew that back in the UK it would be cold so after cleaning up the galley once dinner was over I had the afternoon off for a make and mend and it was my last chance to get a bit of colour on my face. I went up the fo'c'sle wearing just shorts and flip flops and placed my towel on the deck where I lay down to sun bathe. After no more than ten minutes, just as I was drifting into a nice warm sleep a voice stirred me into life.

"Well I'll be buggered!"

I recognised the West Country twang of Ginge's voice so I sat up to see him looking over the side of the ship. A seaman was standing next to him and they appeared to be watching something so I got up and joined them. In the distance I could see what looked like an old, rusty and pretty large cargo ship of some type. The seaman was explaining to Ginge that he had been up on the bridge delivering some message or other and that the Captain and Jimmy the One were in a bit of a tizzy about the cargo ship. It was flying no flag, no one could be seen onboard, it was not answering any signals that we were sending it and its speed and course were taking it into a direct collision with us.

"We are in the Bermuda Triangle, maybe that's a ghost ship and it's going to take us all down to the gloomy depths of the Saragossa Sea," offered Ginge in a ghoulish voice.

Ginge was joking but the three of us thought about this for a moment and then we suddenly became collectively very scared when the realisation hit us that something must have caused all of those ships to sink in the deadly Bermuda Triangle! We stood, transfixed, watching the inevitable collision as the ghost ship came ever closer to ours. After a very short while it was so close that you could make out every detail but on the bridge and on the decks and through the portholes not a single living person could be seen. Finally, our Captain must have made the decision to break orders and change direction as we sharply veered to starboard and to my calculation, very narrowly missed the cargo ship.

As we put some distance between us and the ghost ship I noticed that a group of dolphins had now joined us, diving to and fro across our bow.

"A good omen," I thought to myself.

Proceeding safely back on course Ginge and I took a deep breath and went off to make a cup of tea before I resumed my sun bathing. When I got back in position on my towel I did what sailors do when they sense danger and I kept one eye open until we were well clear of the Bermuda Triangle. We had been away from home for a long time and a week after leaving Bermuda we neared the coast of Cornwall and picked up a British station on our radio in the galley. A very appropriate song from Simon and Garfunkel "Homeward Bound" was playing, a song that everyone onboard had been singing with gusto for a number of days!

CHAPTER TWENTY SEVEN

THE BATTLESHIP POTEMKIN

Back home on Christmas Leave it was indeed cold in London and although my hair was short I stood out from the crowd for another reason as I was the only person in Finsbury Park with a sun tan!

I went Christmas shopping and arranged to see as many of my old friends as possible to let them know about my Bermudan adventures. I did think of writing to Terry Neil as well to let him know that I had survived the Saragossa Sea but probably the story would be lost on him even though he had been in the Manor Gardens Library when I did my research.

Some months earlier I had returned a form in the Morning Star to enquire about meetings they might hold locally and I had received a reply. The letter from the local Communist Party asked me if I would like to contact one of their members in the area who would tell me about meetings that they hold and gave me a phone number to ring. I decided that I would get in touch after Christmas and before I returned to Plymouth.

On Boxing Day I was at Highbury to cheer Arsenal from the North Bank as we beat Southampton 4 -1 and the next day I went to a phone box and rang the number I was given for the local Communist Party. An elderly sounding woman answered and said I could visit her that afternoon. The address was a flat in Stapleton Hall Road which was no more that fifteen minutes walk away so I agreed.

When I arrived at the flat I was greeted by a woman who was in her eighties. She made me a cup of tea and produced a plate of biscuits and we had a good old chat about politics. She was very interesting and full of knowledge about a whole range of issues and all in all she was a very nice person to speak to. She knew from personal experience all about the Suffragettes, the Jarrow March, the General Strike and the Campaign for Nuclear Disarmament. We talked about authors and when I mentioned George Orwell she said she wasn't keen on him. I told her that the main reason I had filled in the slip in the Morning Star was to see if there were any meetings I could attend when I was on leave as I was very interested in left wing politics and I wanted to know what all the different socialist groups and parties stood for.

"On leave from what?" she enquired.

"I'm in the Royal Navy," I replied, "that's why my hair is so short."

"Oh, I'm terribly sorry she said, "The Communist Party doesn't allow members of the Armed Forces to join."

"What about the Battleship Potemkin?" I was about to say but I just said what was in fact the truth, that I had no intention of joining any Party, I was just interested to hear the Communist Party's views on current issues. She did say that she would keep me informed of any meetings and she also told me that fund raising to help produce the newspaper was very important and she gave me the date of the next Morning Star jumble sale at the Hornsey Town Hall.

These were radical times and I was becoming more and more drawn to revolutionary politics and the place to be in North London was Crouch End, particularly the Queens Pub, a fine old Gin Palace on Broadway Parade, which was a magnet for socialists and anarchists of all types. Entering, the Queens for the first time with my brother Geoff and a group of his friends' one of them pointed out to me the people who were drinking in the various bars that made up the Queens.

"If you look in all the bars at this minute you will find members of the International Marxist Group, Anarchists, International Socialists, Maoists, the Communist Party of Great Britain, the Labour Party, Young Socialists, the Socialist Party of Great Britain and the Socialist Labour League."

My head began to spin taking in all of this information and I began to think that socialists were like Heinz, there were 57 varieties of them!

"All these socialists need something to unite them," I said.

Over the coming year it was their opposition to the war in Vietnam that was to unite them. For now, whenever I was on leave I came to Crouch End and attended as many meetings of the various groups as I could. It was an amazing time and the talk was all about overthrowing capitalism and establishing socialism! But what sort? I was confused.

I had arranged to meet up with Sparky on New Year's Eve and so it was that on Saturday I introduced him to the Queens. Before we had a drink in the pub I took him along to the Hornsey Town Hall, just up the road, for the Morning Star jumble sale where I bought Vincent Van Goth's painting of the Sunflowers for two shillings; not the original I hasten to add but a very attractive copy. In the pub Sparky informed me that he wouldn't be going straight back to the ship after the Christmas Leave as he had been given an appointment by his Navy Doctor to see a dermatologist at a Hospital in London.

Over the next couple of weeks of my leave I spent some of my time in the Queens Pub in Crouch End talking to the different socialist groupings that drank and chatted there and I was heartened that they were very laid back about me being a member of the Armed Forces and were very supportive when I told them I wanted to get out of the Navy.

One person I became friendly with was Mike, a socialist printer and he suggested that I have a chat with campaigning journalist and International Socialist Paul Foot. Mike took me to meet Paul at a pub on Kingsland Road near Shoreditch and after a long and helpful chat he said that he would put me in touch with Tony Smythe, the General Secretary of the National Council for Civil Liberties (NCCL) who he knew was doing some work on the plight of young Reluctant Servicemen.

After being given his number I telephoned Tony Smythe from a phone box and arranged to meet him but he asked me not to come to his offices as he didn't want me to be seen by anyone who might be watching the NCCL offices, particularly as I was a serving member of the armed forces which could get me into trouble.

We met up in a flat in Crouch End near the Railway Public House. Tony was very supportive and he told me that the NCCL, which later became Liberty, were campaigning to raise awareness of the difficulty faced by Reluctant Servicemen, people like me in the armed forces, who had signed up as boys then realised they'd made a mistake but were prevented from discharging themselves.

The campaign sought to allow boy servicemen to leave if they wished to and from the first moment I met Tony I also became involved in this campaign. The NCCL campaign called on the Government to allow servicemen the opportunity to leave up to six months after they joined and at the age of eighteen and they also called for shorter signing on periods. In the 1960's boy sailors signed on for 12 years and there were cases of boy soldiers signing on for 16 years.

Over the coming days we were to have several meetings in venues in North London and during this time I spoke to Tony and other members of the NCCL and commented on their forthcoming pamphlet entitled "The Reluctant Serviceman." Among the MP's and members of the House of Lords supporting the campaign was the Liberal MP, Eric Lubbock, who wrote an excellent forward to the pamphlet. In particular he said:

"It is strange that manning requirements of the service should be singled out before all else, including the civil rights of servicemen who are already at a disadvantage compared with other members of the community."

Tony showed me some of the cases that the NCCL were taking up. I had felt sorry for myself but some of the stories that the NCCL had compiled were heartbreaking. One story said:

"The National Council for Civil Liberties provides a relief for me because if I don't inform somebody of my predicament I'm afraid I will be on the verge of a breakdown. I am very near to it now incidentally. The reason why I have stayed in up to now is because of my father's behalf. He was terribly proud of his only son joining up in the Royal Navy. I have never really liked the life, and the past eighteen months have just gone from bad to worse.

So acute is my depression that I recently went on a long weekend to my home with the full intention of not returning to the ship and deserting.

On the night I was supposed to return I was that depressed with my life that I felt I just could not go on living so I picked up a razor blade and slashed both my wrists. After seeing a civilian psychiatrist and spending a week in the hospital, a medical escort came to collect me and take me to the ship. I am now back onboard. I am still in a state of deep depression and I am afraid if I am not released from the R.N. soon I will desert. In the civilian hospital I was treated like a human being, but when I arrived back I was treated as an animal. The 'doctor' onboard treated me for depression and my interview with him lasted no more than three minutes. Surely this is not the state for an 18 year old to be in. I have been denied all the rights of a young person in civilian life."

The case Histories that went into the Reluctant Servicemen [4] pamphlet told many grim stories of young boys being denied their freedom and as I read through them I was amazed to read the story of one sailor who applied thirty times to be discharged as he had a mentally ill sister and his mother needed him at home to help. After years of trying he was eventually discharged on "Compassionate Grounds" but still had to pay £125 to be released!

I empathized with my fellow Reluctant Servicemen. I had spent much time since joining the Navy being afraid of what each day held in store for me and also how my political views seemed to mark me out as a target for the powers that be. I now felt so much happier knowing that someone was at last on my side, in fact the National Council for Civil Liberties and the socialists of Hornsey were becoming my true friends and this made facing the future so much easier for me.

CHAPTER TWENTY EIGHT

SPINGO AND FLORAL DANCING

Returning to HMS Hecate from Christmas Leave I was told that one of the two men who were the ships helicopter fire fighter was being drafted elsewhere in six weeks time and therefore a new fire fighter was needed.

It was a part time job and the duties really only involved being on the flight deck when the helicopter took off and landed. I was asked to apply for the position but didn't care too much for it until I was told that it entailed being trained at a Royal Naval Air Station for a month while the ship would be on manouvers in the Atlantic. The choice between being on dry land for a month or being tossed about at sea left me with an easy decision, I volunteered for the post of HMS Hecate Helicopter Fire Fighter and I was accepted.

In mid February, as the Hecate was being prepared for sea my papers to join the fire fighting course came through so I packed my kit bag and left the ship the next morning and found myself on a train leaving Plymouth for Redruth in Cornwall. Alighting at Redruth Station I was picked up by a mini bus that took me to HMS Seahawk which was the name of Royal Naval Air Station Culdrose the Royal Navy Airbase near Helston.

It was February 1967 and Cornwall seemed pretty much deserted at that time of the year as the minibus took me through quiet country roads and the empty looking town of Helston before depositing me at the Naval Air Station.

I was shown to my quarters and was surprised to be given a room, albeit a tiny one, of my own, but it was in a miserable looking accommodation block. I noticed that behind my bunk there was mildew and a large damp spot, the ceiling was similarly stained and the air inside the room smelt and tasted mouldy. Even though it was February I opened the window to allow fresh air inside. A Chief Petty Officer then appeared at my door and told me to change into my number 8s and report to the main gate in thirty minutes time. At the gate, along with half a dozen others who had volunteered to be fire fighters on their respective ships the Chief Petty Officer informed us that he would be our trainer for the coming month.

Over the next four weeks I was introduced to the theory of fires and the practice of putting them out at various remote areas of the air base; oil fires, wood fires, electrical fires and even chip fat fires which I was told were very common in the married quarters. I became competent in the whole fire thing using an array of fire extinguishers, water, powder, and foam and fire blankets. The other part of the job involved rescue. Over and over again we practised how to rescue a pilot from a burning helicopter. We started off with dummies then went to the real thing as our pilot would be strapped in and pretend to be unconscious and I would have to climb into the cockpit, thump the release button on his belt and throw him over my shoulder and carry him to safety. Although this was hard work in a cold place I consoled myself that at least I wasn't at sea.

At Culdrose we were allowed to go ashore most evenings but there was not much to do in the winter in such a remote part of the country. The nearest town was Helston and realistically it was the only place that could be got to and back again in an evening. I had befriended a young lad called Jim from Southampton who had been sent on the course from another survey ship. We decided to get the bus one evening from outside the Air Base into Helston which was only a few miles up the road.

We wandered around deserted streets peering into shop windows whilst waiting for the pubs to open. There were a few pubs and we tried them all. They seemed unfriendly, dour establishments but we both liked playing darts so we made the best of them.

The beer was the same insipid stuff that you got all around England at that time, Watney's and Whitbread's keg beer that came from a barrel that was simply connected to a cylinder of gas which piped up the gassy and horrible stuff.

On our second run ashore we found a little oasis that transformed our view of Helston, we landed in a pub called the Blue Anchor. It was jolly inside and the clientele were of mixed ages and friendly. They told us that the pub was one of the oldest original Inns in Britain that maintained a working brewery dating back to the 15th Century. In this pub they made the beer in a back room and called it "Spingo." The beer was lovely, unusual and a bit swirly yes, but lovely.

After his first four pints of Spingo Jim was going to get up to buy a fifth but he told me that his legs had stopped taking instructions from his brain. I decided to try and get up but realised I was suffering from the same condition. We both looked sober and our speech was OK but we were getting slowly drunk from the feet up. We agreed that perhaps four pints was sufficient and after a great deal of effort we made our way to the door and staggered to the bus stop doing a passable impression of Bambi on Ice. From then on we made the Blue Anchor our regular haunt but we tried, more often than not successfully, to limit the alcohol intake.

The locals in the pub told us that Helston's greatest claim to fame was the festival of the Furry, or Flora Dance which is held every year on May 8th when the whole town comes alive with a dance that sees men, women and children shuffling along the streets dancing with their partners from dawn to well into the night. It was a simple dance where the steps are repeated over and over again, a bit like Dorothy following the yellow brick road in the Wizard of Oz and there was a song as well that we were taught the words to. So, after three or four pints of Spingo, Jim and I could be seen on a cold winter's night in early 1967 doing the Furry Dance up Coinagehall Street to catch our bus back to the Culdrose Air Base merrily singing:

"Up and down, and round the town, Hurrah! for the Cornish Floral Dance."

The day before I finished my course at Royal Naval Air Station Culdrose I was called in by the Master at Arms and told that my ship, HMS Hecate, had been delayed and would not be getting back to Plymouth for another week.

"That's OK." I said, "I'll go home to London and they can write to me when they want me to return."

The Master at Arms gave me a weary look and said:

"No lad, we've got something better for you than that," and so it was that two days later I reported for duty in the galley at HMS Raleigh in Torpoint, Cornwall.

**

HMS Raleigh was a large shore establishment that trained new recruits to the Royal Navy. It had a large galley and after being billeted in an accommodation block I was instructed to report to the Chief Cook and start work there whilst awaiting the return of my ship. My new mess was another soulless habitat, with sailors in transit who did not want to strike up a conversation and a number of Royal Marine bandsmen but no cooks, the regular chefs at Raleigh had their own mess. I was only required to cook breakfast and dinner and clean up afterwards so effectively that meant working from 06.00 to 15.00 each day. I knew no one here and I wasn't going to be here long enough to get to know anyone so I just turned up each day to do my job and in the evening I got the Torpoint ferry to Plymouth where I would head into a pub on Union Street for a couple of beers.

In the galley I did my job and kept to myself but I did notice that I was never given the job of cleaning the pots and pans. This lowly task was allocated to civilians at HMS Raleigh which was a relief to me as it was not my favourite task. I did notice though that one of the pot washers had an uncanny resemblance to Dick Head, the sadistic Chief Petty Officer Gunnery Instructor at HMS Ganges who had made my life a misery on many an occasion. I had to go up to him one afternoon to give him some dirty dishes to wash so I decided to ask him his name.

"Pete Head," he informed me.

"Do I remember you from HMS Ganges?" I asked.

He confirmed to me that he was indeed the dreaded Gunnery Instructor who had been there but when his 32 year naval career came to an end he moved back to Cornwall which was his home but he couldn't find a job anywhere.

"I don't suppose many firms have the need for people who shoot guns," I quipped.

Ignoring my unsubtle comment he went on:

"Someone told me that they needed pot washers here so I applied. The money is not too good but at least it supplements my pension."

I was shocked that someone could go from the position of power that Dick Head held at Ganges to washing dishes for a living.

"Always be kind to those you meet on the way up as you are bound to meet them again on the way down," I said to myself as I went off to find the most disgustingly dirty and burnt pots and pans I could to give to Dick Head to wash.

**

Among the letters awaiting me when I arrived back on the Hecate was one from Sparky. He told me that following his consultation at the hospital in London he had been sent to work in the shore establishment HMS Collingwood for a few months but as his dermatitis had worsened he had been discharged from the Navy on medical grounds. He hoped that we could meet up again when I was back in London. I felt so sad to be losing Sparky as a mate onboard ship but I was overcome with happiness for him that he had managed to escape.

Onboard HMS Hecate I was now a fully trained and certificated helicopter fire fighter and was glad to hear that I had missed a period of pretty foul weather in the Atlantic. I didn't rub it in by telling people that I had discovered Spingo though, but I was soon to find out the downside to being a ships helicopter fire fighter. Even on my afternoons or evenings off, if the helicopter had to take off and land I had to be on the flight deck doing my job. I also found out that a rescue had to be practised every week and as soon as we had sailed off on our next venture we had barely cleared Drake Island when I was called upon to demonstrate my newly found skills.

Once I had learnt the knack of rescuing someone from a helicopter during my training it all seemed easy enough, but that was on dry land. When you put into the mix a rolling sea and my spindly legs and my ten stone nine pound frame, trying to drag someone out of a helicopter was no mean feat. Luckily for me the pilot on HMS Hecate weighed no more than eleven stone himself.

My main job on HMS Hecate was still that of a ships cook but as my part time job on the ship was to act as the helicopter fire fighter a lot of my free time was given up as I stood on the flight deck just outside the hanger wearing a blue and almost flexible, head to toe "Fearnought" suit with a plastic visor. In my hand was a hose connected to a large drum of foam. I was at the ready to extinguish any fire that might happen when the helicopter took off or landed. Luckily for me and probably even more so for the pilot, I never had to put my skills as a fire fighter and rescuer of stricken pilots to the test in a real life situation.

CHAPTER TWENTY NINE

HOPE ON THE HORIZON

One piece of hope for my attempt to get out of the Navy was in the work of the National Council for Civil Liberties and some supportive Members of Parliament including Lord Brockway who initiated a debate in the House of Lords on 16th March 1967, one of many over the coming years, on boy service in the Armed Forces. [5]

Lord Brockway asked Her Majesty's Government:

" What is the nature of the commitment required for boy-service in the Armed Forces at the age of fifteen years and for those who accept man-service at the ages of seventeen and eighteen years."

He told a story whereby some years ago, he happened to be travelling in the same railway carriage as three boys who had been for several years at an orphanage, and who were then being transferred to the Navy. They were 15 years of age. He asked the Officer who was accompanying them for how long they were to be committed to the Navy, and, to his astonishment, he said: "For 15 years". This meant that those boys of 15 would be 30 years of age before that commitment would be concluded. Lord Brockway said he was startled. He said he had initiated this debate on the advice of the National Council for Civil Liberties and the Continuing Committee of the Board for Conscientious Objectors.

They had sent him cases of boys, teenagers, from the Army who for the last two years have sought to leave the Armed Forces and who had gone down in despair and frustration because they had not the opportunity to do so. He said there were 42 such cases, in great detail, in his hands and they have been forwarded to the Minister of Defence. He said that he had rarely read such tragic human documents, showing deep unhappiness and utter frustration; leading, ultimately to some of these men becoming deformed characters as a result of what they have gone through.

Lord Brockway also said:

"I conclude with some quite positive proposals. First — and this is what I have been saying — the principles of law relating to civilians should be applied in the military sphere. Second, boys of 15 should have the opportunity annually to obtain discharge, and without monetary payment. Third, they should not be committed to long-term service until they are at least 18 years of age. Fourth, they should have the opportunity to choose civilian life when they become adults at 21. Fifth, any Serviceman who claims conscientious objection should be able to go direct to a tribunal and at least should be informed of his rights. Sixth, the decision in individual cases should be with the commanding officer of the regiment, subject to appeal, rather than a decision by the Ministry. Seventh, the establishment of a military ombudsman to whom appeals could go, and unobstructed access of Members of Parliament to submit cases to him. Above all, I am asking for a full inquiry into the present discharge machinery, possibly by reference to the Committee on the Age of Majority, under Mr. Justice Latey, whose terms of reference include examination of teenage contracts.

My Lords, I have raised this matter because I believe it is a matter of freedom and of democracy. We pride ourselves on our record in this country as a free and democratic society. We are proud of it. But this freedom is refuted by this denial to the path of life by these boys even before they have taken their first unattended steps on it. Democracy will be denied unless the Government will reconsider a tradition in the military sphere which is outlived in the civilian sphere."

The debate went to and fro with support from Lord Gifford and the Bishop of Norwich but with objections from the Government and the Conservatives to a number of points raised by Lord Brockway. In his summing up the spokesman for the Government in the debate, Lord Shackleton said:

"The power to hold a Serviceman derives from the Service Acts. Parliament has made it an offence to desert or be absent without leave and has laid down penalties in these Acts, but noble Lords must face this. We may not like having Armed Forces. We may abhor war. There are those who in fact carry their hatred of war to the point where they can conscientiously object. But many of us cannot conscientiously object and have to face the consequences of the fact that there are fighting Services with the unique task of defending the country, and Parliament has recognised that the Serviceman should not have the right to leave at short, or comparatively short notice, and has provided penalties if he leaves unlawfully.

Your Lordships may also wonder whether a large number of men would leave if we gave them the right to go at, say, 21. We do not really know the answer to that question. As I have said, we hope that the vast majority are content with life in the Services. We know, however, that some wives of Servicemen may not be. I would draw your Lordships' attention to the fact that the average age at which a Serviceman marries is going down, and this is in line with the rest of the population."

In short, despite the best efforts of some good people in the House of Lords, I was still stuck in the Navy and I could see no likelihood of an early release; for me there was no hope on the horizon.

CHAPTER THIRTY

MONTE CARLO OR BUST

At the end of March 1967 we left Plymouth with the Admiral Hydrographer of the Navy onboard for a journey that would take us to Monte Carlo for a conference he was attending.

Then a ship called the Torrey Canyon came into our lives. The Torrey Canyon was a super tanker that had been carrying a cargo of 120,000 tons of crude oil and was shipwrecked off the western coast of Cornwall. On 18th March 1967 on its way to Milford Haven the Torrey Canyon struck Pollard's Rock on Seven Stones reef between the Cornish mainland and the Scilly Isles. When we sailed near the area where the oil slick had reached we were told to keep a wide berth to avoid getting the oil on our ships paintwork but in the distance all hell was breaking loose and it was as if we had entered a war zone.

The Royal Navy's Fleet Air Arm was sending their Buccaneer planes to drop 1,000 lb bombs on the Torrey Canyon. After they did this they turned and flew over us and gave a little aeronautical wiggle to show off. Their other trick was to reach the sound barrier when they were just overhead which gave an enormous sonic boom and I could feel my ear drums bounce in and out as they did so. The pilots waved and laughed as they flew overhead, presumably they thought it was a good laugh to try and scare us.

As ordered we were giving the Torrey Canyon a wide a berth as possible and sailed around the oil slick but we could still hear and see the Royal Navy and Air Force planes continuing to drop bombs and we were later told liquified petroleum jelly also. The Ministry of Defence furiously denied that they had stockpiles of a terrible substance called Napalm that the USA were bombing Vietnam with but people were suspicious that the UK's liquified petroleum jelly was very similar. Anyway, the bombing continued before the Torrey Canyon finally sank and as daylight broke the next day the ships' company onboard our ship were horrified to see a dirty rim of crude oil around the bottom few feet of the Hecate. Seamen were lowered on boatswain's chairs with buckets of soapy water and scrubbing brushes and it took a while before they could start painting over the off white colour that part of the ship's hull had become.

Then we set our course south for Gibraltar and on to Monte Carlo. The sea was heavy and rough for the entire trip to Gibraltar and I was sea sick on our way south. I had looked at a map of the world and saw that the Mediterranean Sea which we would soon be sailing into looked like a large lake. I was pleased about this as to my knowledge you don't get big waves and rough waters in lakes. My lake logic held up as HMS Hecate sailed majestically through the Strait of Gibraltar into the calm waters of the Mediterranean Sea. On my first night in the Med I went onto the upper deck to have a look at the stars. We had left the Spanish and North African coasts behind and around me as far as I could see was only water. There was no light pollution so every star in the universe was above me to wonder at. The night sky was a mass of stars, some shooting and they seemed so close to me I felt I could almost touch them.

My thoughts drifted to my childhood days in Finsbury Park and for the first time I understood the effect they were trying to capture on the ceiling of the Astoria Cinema. I remembered my school trip to that cinema from Pooles Park School Nursery one afternoon. It was daylight when I entered and inside the walls of the cinema were decorated like a scene from the Arabian Nights. The ceiling was painted black and small white lights twinkled like stars.

It was very realistic and it completely fooled all of us nursery children.

The teachers told us and we believed them, that by the time we took our seats it had become night time and that the cinemas had no roof and we were really looking at the stars in the night sky. Two hours later when we emerged into the light again outside the cinema we couldn't understand what had happened and it was years later before I realised that the ceiling at the Astoria was made to look like the night sky, it wasn't the real thing! These were the thoughts going through my mind now as I stared into the heavens and chuckled at my childhood innocence to believe such things.

**

It was a warm April day when we arrived at the Quai des Etats Unis in Monte Carlo. In most places where we docked there was a scruffy dockyard between the ship and the town but here we were right in the town and what a town it was! Around us were Marinas where expensive boats belonging to the wealthiest people in the world bobbed up and down. Just along from the quay was a fabulous looking beach and beside us the Avenue Président J.F. Kennedy was lined with trees attached to which were hundreds of twinkling coloured lights.

On our first evening there I was on duty but after cooking tea and cleaning the galley I made my way to the upper deck just to watch the world go by and take in the sights, sounds and smells of Monte Carlo. Along the water front rich and contented looking people promenaded in their designer clothes whilst walking their well groomed poodles. A warm and gentle sea breeze caressed the promenaders and sailors alike and seemed to give everyone a feeling of well being.

The same couldn't be said for a young seaman who came up to stand beside me who let me know his tale of woe as we watched the world go by together. He told me that whilst on leave in the UK he had contracted Gonorrhea from his girlfriend. As a means of both punishment and insurance that he didn't spread the disease any further he was banned from going ashore whilst we were in Monte Carlo.

The next day the Admiral Hydrographer was to have dinner at the palace with Rainier III, Prince of Monaco.

I watched as the Admiral strolled off the ship and into a waiting limousine and as he got into the car I noticed that he had red socks on. I thought this was strange as we were told to wear navy blue socks at all times and not to do so would mean being placed on a charge so I guessed he might have been an Arsenal supporter or a secret member of the Labour Party. I would ask him if I ever got the chance but I doubted that he would ever talk to me personally and in fact he never did. A couple of days later we were all given passes that the Admiral had brought back for us from his dinner that allowed us into the Monte Carlo Casino and as I was off duty that afternoon I decided to pay the place a visit and see as much of the rest of the Principality as I could. I set off down the ships gangway along with my mate Legs and before long we discovered what a hilly place this was. It was interesting to see that the roads were built like a racing car track and as we sat on a bale of hay considering this a local stopped to talk to us. In very good English he told us that the streets are transformed each year into the circuit for the Monaco Grand Prix, a Formula One Race, which was to be held on 7th May. The man was a mine of information as he told us that the building of the circuit takes six weeks and the dismantling after the race another three weeks. The race circuit, he went on, has many tight corners, is narrow and the racing cars have to complete one hundred laps.

It was a disappointment for us to realise that we would be leaving Monte Carlo on May 1st as we would miss seeing the 1967 Monaco Grand Prix but when I read later that the formula one driver Lorenzo Bandini had died from burns after his car had clipped a chicane and crashed upside down in flames amongst the straw bales that could well have been the ones Legs and I had sat on I was glad not to have been there.

After our informative chat about motor racing Legs said that we should go into a bar we had noticed that was situated right on the corner of one of the bends on the circuit. However, when we saw how much the drinks cost we left without buying anything. We then walked from the race track up to the Casino which was very grand indeed.

We watched people playing roulette and some card games but again we couldn't afford to take part and we didn't have the money that they were asking for a beer so we left feeling very poor and very thirsty. We found a small shop and bought ourselves a bottle of orange pop and sat down again by the road watching the construction of the race track.

After a short discussion we then took the decision to find somewhere cheaper than Monte Carlo so we looked for and found the Bus Station and we took a bus to a place called Nice. The bus driver charged us very little for the return ticket and he deposited us about forty five minutes later on the sea front in Nice. The main concern that Legs and I had on the journey was the road we took to get to Nice, it was often high above the sea and it was narrow with no obvious barriers to stop the bus plunging off a cliff if the driver had decided to nod off for a few seconds. Therefore as we got off the bus our first thoughts were to get ourselves a stiff drink to recover from the scary journey. We went into the first bar we came across and ordered Cognac with beer chasers which were surprisingly cheap so we helped ourselves to a few before we set off to explore the town. We were in a jolly frame of mind now that we had found somewhere that we could actually afford and Nice became our regular run ashore whilst the ship was tied up in Monte Carlo.

"Nice is nice," chuckled Legs, enjoying his discovery that the two words were spelt the same. Indeed it was nice, with its fine beaches, broad tree lined boulevards and decent looking shops. Importantly it was cheaper than Monte Carlo and we discovered a small square where we would sit outside a bar on warm evenings drinking wine which we found out was very cheap and of reasonable quality as we watched the world go by. It was quite a bustling cobble stoned little square with the occasional bicycle or moped dashing across it but mainly it was just people.

Over the coming weeks we observed a small gang of pick pockets at work in the square and we were able to give their descriptions to the police one night when they robbed one of our drunken ship mates.

There were also the prostitutes inviting men into little hotels around the square.

I was always surprised that they seemed to finish their business within about ten minutes before they were back out onto the streets again. Then there were lots of people like us, just drinking wine, beer or the occasional coffee, smoking disgusting French cigarettes, chatting and enjoying their leisure time and at peace with the world.

One day on the square we were sitting outside our favourite bar drinking a glass of wine when a small orchestra set up on the nearby Promenade Des Anglais and played some lovely classical music, up until then I had only really listened to pop music but listening to a soprano sing Saint-Saëns "Softly Awakes my Heart" from Samson and Delilah I was impressed.

On the bus back from Nice to our ship on our last run ashore the driver suddenly stopped. Looking out of the window we saw a Citron 2CV car upturned and precariously balanced on the edge of the road, inches from a sheer drop into the sea. The bus driver summoned us all to get out of the bus and asked the younger males onboard, which included me, to get to the side of the car and lift it back over onto its tyres. Positioning ourselves by the car I looked inside to see the driver hanging upside down in his seat belt smiling at us. There were about ten men who took hold of the car and after two or three pushes we flipped it over back onto its wheels. The driver wound down the window and called out "Merci!" before he just drove off again into the night.

"A common occurrence, they take these bends much too fast," explained the bus driver.

I liked Nice a lot and was sorry that our time had come to go back to sea again.

**

The next day was May 1st and we sailed away from Monte Carlo into a beautiful calm sea overlooked by the bluest of skies and a big beaming yellow sun. I was on duty that day which meant that the next day, May 2nd, my eighteenth birthday; I would have a "make and mend," in other words, the afternoon off.

The tradition was that on your birthday you would go around to each mess when the rum was being issued and most people would give you sippers but as this was my eighteenth birthday most people gave me gulpers.

Even the Captain invited me to his cabin where he gave me a drink and shook my hand and wished me all the best.

Let me explain about rum and the Royal Navy. The slang name for Royal Navy rum is "Nelson's Blood" which is based on the story that Nelson was preserved in rum after being killed at the battle of Trafalgar. He was actually preserved in brandy but never let facts get in the way of a good story. In the Royal Navy each day at noon every rating onboard ship who was twenty years or older would be given a standard naval tot of rum which consisted of an eighth of a pint of rum which was over 50% proof. Chiefs and Petty Officers had their rum neat but Junior Ratings had two in one which meant that it was mixed with two parts water to one part rum. The rum ration was served from a barrel known as the Rum Tub which was ornately decorated and reinforced with brass. Every mess would send a rum bosun to the barrel where an Officer would oversee that he was given enough rum in a pot to take back to his mess for his eligible sailors to get their rum ration or tot as it was known. For any favours rendered rum was a sort of payment. You would give someone either, sippers for a small favour or gulpers for a big favour. Also, for birthdays sailors were known to be generous by giving the person whose birthday it was gulpers. Therefore, being encouraged to drink so much rum on my eighteenth birthday I was completely drunk by 14.00 and was carried to my bunk and a basin was kindly placed next to me by someone.

That night my theory that the Mediterranean Sea was a big calm lake was blown out of the water, literally, as one of the worst storms I had ever encountered came upon us. After swallowing a handful of headache and sea sickness pills and being sick into a basin for some time I decided to try and get onto the upper deck where the air would be fresher.

The sight that I beheld was amazing, almost biblical. Along with the usual gigantic waves and crashing water all around me the sky was lit up with an electrical storm and great streaks of lightening flashed downwards out of the heavens. It was like the films I had seen where a Roman God points his fingers down to some poor fellow walking along the street and a great flash emanates from the God's finger tips and reduces the mere mortal to ashes. This act was multiplied many times over and after a while I thought that for safety reasons I had better go below decks after all. So there I was, on the evening of my eighteenth birthday with my head down the pan crying out into the small hours for Hughie.

CHAPTER THIRTY ONE

THE OUTER WHERE?

After the warmth and sunshine of the South of France we were told that for our next job we were to spend the rest of the year surveying the Outer and Inner Hebrides, islands off the North West coast of Scotland.

This news was met with disappointment and general dismay by most people onboard ship as we had been looking forward to a warmer and more exotic posting such as Singapore or Rio de Janeiro. One of my friends, Dinger, was particularly disappointed as he was from Scotland and he told me that he had not joined the Navy to be so near home. We were told that our job was to include surveying the Atlantic coast of the Outer Hebrides and at some point I was to spend a month on an uninhabited island called Mingulay. First of all though, we were to survey the waters around the islands of the Inner Hebrides, the Minch and Little Minch.

We left Plymouth for a journey that would take us up the Irish Sea and before we made our way to the Hebrides to start our job we were to sail up the River Clyde and call in for a few days to the Yarrow shipyard for a few minor repairs.

Being in the shipyard enabled us to have a couple of nights out in Glasgow. We had to leave the ship wearing our naval uniform but we didn't want to go into bars and clubs dressed as sailors so we took a bag ashore with us with our civvies in.

After getting the train into Glasgow Central Station we went to the toilets to change in a cubicle and then deposited our uniforms in a left luggage locker and reversed the process going back to the ship. In the pubs of Glasgow we were introduced to beers called "heavy" and "light" and a pint of heavy became my favourite drink while we were there. On the second night Legs and I found a folk club where a singer called Matt McGinn entertained us with some lovely songs about life and politics. There was also a duo who sang a number of songs including one called the *"Mingulay boat song."* I had never heard of Mingulay until a couple of weeks ago and now as well as being told I was to visit the island I had discovered that there was a song about the place too! The folk singers encouraged us to sing along with the chorus and the entire audience at the folk club seemed to know the song by heart so before long we were all singing the *"Mingulay boat song"* together.

Back onboard ship I listened with trepidation to the shipping forecast as we were to sail next morning to unknown waters around the islands of the Hebrides.

"Here is the shipping forecast for the Minch. Wind north or northeast 3 to 4, becoming variable 3 or less, seas smooth or slight, showers in the far north, visibility good."

"That's not too bad," I muttered to myself and I went to my bunk a little drunk on the several pints of "heavy" I had consumed but not fearing the sea conditions for the next day.

Over the coming weeks our mission was to survey the islands of Skye, Mull, Rum, Eigg and Islay and we set sail on 24th May up the River Clyde en route to the Isle of Skye. As I was duty cook the next morning I had to be up at 04.00 to prepare breakfast. In the middle of the night whilst I was in bed fast asleep the ship anchored off Portree, the largest town on Skye.

Daylight came early this far north and after opening up the galley and making myself a cup of tea and a piece of toast I wandered onto the upper deck to see what Skye looked like. I wasn't prepared for what I saw.

Standing on my own the view before me made me feel that I had been transported to some sort of paradise. An early morning sea mist was rising over the island giving it an eerie but magical quality.

Looking down into the calm still water I saw the heads of several seals bobbing up and down and in the sky a sea eagle flew over the mountains that were rising from the mist. Everything before me was painted in beautiful shades of green and blue; breathtaking was an inadequate word to describe what I was witnessing. I had been amazed at the beauty of Bermuda but this picture before me took beauty to another level. In fact the two most wonderful views I ever saw were both waking up to see the Isle of Skye before me, this time looking towards Portree from the ship and a later time rising one morning to see Skye from the Kyle of Lochalsh.

I was conscious of the fact that apart from a few people in the boiler room and a couple on the bridge I was one of the few people onboard who was awake and I was on my own on the upper deck so I could sing as loudly as I wanted to without anyone hearing. I remembered some words I had been taught at school to the *"Skye Boat Song"* with which I serenaded the mystical island before me:

"Speed bonnie boat like a bird on the wing, onward the sailors cry."

**

That afternoon I was off duty and I was allowed to go ashore with Legs and a few others. Portree did not have a big enough jetty to allow the ship to berth alongside so we remained anchored in the bay whilst a launch ferried people to and from the ship while the other ships boat began the task of surveying the waters around the island. There was a nice homely pub on Quay Street named the Pier Hotel where we were to spend many happy hours over the coming days. On 28th May we were in the pub watching the tiny black and white television set in the bar perched high on a shelf as Francis Chichester arrived in Plymouth in his yacht, Gypsy Moth IV, after completing his single handed voyage around the world. As he crossed the finishing line nine months and one day after setting off hooters and sirens sounded as fire boats sprayed red, white and blue water and the Royal Artillery sounded a ten-gun salute. In the bar we all cheered and got in another round of pints of heavy to celebrate.

Another watering hole for us was the Royal Hotel with stunning views over the bay and we were told the hotel was built on the site where Bonnie Prince Charlie bade farewell to Flora MacDonald in 1745.

Skye was also good for walking around and ashore with Legs and Dinger one day we met up with a group of ramblers on holiday and spent the rest of the day with them as they showed us around the island, on foot.

My first Saturday night on Skye was a real hoot. The three of us were talked into going to a barn dance in the local hall in Portree, whereas the rest of the ships' company thought this would be boring so they elected to go to the pubs instead. The "barn" for the dance was a tiny venue and on stage were men in kilts and women in tartan dresses who had an assortment of instruments; accordions, violins and even bag pipes. Some of the male dancers also wore kilts although most were in suits. There was no alcohol on sale or allowed at the dance and this was emphasised by a big sign on the wall declaring that alcohol was banned at the hall. After the band tuned their instruments the music began and the dancing commenced. We started with the Gay Gordons and people just grabbed hold of partners until everyone was on the dance floor. A local woman who told me she was eighty four years old decided to show me the ropes. Luckily for me, as well as having a partner who knew the dance steps a man on the stage called out the moves as I set off, rather shakily at first, but my country dancing skills from my school days soon kicked in as the caller shouted out:

"Right hands joined over lady's shoulder with man's arm behind her back and left hands joined in front, walk forward for four steps, starting on the right foot. Still moving in the same direction, and without letting go, pivot on the spot with left hand behind the lady and right hand in front and take four steps backwards, repeat in the opposite direction, now drop left hands, raise right hands above lady's head, OK Ladies pivot on the spot, join hands in the ballroom hold and now polka round the room."

As the evening wore on I noticed that the dancing got faster and the whoops from the crowd got louder and as we reeled and swung each other around to the tunes of various dances people started bouncing off the walls and some even fell over squealing with laughter. As no alcohol was on sale I couldn't work out this turn in events at all. Maybe the excitement of dancing produced a sort of drunken state in people.

However, going to the outside toilet I discovered that all of the local men had half bottles of whiskey hidden in their pockets and these were being passed around.

Several people offered me a drink and I soon got into the mood and began dancing as wildly as everyone else. It was my first encounter with whiskey and my sore and throbbing head when I woke up next morning and the bruises on my arms and back where I had bounced off the walls suggested that I had better be wary of taking too much of this drink in future.

On Monday we weighed anchor and spent the coming weeks sailing around and surveying the smaller islands and on Saturday 29th July 1967 we sailed into a sea water Loch called Loch Fyne and anchored in sight of a place called Inveraray. I was duty cook that evening and after I had cleaned the galley I went up on deck with Ginge to do some fishing. We would often go on the upper deck when we were at anchor somewhere and drop our home made fishing equipment, a bent safety pin on the end of a length of string with a piece of wet bread on it as bait. To attract the fish we would throw in a handful of cooked rice or any scraps left over from the galley and our normal catch would be mackerel which we would take back to the galley to grill as a tasty treat. On this occasion, much to my surprise, I landed a small cod. Ginge and I immediately took it to the galley where we cut it into steaks and grilled it with a knob of margarine on top. It was the freshest and most delicious fish I had ever tasted.

The next morning the entire ships' company was told to assemble on the upper deck at 11.00 in our best uniforms where we were to be addressed by the Ship's Captain. We had heard unofficially that he was to tell us something about the law on homosexuality being changed. When we were duly assembled I stood behind a couple of the people onboard who I knew liked each other, Dave and Peter, who held hands and exchanged delighted looks as the Captain said:

"The Ministry of Defence have just informed me that an Act of Parliament called 'The Sexual Offences Act 1967,' had been passed in Parliament which has decriminalised homosexual acts in private between two men, both of whom have to have attained the age of twenty one."

Their hands fell apart and the smiles on their faces disappeared though when the Captain added:

"The Act applies only to England and Wales and does not cover the Armed Forces therefore anyone practicing Homosexual acts in the Royal Navy will still be breaking the law."

When I asked them later what they thought they told me that the law was:

"Bloody unfair!"

Our next Port of Call was a place called Stornoway on the Island of Lewis. It is the largest town in the Western Isles with a population of around 9,000 but I rarely saw more than a dozen people out at any one time and the main excitement on offer to us on a run ashore was either watching the Caledonian MacBrayne boats come in and leave again or drinking in one of the few pubs, the downside to that activity was that the pubs closed at 21.00.

We called into Stornoway on numerous occasions over the coming months as we surveyed the Hebrides, Inner and Outer. It was lovely talking to the locals as the people of the Hebrides had the most clear sounding British accent I had ever heard and their singing voices were just as lovely. My favourite song at that time was the Otis Redding number, "*Sitting on the Dock of the Bay*" which was very appropriate for our situation as, with nothing better to do, Legs, Dinger and I sang the song with our legs dangling over the harbour side watching the Cal Mac boats sailing by. We were joined by young women who cleaned and smoked fish nearby who added their more refined voices to our makeshift choir as we sang about ships coming into Stornoway and going out again.

There were some saving graces to Stornoway, a really good fish and chip shop where you could get a cheap but lovely dish of white pudding and chips and there was a local dance in a community hall held once a week where current pop music would be played and people danced about wildly. There was no alcohol allowed though at the dance but I enjoyed visiting the local pubs for a pint of heavy and a wee dram before the dance started. Speaking to a group of young people at a dance most told me that they had never left the Island although many invariably would do in the end as there was little employment in Stornoway.

On Sundays in Stornoway there was a strict observance of the Christian Sabbath which meant that the pubs were closed all day, Sunday newspapers were not available and the shops were closed too!

One Sunday I was sitting on a wall that was situated between a local Church and a pub with a small group of sailors from the ship where we were bemoaning the fact that we couldn't get a drink. As the Church service finished we couldn't help but notice that men dressed in their Sunday best shuffled over to the Pub's back door and furtively looking all around they gave the door a tap. A small shutter opened into which they whispered a few words and miraculously the door opened and in they went. We watched about twenty such incidents and decided to give it a go ourselves. I knocked on the door and the shutter opened.

"We're closed," said a voice from the other side as the shutter was abruptly pulled down and not opened again that day.

CHAPTER THIRTY TWO

REVENGE OF THE RABBITS

Our next mission was to survey the Atlantic coast of the Outer Hebrides; the idea was to set up two shore bases, one as southerly as possible and one as northerly to communicate with the ship as it sailed up and down between the two locations.

The island of Mingulay was the southern base and the Butt of Lewis was the northern one. It was at this time that I was called in by the Supply Officer to tell me that I was being promoted from Assistant Cook to Cook and also to confirm that I would be spending a month working at the base camp on Mingulay. We set sail and by mid afternoon we were off the island of Mingulay. The four of us who were to go ashore with the job of setting up base were briefed about what our role was on the island and a bit about the history of the place. We were told that Mingulay was an uninhabited island twelve miles south of Barra, just north of Barra Head which was a tiny Island that was much too small for us to land a helicopter on or set up a base which made Mingulay the southernmost Island to use measuring two and a half by one and a half miles. The ships helicopter made a number of trips from Hecate to Mingulay taking the four of us who were to live there for the next month with the equipment we needed and a team to build three huts as well as food. Also, a photographer and a journalist from the newspaper "The Scotsman" were landed to spend a day with us to report on what we were up to.

As I listened to the Officer giving us the briefing about Mingulay I became excited as I was a keen bird fancier, albeit mainly looking at pictures of them in books. We were told that the island was known for its birds and for the first time in my life I was going to see Puffins, thousands of them I was told and black-legged Kittiwakes, Guillemots and Razorbills which nested in the sea-cliffs, and also a pair of Golden Eagles. In the bays and on the beaches we were to see seals. I was surprised to hear that there was an abandoned village on Mingulay which once housed a mill, a Church and a school and we were told that in 1891 the population of the island was 142 people occupying 28 houses in which three generations sometimes shared one single small house. The islanders' livelihood used to be based on fishing and crofting of land on which sheep, cattle, ponies, pigs and poultry were kept. However, despite there being a continuous population on Mingulay for at least two thousand years, evacuations began in 1907 and the island was completely abandoned by its residents in 1912. The Officer told us that there were many theories as to why this was but he felt that probably the ferocity of the weather and the lack of a sheltered landing meant that the island could be unreachable for weeks at a time must have played their part. Also, fishermen losing their lives at sea and the opportunity to have a less arduous and remote existence in other parts of the Hebrides or on the mainland must have contributed to their decision to leave the island for good.

The three people I was to live and work with on the island were a Decca engineer who we called Desmond, Legs and an engineer from Derby who was called Roller after he told us that most of his family worked at the Rolls Royce plant there.

Every day whilst we were on Mingulay we would take turns doing each other's job and the rota that was given to me was: Day one, duty cook; Day two, general dogs body – fetching water, topping up the generator and cleaning up; Day three, night watch as the Radio Operator in the communications hut; Day four, sleeping until midday then cleaning up and doing any other job that needed doing.

There were three huts, the accommodation hut we built in a dip to give us some protection from the wind but the communication hut was on the highest point on a cliff so that we had a clear signal between land and the ship and the generator hut was built in between the two, about fifty yards away from each of them.

We couldn't help but notice that there were a lot of rabbits on the island who seemed a bit puzzled by our presence. We were probably the first humans that had been on these cliffs in their life time. Seeing so many rabbits I suggested to Legs that maybe we could set a trap to catch some as one of my specialities was cooking rabbit pie.

On the first day I cooked all the meals for the others which we ate in our living accommodation hut that we had made very cosy. It was the end of summer time and a strong wind blew in from the Atlantic and made everything rattle but outside the sky was blue and a reasonably warm sun shone on us each day and it still stayed lighter much longer than I had known in London.

Between dinner and tea I went off with Legs in search of fresh water. We both carried two empty jerry cans on our backs and our binoculars around our necks as we set off in search of water that we knew was available on a hillside about a mile from our base. To get to the hill we had to walk over a natural sea arch and as we did we looked a long way down at waves that crashed and swirled against the rocks below. I was certain that if we had slipped off the arch we would fall to our death so I took great care in getting from one side to the other. On the other side of the arch I noticed another mass of Puffins on a hillside and I sat down with my binoculars to watch. This was a beautiful site, Puffins are such lovely creatures and as I watched them the words of a song by Dusty Springfield's old group, the Springfields, came into my head that I thought suited the occasion admirably. I asked Legs if he knew the song and he did, so together we sang out loud to the thousands of Puffins on the hill the words to the *"Island of Dreams."* They seemed impressed.

Apart from birds and rabbits the only other life we encountered on our walk to the hill were sheep that had been brought to the island to graze in the fields.

When we got to the hill we searched for a stream of water and after we climbed about fifty yards up the hill we found tiny streams of water that flowed down around us.

Putting the jerry cans at an angle we filled them up and then sat down to drink some of the delicious fresh water and rest before we returned to the huts. From the hill I used my binoculars to look at the cliffs in the North which were alive with Puffins. This was an amazing site and as I was lost in the magic of seeing such a natural wonder Legs tapped me on the shoulder and asked me to look down into Mingulay Bay which was on the sheltered east coast of the island. The bay was stunning in its beauty, a clean and empty sandy beach with a sea that was as blue as the waters off Bermuda in parts and in others was bottle green and crystal clear. The waves were gently rolling onto the beach where a baby seal played in the surf. However, the main reason that Legs had drawn my attention to the bay was that anchored in it was a trawler. I trained my binoculars onto the boat and was surprised to see that the trawler looked top heavy with aerials and telecommunications equipment. Looking closer I could see that it flew a red flag with a hammer and sickle on it.

"That's the flag of the Soviet Union," I said to Legs.

"Shit!" said Legs.

We were both shocked by this presence and we decided to get back to the others as quickly as we could to report our discovery.

When we told Desmond and Roller of our findings it was decided to make radio contact with the ship and tell them. The intelligence was given to the Duty Officer who decided to talk to us over the radio in person.

"Don't worry about the trawler" said the Duty Officer.

He went on: "The Soviets like to keep an eye on what we are up too and that boat is as much a trawler as my left testicle. They will listen into all of our communications but as soon as they find out that we don't have a military purpose and we are just conducting a survey they will soon bugger off. We could send a couple of Launches around to worry them but I don't think we will bother. They will only tell us that they are a harmless trawler and will be off again to continue fishing once they have had a rest."

That evening in the accommodation hut we drank cocoa and played cards and frightened ourselves by making up stories about the ghosts that would come up from the burial mounds in the abandoned village or the Soviet sailors who would creep up and cut our throats in the middle of the night.

As the huts windows and doors rattled in the wind I slept uncomfortably that night with one eye open in case there was a visitation from the village or the trawler.

The second day on the island I was given a short course by Desmond on how to work the equipment in the communications hut. He told me that:

"The radio position finding systems operate on hyperbolic principles and allow distances from shore based transmitter stations, like our one, to be obtained using special receiving equipment that is fitted onboard the ship."

"OK," I said but in the main this information went straight over my head and I just made sure I knew how to take readings from the dials and how to make calls to the ship.

Roller showed me how to top up the generator with diesel from large cans we had brought with us and how to check the gauges to make sure everything in the generator hut was in order. I was told that under no circumstances was the generator to be allowed to run out of fuel as this would mean that we would have no electricity for the huts and importantly the communications equipment would stop working. I spent the rest of the day doing my dogs body jobs looking after the generator and topping it up at regular intervals, helping prepare the vegetables, fetching water, cleaning up the huts and trying to make a trap to catch a rabbit. The next night I reported to the Communications hut at 20.00 to take over the night watch. I was to radio into the ship every hour and give them the readings from the various bits of equipment in the hut. I had only ever seen people operate radios on films before now so it was with great delight that I did my first radio job.

"This is Mingulay calling Hecate, come in Hecate, over."

A voice crackled onto the radio.

"This is Hecate, thank you Mingulay; we are ready to receive your readings, over."

After I had given all my readings from the various displays on the communication equipment I was able to say:

"This is Mingulay to Hecate; I will call you again in one hour, Roger, over and out."

"Who the fuck's Roger?" was the reply.

My imagination ran riot being on my own and when the sun disappeared I started to get really scared. I was in the dark, on my own, on an uninhabited island with the only other people a hundred yards away and they were fast asleep. The wind was howling around my hut and my thoughts went to the Soviet spy trawler in the bay on the other side of the island and I wondered if the sailors would wander the island at night. When I began contemplating my next task, topping up the generator, I opened the door slightly and peered out to see if the hut was visible, it wasn't. It was dark outside, not just ordinary dark but pitch black and not only couldn't I see the hut, in fact I couldn't see a thing. I was now scared beyond mere terror and I could hear my heart thumping and I could hardly breathe. I would have to go out soon, on my own, with only a torch, in complete darkness and walk fifty yards to the generator hut to top up the generator with diesel. Roller's warning about the need to keep the generator topped up with diesel went through my head; it was a job that had to be done otherwise there would be no electricity and the communications equipment would fail and I would be on a charge. More importantly for me the lights in my hut would go out. I closed the door and was summoning up the courage to go down to the generator hut when suddenly there was a totally unexpected knock at the door, actually more of a thud. My heart stopped as did my breathing. I tried to think logically but I was too scared to apply logic; there was nowhere to hide so what should I do? There was another thud. I started thinking, maybe it was one of my fellow sailors or the Decca engineer come up to collect something. Maybe it was the Soviet sailors come to kill me or maybe it was a ghost from the graveyard in the deserted village come to see what I was doing on their island. Another thud quickly followed by another, I convinced myself that it was probably Desmond who had come to the hut to pick something up. I would have to open the door but how could I protect myself in case it wasn't Desmond? I picked up the fire extinguisher to use as a weapon in case someone or something meant me any harm. I also started praying:

"Please, oh please, oh please God, protect me from whatever evil lurks outside!"

Then summoning every ounce of courage I gently opened the door and looked out, there was no one there. I put down the extinguisher and picked up my torch and standing just outside the doorway I slowly scanned the darkness. I could hear more thumping but this time it was just my heart and then the light from the torch picked up a flash of something small running under the hut, then another and another.

"Bloody rabbits!" I shouted out loud to myself with a degree of relief.

"What are they doing up at this time of night?"

I went back inside the hut and firmly closed the door. Another thump and then another and I realised that the thumps were not against the door but the deck. The hut was built on piles of bricks on each corner and the rabbits were running about beneath the hut and bashing the floorboards as they did so and scaring the life out of me in the process. As the intensity of noise from the rabbits banging the deck below me increased I began to fantasize that these rabbits might be relatives of the ones I had put in the pie at HMS Pembroke and were seeking to extract revenge by frightening me to death or maybe they would attack me when I went down to the generator hut and bite me to death.

I was scared but I couldn't leave the generator untended any longer so leaving the hut and striding down the hill with my torch swiftly moving to and fro to pick out any movement and my ears pricked to pick up any sounds I made my way to the generator hut. I quickly closed the door of the hut and then poured diesel through a funnel into the generator and checked all the gauges before running as fast as I could back to the communications hut where once inside I slammed the door and stood panting for several minutes before calling up the ship again to give my report.

In the morning I had a chat with Legs who said I should start setting my trap to catch a rabbit so we could have rabbit stew but I had made up my mind that I didn't want to upset the rabbits anymore and replied that I'd gone off the idea. I offered the suggestion that we could perhaps try and catch a lamb instead.

The next time I was on night watch in the communication hut I was fantasizing again about being attacked by crazed rabbits or Soviet sailors and worrying about having to go down in the darkness to top up the generator when the radio crackled into life with a voice saying:

"Hecate to Mingulay, come in Mingulay, over."

"This is Mingulay receiving you loud and clear, over." I replied.

"We have a communications test to carry out, over." The voice at the other end said.

"Repeat the following words after me: 'I cannot hold a hot potato in my hand'."

"I cannot hold a hot potato in my hand." I repeated.

"Then stick it up your arse! Ha Ha Ha Ha Ha Ha!"

The radio operator onboard ship obviously thought that this was a great joke to play on me but at least it kept my mind off the killer rabbits.

The next day when I was collecting water from the hillside I noticed in the field below that a baby lamb was lying down on the grass. I watched for a short time but after a while I deduced that it was not moving at all and had probably died. As I watched through my binoculars an eagle appeared from over a hill and was swooping down from the sky above. With its claws extended it gripped the lamb and lifted it into the air taking it off to a distant hill for its dinner I presumed. After witnessing this I thought it best not to have a sleep in the open whilst on this island just in case one of the eagles took a fancy to me.

There were a limited amount of adventures that we could partake in on Mingulay but over the four weeks working there we spent time on a number of antics. We would creep up as close as possible to peer at puffins and seals which was fun and eventually we got up the nerve to go down to the bay and shout at the Soviet trawler.

No one appeared on deck to shout back at us but we thought we were doing our bit for the cold war. We would also visit the deserted village and walk in and out of the buildings trying to imagine what it had been like to have lived there.

However, our time on Mingulay went very quickly and when our four weeks were up we were taken back to the ship in the Wasp helicopter for a short voyage back to the River Clyde and a week's leave for the ships' company. Leaving Mingulay I would miss seeing the lovely Puffins everyday but I was looking forward to a spell of leave.

I had become good friends with Dinger during our time onboard ship and he had suggested that rather than going home to London for the week of leave we had been given I should stay at his parents' home in a town called Thornhill near Dumfries which I readily agreed to.

As the helicopter deposited me back onto the flight deck of HMS Hecate after my month on Mingulay I was aware that the ship was rolling in a heavy sea. I had got used to walking on land that did not roll and pitch under me whilst on the island but I was now onboard ship again, the dreaded moving ship. I reported to the galley where I was given the task of peeling several large bags of onions that were to be fried to accompany the sausage and mash that was the evening's tea. I asked if it was OK to peel my onions on the upper deck in the fresh air and as I sat on the quarter deck peeling my onions I very soon regretted this as I began inhaling diesel fumes that came up from the engine room. As tears rolled down my cheeks from peeling a large quantity of onions and as the ship rolled I became quite distressed and I was feeling very queasy when the lyrics of the debut song from Procul Harum, *"Whiter Shade of Pale"* drifted out of a transistor radio nearby. I was feeling a bit more than kind of seasick as I ran to the side of the ship and threw up. Thankfully though, we were soon sailing up the River Clyde and the ship had stopped rolling about and my sea sickness was receding. The next morning we were allowed ashore to start our leave and Dinger and I got a train from Glasgow to Ayr. We had a brief look around the town and he showed me a statue of the great Scottish poet and lyricist Robert Burns before we boarded a bus to Dinger's home in Thornhill. The bus passed through Cumnock and New Cumnock in the Southern Uplands and for the first time in my life I saw coal mines.

Thornhill was a small place and there was not much to do but it was different and I enjoyed myself.

However, when Dinger introduced me to his friends I was shocked to learn that so many were unemployed. It seemed that most of the people I met who had a job in Thornhill were employed at a local pork processing plant. There was little other work to be found and many of Dinger's friends would spend a lot of time hanging around on street corners chatting to each other. I was pleasantly surprised how politically aware some were compared with many of my friends back in London. One of his mates was a communist and a couple were members of the Scottish Nationalist Party which was, they told me, more socialist than many of the other Political Parties. I didn't know enough to argue one way or the other but I wasn't a great fan of nationalism which I never thought of as being socialist as to me an integral part of socialism was that it was internationalist. I was impressed though that the street corner discussions were not just about football and sex but about how people could change society.

The town had a charming little cinema and one day during my stay there was a special showing of a film called "*The Brave Don't Cry,*" commemorating the events of September 1950 at the Knockshinnoch Castle colliery where 129 men were trapped by a landslide and thirteen were killed in that mining disaster. I was much moved by this film and not for the first time it came home to me that the world of work was not always a safe place and some industries including mining were particularly dangerous.

The largest town near to Thornhill is Dumfries which I thought was an enchanting place that we visited several times. We once watched the local football team, Queen of the South and since that time I always looked out for their results on a Saturday afternoon.

The River Nith runs through Dumfries toward the Solway Firth and I enjoyed walking over the several pretty bridges that cross the river within the town. I discovered a nice space called the Dock Park which is the oldest park in Dumfries and is located on the east bank of the River Nith. Sitting outside the park café in the sunshine drinking a cup of tea one day I was reflecting on a new craze in pop music known as psychedelic music. I had read that bands and artists were inspired and influenced by this new psychedelic culture which attempted to replicate and enhance the mind altering experiences of psychedelic drugs.

I was not sure that I liked this culture or what it was doing to pop music when from a radio playing in the café I heard a song of this genre by the Small Faces called *"Itchycoo Park."* I decided this song was an exception to my opinion that psychedelic music was not very good and I sang along.

Finishing my cup of tea after my sing song with the Small Faces I wandered next to the River Nith and across a nice little bridge, not the Bridge of Sighs I admit but a lovely one all the same.

CHAPTER THIRTY THREE

THE FREE WORLD

I had often heard people refer to something called "Living in the Free World." What does living in the Free World mean? I was soon to find a very novel take on the concept of freedom.

Anyway, after our short but enjoyable holiday in Thornhill, we joined up with HMS Hecate in Greenock from where the ship went off to continue with its survey of the Outer Hebrides before we sailed back to Plymouth for the last time with me onboard. I found out that after a spell in Plymouth I was to be drafted to a frigate called HMS Exmouth.

When the day of my departure came I said farewell to my ship mates, leaving HMS Hecate and Devonport Dockyard behind me. It was 11th December 1967 and with my kitbag on my shoulder I boarded a train and headed to London. The train was full and I had to stand for most of the journey but the thought that I had managed to wangle a night at home before having to join my next ship in the morning kept me cheerful. I only became miserable again when I remembered that the next ship I had been drafted to was another seagoing one that would no doubt be shortly off to sail the ocean waves which for me meant only one thing - more sea sickness!

My orders were to join HMS Exmouth in Chatham Dockyard the next day and I had to be onboard the ship before 09.00.

That gave me time for a nice evening at home.

I even managed to have a game of darts in the Osborne Tavern in Stroud Green Road with my friends Dave and Les.

The next morning I left home early and joined the office cleaners on the smoke filled bus from Finsbury Park to Charing Cross Station. At the news stand I went to buy a copy of the Daily Mirror only to be told that they had not been delivered yet and the newspaper seller said he only had the Daily Telegraph so I bought a copy. I entered an empty unheated carriage on the milk train and sat down on a dusty seat. The train departed the station and soon I was making my way through the gloomy suburbs of South East London heading towards Chatham to join my next ship. As dawn broke and I looked out of the train window and watched the Kent countryside go by I considered my position in life. I didn't like being away from home, I didn't like being at sea, I didn't like Naval discipline, I didn't like the class system of the UK and how it was reflected in the Royal Navy and I didn't want to be part of a military machine when our ally, the USA, was waging an unjust war on the people of Vietnam. Summing all this up I concluded that I still desperately wanted to get out of the Navy.

As the journey continued I decided to read the Daily Telegraph for the first and it transpired, last time. The newspaper was unbelievable, it really was just a right wing rag, the so called news items were biased and not factual and the editorials were a rant against trades unions. There were two pages of obituaries; all concerning people from the top of the social tree, Brigadiers, Admirals, Captains of Industry, Lords and Ladies. It was a paper of the capitalist class written to exchange the sort of chatter they would have at dinner parties in expensive restaurants and it was filled with warnings about disgruntled workers going on strike led by communist trade union bosses. By the time the train had reached Gravesend my fury at reading this vile rubbish had reached an explosive level and in a rage I ripped my copy of the Daily Telegraph to shreds and threw it out of the window so that no one else would be able to read its lies. I calmed down after a while and getting out my notebook and pencil I wrote a poem about my journey. Later when I related my Daily Telegraph experience to a friend they sang to me this little ditty:

"When I think I need a laugh, I read the Daily Telegraph."

Arriving at Chatham Dockyard I reported to the main gate to be informed that HMS Exmouth was not yet ready to take any crew onboard so I was directed to a mess in one of the accommodation blocks in HMS Pembroke, the shore establishment where I had attended cookery school. I warily made my way through the main gate in case the Royal Navy Regulator who had been on duty when I left at the end of my cookery training was still working there. To my relief he wasn't and I made my way to a mess.

In the mess I was allocated a top bunk and told to report to the galley as soon as I had stowed my kit and washed and changed into my cooks' whites. I did so and was told by the Chief cook in charge that I would have to join in the watch system in the galley until I was called to go to my ship and there was no date yet when this would be. This meant that on my first day I would be on duty on the late watch cooking tea then breakfast and as soon as dinner was finished the next day I would be off on make and mend and was not required in the galley until 08.00 the following day. This system suited me very well as it meant that I would be able to get a few afternoons and evenings at home whilst I was at HMS Pembroke and see my friends, go to some political meetings and advance my work on the Reluctant Servicemen campaign which would hopefully get me out of the Navy. Also, as far as I was concerned they could keep me on dry land and away from the dreaded sea as long as they liked.

I felt strange wearing a cap tally with HMS Pembroke on it again. The last time I had been here I was still a trainee cook but now I had practised my trade on the high seas and all in all I felt a bit of an old sea salt. My new mess-mates all seemed to be in transit like me, to and from different ships and my mess seemed like an alien world where people hardly bothered to talk to each other. I knew no one here and I had no friends or time to make them. The Pembroke galley I worked in seemed vast and soulless after the tiny bustling one I had plied my trade in onboard HMS Hecate. Worse still was the Royal Navy bullshit of a large establishment.

There were dozens of chefs in the galley and there was a strict hierarchy enforced by petty orders bellowed out by jumped up Chiefs and Petty Officers.

Onboard ship I had been responsible for cooking complete menus but here, cooking for over a thousand people at each meal the jobs were more basic with a strict division of labour. More often than not I received an order shouted out loudly as if I were deaf such as:

"Make up enough clacker (Short crust pastry) for a hundred pies," or

"Cook roast potatoes for six hundred people," but very often the orders to me were:

"Scrub every pot and pan until they bloody well sparkle!"

The Officers talked to each other like ordinary human beings, the Chiefs and Petty Officers did likewise to their own but the cooks and assistant cooks were the lowest of the low and could be spoken to as if they were sub human. I hated the Class System!

Getting up at 04.00 for my first breakfast duty in the galley I arrived at the doors and awaited the Petty Officer cook who had the keys to let us in. As we entered and the lights were switched on there was a significant and sudden outbreak of activity. On the worktops mice looked at us in surprise while on the ground cockroaches were making a run for it. Within seconds of the lights coming on all of the wildlife had scampered off to their hideaways.

"Right, make up buckets of soapy water and let's get this place scrubbed before we start cooking, just like Fanny Cradock would," ordered the Petty Officer. Apparently, no end of fumigations and mouse traps had made an impression on the animals and insects that lurked in the far reaches of the galley at HMS Pembroke, I was amazed.

**

As it turned out HMS Exmouth was being extensively refitted and it was some months before we actually left for sea. This suited me very well indeed as it meant that I could get up to London often and importantly I would not be sea sick for a while. For some reason at the end of January I was given a HMS Exmouth cap tally and was taken along to the ship, about ten minutes walk from my accommodation block in Pembroke Barracks, where I was told to report to every day until the ship was ready to go to sea.

It was then that I met up with Dicky Bird, a Leading Cook who I had seen in the galley at Pembroke but had not realised that we were both destined for the Exmouth.

Before boarding HMS Exmouth for the first time I stood on the dockside with Dicky and looked the ship over from the shore, it was a rather old fashioned looking grey coloured Royal Navy warship with F 84 painted on the side and it looked to me as if it had seen better days although a posse of seamen were applying coats of paint that would cheer it up immensely. I noticed, with some relief, that the ship didn't have any big guns so it was unlikely that I would be involved in anything to do with fighting whilst onboard.

Walking up the gangway I did notice two small Bofers guns on the upper deck which almost gave the frigate the look of a proper Navy warship without it being too menacing. A Chief Petty Officer was designated to give a tour around the rest of the ship to a handful of us who had turned up that day and whilst doing so he gave us an insight into what the future held for us. He told us that HMS Exmouth had been an anti-submarine warfare frigate of the Blackwood or Type 14 class but was now going to be the first major warship to be powered by gas turbine engines alone and it had Bristol Siddeley Olympus and Proteus engines installed, jet engines we were told, to replace the conventional ones. The ship would conduct sea going trials including subjecting the engines to cold and hot weather to make sure they worked in extremes of temperatures before they were installed into proper ships. There were 141 people onboard so in terms of numbers to cook for it was similar to Hecate with only about twenty more mouths to feed.

However, the ship was still not serviceable and most of the crew were still accommodated at HMS Pembroke and ate all of their meals there. This meant that Dicky and I had little to do onboard so we used to invent games to pass the time. One activity was to scrounge cigarettes from other sailors going by but in the main we just played draughts or cards and chatted. Many of Dicky's views on world politics were different to mine but he was always good for a discussion and at least he did have views. I liked Dicky a lot and over the next two years he was to become my mentor in all things cooking as well as a very good friend.

This was a strange period though as some days we were sent to the ship, to do nothing much at all and other days we were asked to cook in the Pembroke galley.

On 27th February, Pancake Day, it was decided to gather in as many idle chefs as possible and I was put back in the main galley with the specific job of making pancakes. A Chinese chef from Hong Kong and I were given our own cooking range with twelve frying pans and for over two hours we just cooked and tossed pancakes, enough to satisfy over a thousand sailors. During this task someone had made us special badges that we wore which proclaimed that we were: "Royal Navy Tossers."

Dicky Bird at HMS Pembroke

Another time that we were called up to do work off the ship was on the week of Chatham Navy Days when the dockyard and ships were open to the public. Dicky and I were detailed to a small oil fired galley where we had to produce pies and pasties and cakes especially for the event. I had never worked with an oil fired stove before and it was only by experience that I realised that you had to keep turning dishes around as they cooked. My first attempt at cooking a Bakewell tart in such an oven led to one half being burnt black and the other side as white and as runny as when I had put it in.

Whilst we were still waiting to be ready for sea I had a weekend off which I spent in London. That Saturday, March 17th, I attended a big anti Vietnam War rally in Trafalgar Square in London. After the rally we marched to Grosvenor Square, where Vanessa Redgrave delivered a letter of protest to the American embassy. The crowd, though, refused to disperse when told to and a fierce battle ensued between demonstrators and riot police; by the end of the afternoon more than 200 people had been arrested but I was fortunate to avoid getting involved in the fighting.

When HMS Exmouth was at last seaworthy her ships' company were summoned to leave the accommodation in HMS Pembroke and come onboard. A formal commissioning ceremony took place and the local press did a blurb on the ship in which they included a quote from Rolls Royce who made the ships engines:

"HMS Exmouth is the first major warship in the free world to be powered by gas turbine engines," it said.

I mused on this wording and considered what the phrase "free world" meant. Did it mean free to keep people like me in the Armed Forces when I wanted to leave? The 141 individuals who made up the ships' company of HMS Exmouth, whether they loved or hated the Navy, were all tied to contracts of up to twelve years, many of these contracts had been entered into when they were boys of fifteen or sixteen years old and none of them had the right to change jobs, to take their labour elsewhere or even to join a trade union.

In fact they didn't have any of the rights you might expect in a "free world" so why was the ship I was on described as being part of this free world?

In the circumstances, working in a ship which was the first major warship in the free world to be powered by gas turbine engines, against my will I would add, appeared to be a trite statement. If you say things often enough people will believe you I suppose but there was a real irony I thought in the Rolls Royce statement. Was I part of the free world? No I bloody well wasn't!

The next day I wrote to the Managing Director of Rolls Royce and told him that I would love to live in the free world and could he please help me achieve this but he never did reply to my letter.

**

Onboard my new ship I was shown my mess and to my amazement I discovered that on this ship I would be sleeping in a hammock. I thought this type of sleeping arrangement had gone out with Horatio Nelson and my horror at the thought of sleeping in a swinging canvas bag was increased when I was told that my particular allocated space was immediately over the hold to the ships fridge and freezer.

I was given a locker to stow my kit into and after changing into my cooks' whites I was taken to the ships galley where I was introduced to the Petty Officer who said his name was Harry and I met my fellow chefs before being set to work helping to prepare dinner. Working in the galley with me was Petty Officer Harry, my mate Leading Cook Dicky Bird, a Cook we called Father John and two young assistant cooks. Young! I was starting to feel like an old hand.

Unlike the Hecate this ship did not have a dining mess. Sailors had to queue up at the serving hatch in front of the galley and food would be placed onto their trays which were taken back to their mess to eat. After dinner I was asked to help prepare the food for tea when one of the ships Petty Officers appeared with a mean and decidedly glum looking sailor. I was asked if I could knock up something to eat for this individual so I agreed. As I was scouring the hot cupboards for any leftovers from dinner I looked up at the sailor who had been left with me and there seemed to be something familiar about him. He was a rather manic and very angry looking young man and he was addressing me in a Manchester accent.

"Bloody Hell! It's Mad Man!" I said to myself.

The mad punchy boy from Hawke Division at HMS Ganges was standing beside me.

He now appeared to be almost twice the size he was as a fifteen year old boy and I was certainly not going to mess with him and I really hoped that he wouldn't recognise me.

I gave him a tray of food that I had made up and he stood up eating it at the serving hatch. As he ate he decided to engage me in conversation.

"I hate Officers," he informed me.

"Me too," I decided to empathise with him.

He stared at me and after a few moments a light bulb went on inside his head as he said:

"I recognise you, you're Manfred Mann and you were in Hawke Division at HMS Ganges!"

"Shit!" I muttered under my breath.

"So what have you been up to since you left there," I enquired with a smile hoping he wouldn't remember the occasion I had kicked him in the balls.

"I've been in and out of D.Q's since I left Ganges," he said.

"What's D.Q's?"

"Detention Quarters, Navy prison, every time I see an Officer I punch him so they keep locking me up," Mad Man said, cheering up at the thought of punching Officers.

"I'm trying to get out of the Navy so I thought that if I keep punching Officers they might let me out," he continued.

"How many have you punched?" I asked.

"Oh, loads but they still haven't let me out, they just keep sending me to D.Q's. but now I've done my time and they have put me on this bloody ship."

I remembered back to the Annexe at Ganges and how Mad Man had been one of the few who seemed to like being in the Navy, something had changed but I was not going to try and find out what so I just gave him a double helping of spotted dick and custard to keep him happy. As he slowly licked the last drop of custard off his spoon he continued to stare at me in an inquisitive manner.

"Hey, I remember now!" he suddenly cried out.

"You kicked me in the bollocks at HMS Ganges; I'll give you a right good hiding for that when I get you on your own."

Luckily for me the Petty Officer came back and took him off to get him settled into his new mess.

I was grateful to be told that it was not the same mess that I had been allocated.

That evening an Able Seaman in my mess demonstrated to me the knot I needed to master so that I could sling my hammock properly in order that it wouldn't slip and come undone once I was lying on my canvas bed. It was with some trepidation however, that I pulled myself up and swung my body onto the hammock for the first time as the hatch to the hold below was open, it was always left open I was told, and the drop to the iron deck underneath me was a good six yards. Once in my hammock and satisfied that I wasn't going to tumble out I was surprised how comfortable it felt. I opened my biography of Ho Chi Minh, expecting to have a quiet read when I suddenly heard a commotion near the Wardroom. I was told later that Mad Man had flattened an Officer and had been dragged off the ship to be sent back to Detention Quarters again and much to my relief I never saw him again.

Two days later, with a full complement of sailors onboard we set sail to see how the engines would fair but after a couple of days at sea an entire ring of Olympus turbine blades failed in the ships engine and a big tug was sent to tow us back into Chatham Dockyard. These were soon repaired and the next few months we were at sea testing out the new engines. The ship did prove its worth though as eventually the trials were successful but for now though we had to endure a number of occasions when a tug was called upon to tow us back into various ports. We spent the next few months at sea testing out the experimental engines during which time we paid a visit to Exmouth in Devon and also undertook trials in the North Atlantic and then we went to Portsmouth. One Saturday night in Portsmouth I had gone for a curry in town and met up with chefs Dicky and John from my ship in the restaurant. After several pints of beer had washed down a particularly hot Vindaloo we decided to go for a couple more pints at a nearby pub.

Along with my ship mates we headed off in the direction of the Mucky Duck, as the White Swan Public House was known and stopped off at a photo kiosk to have our picture taken. We then proceeded to the pub and were enjoying our stroll there when somebody stopped me and asked me to tell them the time.

I was unaware that apparently a local sport of some of the gangs in Pompey was sailor bashing and they could spot us servicemen a mile off even if we were in our civvies, it was the short back and sides that gave us away. As I looked down at my watch the person who had asked me the question along with four of his mates proceeded to punch and kick me. As numerous boots landed on me I thought that I should try and make a run for it. This I managed to do and as I broke the record for the four minute mile running away from the gang I was aware that they were not interested in my friends but gave chase to me in a car they had got into. They caught up with me in a lonely street and as their car screeched to a halt in front of me a Taxi appeared.

I ran in front of the taxi and hailed it and managed to climb in as the gang of thugs reached us. As the cab drove off at speed I breathlessly explained the attack to my driver who said he would take me to the police station. Turning a corner however, we thankfully spotted a police car that was parked there. I got out of the cab and climbed into the police car to relay my experience to two policemen who asked me to sit down in the back seat. "I'm sure I would recognise their car and some of my attackers if we went looking for them," I told the uniformed officers.

"Were they black?" one of the policemen asked. When I told him they were white he said he would drop me off at the dockyard gate; which he did. When I got out of the car and said goodnight to them the police advised me not to walk around Portsmouth on my own at night and to be careful about whom I spoke to. I met Dicky and Father John onboard and thankfully they were OK. For some reason the gang were after me, probably because I was the youngest and had the shortest hair I guessed.

From left to right – HMS Exmouth Cooks John, Dicky and Me!

We sailed again two days later and were cheered up by the fact that we now had films delivered to the ship and a projector to show them on. Of course there was no cinema onboard so the sheet was taken from my hammock and fixed to the pipes along the bulkhead and this became a screen. We had James Bond films and some others that had been on release in the British cinema several years earlier but one staple were the Looney Tunes cartoons which were by far the favourite. Tom and Jerry in particular received enormous cheers and if in the opening credits the name Fred Quimby was mentioned everyone would shout out loudly: "GOOD OLD FRED!" The reason for this was quite simple, Fred Quimby cartoons were by far the most violent and the poor old Tom cat in the cartoon would be chopped up, blown up, sliced, decapitated and a steam roller flattened him into the tarmac on a frequent basis.

CHAPTER THIRTY FOUR

THE MAN FROM THE MINISTRY

For me the best entertainment on the ship was in the galley with Dicky Bird. He had an uncanny skill of being able to make up his own words to any song that came on the radio, he had us in giggles for hours on end and of course I would sing along with him. The only problem with his versions was they were not for singing in polite company. He also continued to teach me the tricks of the trade and my cooking skills were soon recognised by the ship's Supply Officer who recommended me to take my practical examinations for the rate of Leading Cook.

I had passed educationally some time ago but my Officer now wrote about me in glowing terms saying I was an above average cook whom he highly recommended for the rate of Leading Cook. So it was that I was packed off to HMS Victory in Portsmouth, (the Barracks not Nelson's ship I hasten to add) to take my examinations for promotion. These took place over the space of a week in which time I baked loaves of bread and bread rolls and made three, four and five course meals, all of which were inspected, poked, prodded, criticised and consumed by my examiners.

Cooking my first meal I was told that the food would be marked for presentation and taste. The interesting thing is that once I had served my meal up to the people marking me, three stony faced individuals, an Officer and two Petty Officers they immediately left the food and went into the galley to make sure I had cleaned everything up.

All pots, pans, worktops and decks had to be immaculate and the trick was to clean as you went. I was told that if there was one dirty pot in my galley then no matter how good the food was I would have failed the exam.

My first meal seemed to go well apart from the custard being criticised for being too sweet and the apple crumble being not sweet enough. I was going to argue that the two together balanced each other out but thought better of it and took the criticism on the chin.

The next chef up had a different menu to mine. I asked him if I could stay in the galley and observe him and he said that was fine. He had to prepare broad beans which are not the most attractive looking vegetable and when cooked look more grey than green. I told him of a trick that I used onboard my ship which was to put a small amount of bicarbonate of soda in the water they were cooked in and this would make them appear to be a lot greener. He did this and it worked a treat, the broad beans were a lovely bright shade of green. The examiners though went mad.

"If we wanted you to change the appearance of a vegetable from what it is supposed to look like we would have fucking well told you!" screamed one examiner at my fellow chef.

Unfortunately, on this very fine point they failed his entire meal and he was told he would have to do it all over again the following day. I made myself scarce.

**

The next morning I had taken an examination in bread baking and was just about to get cleaned up when an Officer I had never seen before came into the Cookery School and told me to quickly wash myself and then follow him to the wardroom. As I trotted along behind him wondering what was up he told me that someone from Whitehall wanted to talk to me. I was shown into the wardroom, a spacious and quite magnificent room with a long polished wooden table. The walls were full of paintings of admirals and sea battles and there was a huge picture of the Queen looking down at us. The Officer left and closed the door and a man, probably in his early sixties, wearing an expensive looking three piece civilian suit asked me in a Public School accent:

"Are you Cook Stephen Mann from HMS Exmouth?"

When I confirmed that he was correct in assuming that I was Cook Mann he continued:

"I have come from the Ministry to ask you some questions."

He didn't tell me his name or say which Ministry he was from.

When I heard this opening statement my face must have turned as white as the flour I had just been using to make my bread. I was terrified and my knees went to jelly. He must have seen this and he asked me to sit down.

Before he started questioning me I noticed that he put his hand inside a very nice leather briefcase he had with him and I heard a click, he was obviously taping our conversation.

"I understand you have been talking to people onboard ship about socialism," he said.

For the next two hours he grilled me about who my friends were, what my political beliefs were and where I went when I was on leave. I decided not to tell him too much so when he asked me if there were any others onboard ship with similar views to mine, I said that unfortunately there wasn't and all of those I had spoken too about politics took their views from the Daily Telegraph and the Daily Mail. I saw a look of satisfaction on his face when I told him this lie.

"What about places you go to when you are on leave in London?"

I guessed that they may have followed me and found out where I went to or if not he was just fishing. I gave him the names of a lot of pubs I had visited but none of the ones where I had actually gone for meetings or chats with my socialist friends. I noticed that he jotted all of this down but he didn't offer me a pen or paper to record any of my own notes though.

When my interrogation was over I was taken back to the Cookery School where the others were taking their exams and I wondered why I had been given no warning about what just happened and also why I was not allowed to take anyone in with me. I was also not offered a cup of tea and a biscuit. I was literally suffering from shock after this incident and asked if I could now have a cup of tea and ten minutes to recover. For the first time in years I put sugar, four teaspoons in fact, into my tea.

The next day I was informed I had been completely successful in my exams and that I had passed professionally to become a Leading Cook. Leaving Portsmouth I took the train back to London.

I had been granted a day at home en route back to Chatham where I was to rejoin the Exmouth so I boarded the number 4A Bus outside Waterloo Station to take me to Finsbury Park. Crossing Waterloo Bridge I looked down at the river Thames and the Kinks song *"Waterloo Sunset"* came into my mind and I started singing the song to myself. I will be in paradise when I get out of the Navy I thought.

I had been shaken up by my interrogation in the wardroom of HMS Victory and was really scared and worried about what the Navy would do to me. I couldn't stop wondering what their next move was but I didn't have long before I would find out.

After my night off I returned to my ship with my qualifications for promotion to Leading Cook in my hand and I was told to immediately report to the Captain. In my mind this was to be:

"Well done Cook Mann on passing your exams we will promote you to the rate of Leading Cook next week."

In the Wardroom were a Lieutenant and a Petty Officer. The Officer informed me that he had received a report prepared by "the people in Whitehall." He instructed that from this moment on I was not to talk to more than one person at a time whilst onboard ship.

"If you are talking to someone and another person joins the conversation you will walk away, you must never talk to more than one person at a time, do I make myself clear?"

I was shocked. What was happening to my civil liberties, my rights, did I have any?

"Yes Sir," I replied as it was not worth my while questioning someone in authority in the Navy.

I was told to go back to my duties in the galley and to keep my nose clean.

"We will be watching you at all times," he concluded.

Onboard ship we spent the rest of the year testing the engines out at sea and sailing up and down measured miles to see how fast we were going and all the time I knew I was being watched by someone I gave the nickname Petty Officer Grass to who had been assigned to keep an eye on me.

In October we were back in Chatham and I had a weekend off which I took in London as I wanted to go on an anti Vietnam War demonstration.

Arriving in Finsbury Park on the Friday evening I walked to my parents flat where I could hear the strains of a Pink Floyd song emanating from 133 Haden Court where Syd Barrett was singing a song about riding a bike. My Brother John had discovered what he described as his type of music but my word didn't he play it loudly! John told me that he thought that Mum and Dad would be enjoying an evening at the pub so I set off to join them. They had taken their custom from the Kings Arms as the landlord there had vanished with the Christmas club money amongst which was the ten shillings a week my Dad had put in through the year. They now frequented the Moray Arms and as I approached the pub in Durham Road I could hear my Mum's voice, she was singing *"Those were the Days"* the Mary Hopkin's hit song. Entering the saloon bar I arrived just in time to join in with the rest of the pub's customers in the chorus.

**

The anti war demonstration to be held in London on Sunday 27th was set to be the biggest yet and was organised by the Vietnam Solidarity Campaign. On the Saturday there were headline stories in the Tory press with Conservative MPs saying they hoped it rained heavily to discourage the numbers turning up. However, on Sunday 200,000 people marched through London to demonstrate their opposition to the war. Neil, a mate of mine who was a seaman onboard ship, met up with me and came along too. We had considered marching in uniform but were talked out of it as it would have just been a token gesture and we would have been thrown in D.Q's for our efforts and knowing my luck I would have probably been put in a cell with Mad Man.

Back onboard ship I noticed that I was being watched by Petty Officer Grass even more closely particularly as I had given out anti war leaflets to as many people as I could. I had also written articles for the Morning Star and Socialist Worker newspapers about the views of British Servicemen to the Vietnam war, on the advice of the editors I did this anonymously but I now made a point of bringing copies of these onboard and leaving them around for people to read.

The ship spent a while in Chatham having repairs and modifications done and I was able to get back to London a couple of times a week which was great for me. It was now the winter of 1968 and Christmas was approaching.

My mate Dicky was to be on duty over the Christmas period so I bought him a card with a picture of Karl Marx on the front. I wrote underneath the picture of a white bearded Marx: "Father Christmas" and inside the card I wished Dicky a very Happy Christmas. I felt for him being away from his family at Christmas especially as I had managed to get home for Christmas every year I had been in the Navy.

Back in London a group of assorted socialists from the Queens Pub had bought tickets to see the play *"Close the Coalhouse Door"* that was showing in a theatre in the West End. About fifteen of us had made the trip and we all thoroughly enjoyed the memorable and moving songs of Alex Glasgow which were sung throughout the play. Afterwards we all stood on the pavement in Shaftesbury Avenue and sang the theme song to the play before we raised our clenched fists and gave a rousing rendition of the *"Internationale"* to the passing theatre goers of London's West End:

So, Comrades come rally
and the last fight let us face,
the Internationale unites the human race!

Whilst on my leave in London I met up with Tony Smythe to discuss progress on the Reluctant Servicemen pamphlet and I also gave him an article I had written for him to submit to the publication, "Peace News." During a chat I told him how much I really wanted to get out of the Navy and that I didn't think I could wait for the NCCL campaign to force the Government to change the law to get me out, especially as I was now being watched to make sure I wasn't talking to more than one person at a time.

"You could try and get out by telling them that you are a Conscientious Objector," he offered.

"On what grounds?" I asked.

"You should tell the Royal Navy that you are a pacifist," he advised.

Tony told me that he had been imprisoned as a Conscientious Objector in 1958 for refusing military service.

I thought a lot about his suggestion over the coming days. Was I a pacifist? I certainly abhorred war and I felt that Governments too readily resort to armed conflict to resolve issues rather than engaging in dialogue and diplomacy. From a socialist perspective wars were about imperialism and colonialism.

Working class people had died in their millions over the past century in order that the few who had the wealth held onto it and had created even more wealth by waging war. But what would I have done to stop the rise of Fascism, would I have fought against Hitler and would I have joined the socialists and trade unionists that went to fight Franco in Spain? I probably would have done but I was moved when studying pacifism by reading words of Mahatma Gandhi who advocated peaceful civil disobedience to oppose an aggressor when he said:

"Victory attained by violence is tantamount to a defeat, for it is momentary."

The current major world conflict was the war in Vietnam and I was certainly opposed to that. If British Forces were asked to enter that war on the side of the USA I would object to it and I would not take part, I was completely certain of that. I concluded that I could put my hand on my heart and truthfully say that at this moment in time I was a pacifist and a conscientious objector. I couldn't make my mind up though on what to do especially as Tony had told me that there were three responses the Navy could make to a request for Discharge on grounds of Conscientious Objection: 1. they could refuse the request; 2. they could accept the request; 3. they could put me in prison. Whatever the Royal Navy decided to do they would not make it easy for me was his warning.

**

One diversion from my campaign to get myself out of the Navy was taking driving lessons whenever I was in London. A good friend of my parents, Albert, who drank with them in the Moray Arms, had a Mark 11 Ford Cortina and he had offered to give me free lessons. Whilst out on the roads of North London trying to avoid mounting the pavement and sudden stops, Albert used to chat about all sorts of things. One day he asked me about the sea shanties we sang on ships. A romantic concept I told him but sadly not true. We did sing onboard all the time but only along with pop music on the radio. Sea shanties were working songs on merchant ships which died out when sailing ships were overtaken by steam. In the Royal Navy in the days of sail however, work was carried out onboard ships in silence and orders were piped by the boatswain's pipe or whistle. I proudly told him that I was very good with a boatswain's pipe.

CHAPTER THIRTY FIVE

AT WAR WITH ICELAND

HMS Exmouth was to conduct both hot weather and cold weather trials to test the ship's experimental engines.

The cold weather trials meant us spending some time in the Arctic Ocean and the first stop on the way up North was to be Oslo in Norway. I tried to think of what I knew about Norway. I had recently enjoyed reading a book called "Kon-Tiki: Across the Pacific in a Raft" written by the Norwegian explorer Thor Heyerdahl. Kon-Tiki was the raft used by Heyerdahl in his 1947 expedition across the Pacific Ocean from South America to the Polynesian islands. He believed that people from South America could have settled in Polynesia in pre-Columbian times and the object of the expedition was to test the sea going abilities of the South American balsa raft and to investigate whether it would have been practically possible for the original native population of Peru, the Incas and their predecessors, to have reached the islands out in the open Pacific. The story I had avidly read was that the Kon-Tiki raft had been towed out of the harbour in Peru and left adrift in the Humboldt Current. A hundred and one days later, after crossing 4,300 miles of the Pacific, the raft was washed up on the Raroia reef well inside Polynesia. It was a remarkable story and now I would be visiting Norway for the first time in my life.

It occurred to me that I knew very little about the country apart from reading about the adventures of Thor Heyerdahl and of course the actions of my old Captain back at HMS Ganges when he went to Norway to blow up the German ship Tirpitz.

On my Christmas Leave home I had spent a few hours in the reference library in Manor Gardens to find out more. In my research the facts I found out were, 1. Norway was famous for its fjords, 2. It had a population of less than five million, 3. It shares a border with Sweden, Finland and Russia 4. The capital city is Oslo. I also discovered that Norway proclaimed its neutrality during World War II but was nevertheless invaded by Germany in 1940. Norway was unprepared for the German surprise attack but military and naval resistance lasted for two months. King Haakon and the Norwegian Government escaped to London where they supported the fight against the Nazis through radio speeches and by supporting clandestine military actions in Norway. The leader of the small Norwegian Nazi Party, Quisling, formed a Government under German control and up to 15,000 Norwegians volunteered to fight in German units. However, many Norwegians joined the Allied forces as well as the Free Norwegian Forces and during the five years of Nazi occupation, Norwegians built a resistance movement which fought the German occupation forces with both civil disobedience and armed resistance. I also found out that the Christmas tree I saw each year in Trafalgar Square in London was given by the City of Oslo as thanks for the British assistance during World War II. Bergen similarly gave a tree each year to Newcastle.

Returning from Christmas Leave the ship set sail from Chatham for our trip to the frozen North. Our Petty Officer Harry had gone sick during his leave and wouldn't be joining us so they put our Leading Cook, Dicky Bird in charge. The fact that we were one chef down though was not on my mind, I just wondered what the weather would be like.

Even though we were sailing up the North Sea in January the water had been reasonably calm but I did notice when I went up on deck to throw the gash overboard each day that the air was becoming increasingly colder.

When we arrived into Oslo Fjord I was on the upper deck collecting a bag of potatoes from the vegetable locker when spray from the sea hit me in the face. It was freezing and to my amazement where the water had come into contact with some wire stays it had formed into icicles. I shivered and quickly carried the potatoes down below to get myself warm again in the galley.

In the late afternoon I was allowed to go ashore with my friend Neil, who incidentally swore most of the time. We decided to explore Oslo on foot and because of the cold weather we had been issued with Russian style fur hats, heavy winter coats, gloves and scarves. It was minus 19° Celsius as we stepped ashore and although only my nose, eyes and mouth were exposed to the air they soon froze and I lost all sensation in them, in fact I couldn't even open my mouth to talk as my lips seemed stuck together in the frosty air of Norway.

"My word isn't this place cold!" I thought to myself.

Looking at the grim frozen expression on Neil's face I surmised that he was having similar thoughts but was probably expressing them in a more colourful way. Snow was everywhere and where the snow ploughs had cleared the roads there were high walls of solid icy snow on either side, some of these snow walls were too high to see over. We walked up Rozenkrantz Gate where at the top we spied the Spikersuppa ice skating rink. We couldn't believe it, right there in the middle of Oslo city centre were people skating in public. I'd never seen people skating on ice before and despite the cold we bought ourselves a hot drink from a kiosk and sat down and watched these carefree Norwegians, young and old, for half an hour as they gracefully waltzed around and around the ice circuit. What a lovely facility, I thought to myself, it was public and it was free for participants and audience alike.

We were still too frozen to hold any conversation but I could see Neil was still looking baffled at how much we had been charged for the coffees and he kept checking his change. As we got up to leave the skating rink Neil lifted his hand to his mouth as if taking a drink and then he wobbled his knees. I took it that his sign language meant something along the lines of: "Let's find a pub and get legless."

We walked up and down the streets looking for somewhere to get a drink but we couldn't find a pub so eventually we went into a restaurant to get some directions. We stood under an electric heater in the entrance for a few moments to thaw out and when our lips were once again mobile we asked a waiter if he could direct us to the nearest public house. The waiter laughed loudly for quite a while before informing us that there were no pubs or bars in Norway and alcohol was only allowed to be served in restaurants to accompany a meal. After getting over this shocking piece of news Neil and I decided to ask for a table in the restaurant so that we could get something to eat in order to have a drink. Inside we discovered that it was a fairly ordinary place, there were no fine table cloths, no array of wine glasses or tables full of cutlery, just a knife and fork and a paper napkin, but the place was full of locals who appeared to be enjoying themselves. The menu was in Norwegian and we had no idea what it said. Our waiter who introduced himself as Edvard spoke excellent English, as did most Norwegians we came across and he guided us through this perplexing language. It seemed that the local food involved a lot of dishes made up of raw herrings or cod that had been subjected to some unnatural processes. Our faces lit up though when we were told that hamburger and chips were on the menu although I became a bit concerned when I looked at the prices and saw lots of noughts next to each figure. Before we ordered our meal I did a quick calculation, converting Kroner into Pounds.

"My word isn't Norway expensive" I said to myself.

"Fucking Hell, look at those bloody prices!" said Neil.

We assembled our collective wealth onto the table and found that we just had enough money for a small meal and one bottle of beer each so we decided to stay and we ordered our food and drink. Listening to people on the other tables we realised that the toast when having a drink together in Norway sounded as if they were saying "school!" so we asked Edvard to write down the word for us which he obligingly did. We touched our glasses together before raising them in the air and Neil and I loudly proclaimed, much to the amusement of the people at the tables nearby: "Skål!"

Edvard was very friendly and came up to us a number of times to chat about his trips outside of Norway and when I told him I was an Arsenal supporter he ran off to the kitchen and brought back the chef who was named Knut. He told me that he had served his one year of National Service in the Norwegian Navy and also about his trips to the UK and to my delight he said that he had visited London and in particular had gone to Highbury to watch Arsenal play and that he was a big fan.

"The King of Norway, Olav, supports Arsenal too," he told me.

I was warming to Norwegians, if warming was a word that you could use this far north!

Neil and I savoured our lonely glass of beer for a long time before we eventually left the restaurant for the cold streets of Oslo once more. Before our mouths froze over again I heard Neil complain that we could have got ourselves drunk for a week in Spain on the money the meal cost us. We reflected that it was probably a good thing that there were no pubs in Norway as we wouldn't be able to afford to drink in them anyway.

After our short stay in the Norwegian Capital the ship set sail to travel further north to test out the experimental engines in the freezing cold seas of the Arctic Ocean. Chatting to Dicky as we cleaned the galley after breakfast we wondered how much colder than Oslo it would be and we shivered at the thought. One of the seamen who had been on watch on the Bridge when we had sailed came into the galley to cadge a bacon sandwich. As I prepared it for him he gave us an insight into where we were setting off to. He told us that they had set the course for Tromsø which was 1700 km north of Oslo and almost 350 km north of the Arctic Circle. He had heard that it was one of the best places to view the spectacular Northern Lights in winter but the downside was the sun was not visible between November 21st and January 21st. However, there would be some faint daylight for a few hours when we were there.

He told us that officers on the Bridge had been discussing the people that live as far north as Tromsø and concluded that they were made of stern stuff. A number of expeditions had Tromsø as their starting point and explorers like Roald Amundsen and Fridtjof Nansen used to recruit their sailors from Tromsø citizens.

I hoped that no one would get drunk and pick a fight with any of them whilst ashore but as alcohol was so expensive and so hard to get I doubted if they would. On our journey north we hugged the stunning Norwegian coast for most of the way with frequent glimpses of the mountains and fjords. On the way we sailed past Stavanger, Bergen, Ålesund and the Lofoten Islands before docking in Tromsø.

I was on watch the afternoon that we arrived in Tromsø and as many of my ship mates made their way ashore to discover the town I stood on the upper deck in my cooks' whites watching them and wondering how soon it would be before their money was spent and they were back onboard. It suddenly occurred to me that although I only had my short sleeved T-shirt on, I was only feeling cold but not frozen as I had been in Oslo. There was certainly snow everywhere but amazingly it was only just below freezing in Tromsø whereas it had been minus 19° Celsius in Oslo. As I was musing over this seemingly illogical situation I noticed that tied up near us was a Norwegian fishing boat. I could see that they had just brought in a catch so I leaned over the side and asked them what they had caught.

"Sild!" a Norwegian fisherman shouted back.

"What's Sild?" I enquired; this was a new name to me.

"They are a young herring, they're delicious, try some" was the reply.

"You just need to rinse and dry them and then dust them in some seasoned flour and fry them, your sailors will love them, and we will give you a bucket of them in exchange for some meat."

I went off to seek permission for the Norwegian fishermen to come onboard with their large bucket of still wriggling Sild and once granted I took them to our meat locker.

"I can let you have six T-bone steaks in exchange for the fish" I said.

"Make it eight steaks and we will give you two buckets of fish," was their response.

"Done!" I said, not knowing if I had been done or if they had, I expect it was the former.

For tea that evening I fried up the Sild and placed them in large dishes on the serving counter for people to help themselves as an extra course. I have to say that the Sild went down very well with everyone.

The next day I went ashore in Tromsø for a drink with Dicky this time and we again encountered the "you can only buy alcohol with a meal" scenario so entering a restaurant we ordered cheese sandwiches as the cheapest option to have with our glass of beer. The bread was a local Norwegian type with a crust as hard as a rocket shell. Dicky took one bite and the bread broke his dentures at which point he threw the sandwich across the restaurant, drank his beer and left the restaurant grumbling loudly. For us all, but particular for Dicky, Norway was an expensive run ashore

The respite of tranquil Tromsø soon came to an end as we set off to sail around the coldest parts of the Arctic Ocean before going around Iceland and then coming down the North Sea and returning to Chatham. My God it was rough and for a full two weeks we toiled in a gale that was never less than force eight on the Beaufort scale. When we had encountered similar weather when I was on the Hecate we found it impossible to produce anything but soup and sandwiches for the crew. Many onboard were at this stage like me, pale faced and sick but Dicky took the decision to carry on cooking as near normal meals as possible. We even had chips but Dicky ordered that only he was to work on the fat fryers in this bad weather and he fried smaller amounts of chips in less oil to prevent hot fat from spilling over the top of the fryer.

One disaster I encountered was with my Yorkshire puddings. I made them up in the usual way, combining eggs, milk and flour and a pinch of salt which I beat into a batter. This I poured into trays of hot dripping which I carefully placed into the oven. The ship continued to roll and pitch and after thirty minutes I opened the oven to find empty smoking trays while the entire walls of the oven were covered in an inch thick layer of burnt Yorkshire pudding mix.

Nevertheless, following Dicky's example we did manage to carry on and produce decent meals and even the Captain came down to the galley to congratulate us on our brave efforts to keep the crew fed and he was particularly impressed with Dicky producing the chips.

It was only when we reached the south of Iceland that the weather improved and the sea now just produced a heavy roll which I could get used to. I was looking forward to getting back to Chatham in a few days time when an announcement came over the ships tannoy that Iceland was threatening some British trawlers as there was a dispute about where each country's boats were allowed to fish. There were some British fishing boats in the area that were being harassed by a few Icelandic trawlers and it had been suggested by the Admiralty that as we were in the area we could spend some time showing a presence to warn off the Icelandic boats. I recalled reading that there had been confrontations between the United Kingdom and Iceland regarding fishing rights in the North Atlantic in the past and now I was on the front line in the "Cod War!" It must have soon become apparent to the Iceland sailors in their boats that intimidated the British trawlers by sailing straight at them before veering away at the last moment, that HMS Exmouth had no guns to threaten them with. After a few hours of standing off after our ship first appeared they now ignored us and carried on regardless in their intimidation tactics with the British trawlers.

One afternoon I went onto the upper deck to collect a bag of potatoes from the vegetable locker to take back to the galley when an excited Officer who people referred to as Lieutenant Brazil, because they thought he was a bit of a Nut Case, stopped me.

"Look!" he yelled.

"Look, there's a bloody Icelandic trawler right next to us!"

I looked up and he was correct, a fishing boat was only yards away and lining the deck were several Icelandic fishermen laughing and gesturing rudely at us. One had even dropped his trousers and bent over to reveal his naked buttocks. It was not something I would contemplate doing in this chilly weather but I assumed he must have had a drink or two.

"Open up your bag of potatoes and start throwing them at those bloody idiots" ordered Brazil.

"But I'm a cook not a gunner and I'm opposed to war" I protested.

Brazil momentarily stopped in his tracks.

"What do you mean you're opposed to war? What are you doing in the bloody Navy then?" he spluttered out.

"That's just the point," I replied.

"I don't want to be in the Navy and I'd be grateful for anything you could do to get me out."

He stared at me manically for just a second or two before continuing.

"Never mind all that bollocks just bloody well start throwing them," he insisted, so I obliged.

At first the potatoes I threw missed everyone and as they landed on the Icelandic boat they were picked up and thrown back but after a while I did manage to hit one sailor on the head. He looked at me angrily and I thought that I would avoid going ashore in Iceland if I ever had the opportunity in the future as he might recognise me. After a while I was joined by a couple of other sailors who had been forced to enrol in this ridiculous game. However, when my bag of ammunition, (King Edward Potatoes), had run out the Icelanders changed tactics and they started putting the potatoes we threw at them into a bucket. No doubt it had occurred to them that the potatoes would make pretty decent chips. Laughing at us as they wandered off to take the bucket of King Edward spuds to their galley to no doubt fry them to complement the cod they had caught in these disputed waters.

"Fish and Chips!" they shouted at us.

"Tell Harold Wilson we're going to bloody well enjoy our fish and chips tonight made with our fish and your potatoes, Ha Ha Ha!."

I mentioned this adventure to Neil who had just come down from completing his watch on the Bridge. He had no knowledge of anyone being told to engage the enemy and he thought it was just something that Brazil had decided to do off his own back in a moment of madness.

"He's fucking bonkers!" offered Neil.

After my short spell at war with Iceland the ship continued to make its way to the North Sea and back to Chatham but before we did we had been scheduled to spend a couple of days in Holland followed by a short trip to the German harbour of Wilhelmshaven. Arriving in Germany we were allowed ashore almost as soon as we had berthed alongside the jetty so I decided to explore the town on my own.

After such a period of being at sea in rough weather I could feel myself rolling from side to side as I walked along so I thought I would just find a nice café or park bench and have a sit down to recover. Many of the buildings I passed looked new and were built in the ugly post war architectural style that much of Plymouth, Portsmouth and London had been re-built in. Luckily, I found a café in a park and I sat down at a table and began to read, "*Ten Days that Shook the World*" by John Reed. As soon as I had opened the book up a man who looked as if he was in his late fifties sat down next to me. As I was wearing my uniform he knew I was British so he started talking to me in pretty good English. He asked me what I was doing in Germany and we then talked a little about how cruel the sea could be until he suddenly changed the subject and he told me that two thirds of the buildings in the town we were in were destroyed by allied bombing in the war. We silently dwelt on this information for a while before he rummaged around in his pocket. He took out his wallet and produced from it some photographs.

"This man was the greatest German who ever lived, he did so much good for us," he said, showing me a dog eared photograph of Adolf Hitler.

"I thought that Hitler was Austrian?" I said under my breath and I gave him a nervous smile as he handed me another picture, this time of a young man in an SS uniform.

"That's a picture of me in the war," he told me.

"That was a great time for Germany and we would have beaten you if we had not made war with Russia too."

I decided to try and change the conversation to the weather but he just carried on in this vein before getting up and doffing his cap to me and he said:

"Have a good time in Wilhelmshaven and I am looking forward to reading in the newspapers that your ship has sunk on the way back to England," and with a broad smile he left.

The next day a small group of us took a long bus ride to Hamburg as we had heard it was a good run ashore. Alighting from the bus in Hamburg we asked some locals where the best place to go was. Looking at our uniforms they pointed us in the direction of the Reeperbahn.

A young friendly German lad in his early twenties walked along with us practicing his English language skills. He told us that the locals called the Reeperbahn "die sündige Meile" the sinful mile. This seemed to excite a few of my ship mates. When we arrived at the Reeperbahn there was a real buzz about the place and while three of my group went off in search of the brothels, Neil and I entered a night club that was pumping out pretty good rock music. Inside we bought a couple beers and settled down to the Beatles like music of a German band which was very acceptable indeed. After half an hour the others came in and found us, they were bemoaning the fact that the prices in the brothels were beyond them so they suggested drawing lots in order that one of them could go if the rest of us had a whip round to finance this venture! As they went off again Neil and I went into one more night club before we had to get the bus back. We agreed that we liked Hamburg which was a lot more cosmopolitan and lively than Wilhelmshaven and to my relief nobody there showed me a picture of Hitler.

After our short stay in Germany we left and made our way back to Chatham where the ship was docked to make some repairs after the recent buffeting we had taken at sea. The Captain placed an article in the Chatham News commending the ships cooks and in particular the Leading Cook, for the amazing job we had done whilst we were in the Arctic keeping the ships' company fed and watered in exceptionally bad weather.

"Dicky deserves that commendation," I thought to myself.

When the mail bag was brought onboard I had a number of letters handed to me that were from friends and family which I noticed had already been opened. That was the last straw for me. I had been doing a lot of thinking whilst I was in the Arctic and before I went home to London on leave I made a momentous decision to put in a formal written request for "Discharge from the Royal Navy on grounds of Conscientious Objection."

CHAPTER THIRTY SIX

MORALLY INDEFENSIBLE

On my next leave in London I went to a couple of political meetings including the International Socialists and an anarchist group in Hornsey

My younger Brother John had become an anarchist, the pacifist type, he was at pains to tell me and when he could he would drag me along to anarchist meetings. However, I was much more in tune with socialism and I preferred going to their meetings. It was a good decision on my part as it was at a socialist meeting that I met Jennifer, a beautiful young woman who was training to become a teacher and we started going out together.

Whilst on leave I met up again with Tony Smythe and he told me that on the 23rd April 1969 Lord Fenner Brockway had taken up the matter of Reluctant Servicemen once more by initiating a debate on the release rights of boy entrants in the armed forces when he raised the question in the House of Lords: [6]

"To ask Her Majesty's Government on what grounds, in view of the decision to make the age of majority eighteen years, boys enlisting into the military services from fifteen years upwards do not have the protection of the Infants Relief Act 1874, and are legally bound to serve, with limited opportunities of discharge, until thirty years of age."

Lord Winterbottom, the Parliamentary Under - Secretary of State for Defence replied to the debate and said:

"My Lords, my noble friend is concerned with two different concepts. The Infants Relief Act 1874 deals with contracts made by persons under the age of majority so as, with certain exceptions, to make them void. A person, of whatever age, who enlists in the Armed Forces in law, does not thereby enter into a contract, either with the Crown or with anyone else, as regards the service he agrees to undertake voluntarily."

Strange semantics I thought which basically meant that there was still no way out of the Navy for those like me who had signed on for twelve years from the age of fifteen. The campaign for Reluctant Servicemen however, was carrying on and Tony told me of yet another challenge by NCCL supporters in Parliament which was on the 7th May when there was a House of Commons Debate on Young Servicemen (Morale and Conditions) [7]. The actors in this bit of parliamentary theatre were John Biggs-Davison the Conservative Member of Parliament for Chigwell, Gerry Reynolds the Government Defence Minister who was also Labour Member of Parliament for Islington North and Tom Driberg the Labour Member of Parliament for Barking.

The debate went as follows:

Mr. Biggs-Davison

"What representations has the Secretary of State for Defence received from the National Council for Civil Liberties about morale and conditions in the Services; and what reply he has sent?"

Mr. Reynolds

"The National Council for Civil Liberties has asked to be associated with a recent request from the Parliamentary Civil Liberties Group to discuss with me the question of young Servicemen. I have advised the Group that I am prepared to examine and subsequently discuss with it detailed complaints; and I have kept the National Council for Civil Liberties informed."

Mr. Biggs-Davison

"Are the Government aware of a report and connected activities which tend to tamper with the morale and loyalty of Her Majesty's Forces? What advice has been taken from the Law Officers of the Crown?"

Mr. Reynolds

"I am aware of quite a number of things, but on the information that the hon. Gentleman has given the House now I would not like to say it has anything to do with what he is talking about. If he cares to let me have details, I will certainly look at them."

Mr. Driberg

"Does my right hon. Friend agree that it is not tampering with the morale and loyalty of the forces to recognise that 15-year-olds who sign on for 12 years without really knowing what they are doing should be released, or given the option of release, at 18 in accordance with the Report of the Latey Committee?"

Mr. Reynolds

"This matter, as my hon. Friend well knows, has been and is still being examined by the Government. Despite all the publicity there has been, I am still surprised at the very small number of such cases in which there is hardship which has been so far forwarded to me in the last two years."

Reading the transcript of this debate it occurred to me that if there were only a small number of cases of servicemen who wanted to leave then why not let me out?

**

I mentioned that my Dad worked in the stores of a garage on the Holloway Road with a pub situated between the stores and the actual garage. It was common for policemen to clock on at the local police station and then walk to the garage and sit in the store room whilst my Dad or one of his colleagues got them pints of beer. Sometimes they would have a few pints and then go off to work, other times they would stay there drinking until their shift had finished. A strange thing happened after my next driving lesson which only came to my knowledge because of the relationship between my Dad and these policemen.

The person teaching me to drive, Albert, was having his car repaired so my Dad's garage loaned him a car for a couple of days. One evening when Albert called to give me a driving lesson I mentioned to him that I would like to go to an anti war meeting in Hampstead Library so Albert suggested I drive us there as part of the lesson. I parked up the borrowed car, a Vauxhall Viva, outside the library and Albert and I went in.

After the meeting, which Albert said he had enjoyed, we left and I drove us both back to Holloway Road where we dropped the car off on the forecourt of my Dad's garage.

The next day the local CID, great drinking pals of my Dad, visited the garage and enquired about the car that had been seen at the Library.

When my Dad asked what the problem was the reply came back that the Special Branch had contacted them and wanted to know who had been using the car as it was registered to my Dad's garage. My paranoia deepened.

CHAPTER THIRTY SEVEN

THE ROAD TO RIO

Back onboard ship we were informed that our next task was to test out the ships engines in hot weather.

A loud cheer went up when this was announced on our Daily Orders notice board. We were to sail to Gibraltar and from there we would pass the Azores and on to visit Gambia in Africa before crossing over the Atlantic Ocean to Rio de Janeiro in Brazil.

A Royal Navy Doctor came onboard and gave us a lecture in how to survive in the tropical heat we were to be subjected to.

"Keep out of the sun as much as possible and drink plenty of water and take luke-warm showers to keep you cool but don't take too many and don't use soap each time; it will wash the natural oils out of your skin and do you no good," he warned.

He also issued us with salt tablets to replace the salt loss from perspiration as we were told we would spend a lot of our time sweating in the heat.

I had a short weekend at home before having to leave on our trip to the tropics to test out the ship's engines. I met up with my mate Les in the Osborne Tavern in Finsbury Park and as we played darts he told me that he had booked up his summer holidays at Butlin's Holiday Camp in Clacton. I didn't want to boast but when I told him that I was off to Rio his eyes almost popped out.

"You lucky bastard!" he said.

I did inform him that I would swap places with him any day to get out of the Navy although I had to admit there was a part of me that was secretly enjoying the thought of sailing to Brazil.

Leaving Chatham our first stop was Gibraltar which was very pleasant and seemed to me like being in England with sun. What stuck in my mind was remembering a newspaper article I read saying that John Lennon had married Yoko Ono in Gibraltar earlier in the year so I would have to have a good look around the place to find out why. As I walked the streets of this British overseas territory it seemed a strange place, all red pillar boxes and British Bobbies and a big rock with apes running around stealing food from people, but we were not there that long before we set off on our trials in the South Atlantic.

Soon after sailing away from Gibraltar we were making our way down the coast of Africa to Gambia when the inevitable happened, the engines packed up and a big tug towed us back to Gib! We spent the next month or so back in Gibraltar whilst repairs were made to the engines and I decided to make the most of my leisure time there by going to the beach and swimming in the warm sea. It was here that I encountered my first experience of sun burn. One afternoon, off duty, Neil and I took our towels and swimming trunks onto the beach but we stopped off first in a bar and had perhaps one too many beers. Before leaving the ship I had already done my rounds of the messes to receive my sips of rum for favours rendered during the late evening and early morning to seamen and stokers on watch who had looked into the galley for some hot soup or sandwiches. Once my rum intake was topped up with several beers I was feeling the worst for wear. I felt a little too drunk to swim so I laid my towel on the beach and proceeded to fall into a lovely deep sleep. My nice dreams suddenly changed and I was now dreaming that someone was rubbing my back with sandpaper when I awoke to find a local boy doing just that. He had noticed that my back had developed a large blister filled with liquid and he decided to rub sand into it to burst it. He succeeded and I was in agony.

I somehow managed to put a shirt on over my back and returned to the ship where Neil said that I should stand under a cold shower to take the heat out of the burn. I stood under ice cold water for fifteen minutes but when I turned the shower off the pain returned. I needed to see a doctor but the injuries I had would be classed as self inflicted and I would be put on a charge. I pondered this dilemma for a while but then took the decision that I needed to seek medical advice as the pain was so bad. As predicted when I saw the doctor I was placed on a charge. My punishment was a week's stoppage of leave and extra duties.

During this time the United States of America's Mediterranean fleet arrived in Gibraltar for some reason or other. They never travelled light; there was an aircraft carrier, several destroyers and a couple of frigates and some support vessels. With so many ships docked in Gibraltar space was at a premium and the next day an American destroyer with a name that sounded something like USS Tutti Frutti berthed next to us. It was amusing listening to the orders being piped over their ships tannoy. One I loved was to call their sailors for inspection on the upper deck before going ashore:

"Liberty guys to glamorise and materialise abaft the after smokestack!"

Another piped order announced payday when the American sailors would be lined up to receive their wages with the announcement that said:

"Crew of the USS Tutti Frutti to assemble for your pay, the Eagle has shit!"

I liked having the American Navy berthed next to us in the harbour as they were pretty friendly and the ones I spoke to about the war in Vietnam, similar to the servicemen on the base in Bermuda, were opposed to it.

When my punishment for getting sunburn was over I was allowed to go ashore again so I went for a drink with Dicky to Sugar's Bar. Sugar was a larger than life character, very camp, who owned the place.

His bar was a great favourite with British sailors and always appeared to be heaving with them. Dicky and I were welcomed at the door by loud speakers which boomed out the song "*Sugar Sugar*" by the Archies.

That night a large number of American sailors also visited Sugar's bar. As Dicky and I stood at the bar having a drink and chatting one of the more patriotic and fairly drunk American sailors shouted over to us:

"Hey, when are you Limeys going to join the war in Vietnam?"

Quick as a flash Dicky answered back:

"There's no need to mate, the Vietcong are doing a good job as it is."

That was it; chairs were crashed over heads, glasses were thrown and it was just like a western bar room brawl from a John Wayne film. Dicky and I quickly exited through the back door to find a quieter establishment and we left those who liked to fight to get on with it. As we strolled down Main Street, jeeps and vans full of Royal Navy Regulators and American Military Police sped by in the opposite direction.

When, after a few days of having the Tutti Frutti berthed next to us, it left with the rest of their fleet to go to sea, a small group of sailors from HMS Exmouth reignited the rivalry between the two Navies as they waved the Americans goodbye and sang:

"There's a buzz going round the harbour,
that the yanks are going to sea,
with crates of Pepsi Cola,
and a bloody great tub of ice cream.
They are all good kids in harbour,
but oh my Christ at sea,
yes they're fucking good kids in harbour,
but oh my Christ at sea."

"That doesn't bode well for Anglo American relations the next time we all meet up in Sugar's bar," I thought to myself.

On June 6th there were very few people on duty onboard the Exmouth as most of the ships' company had gone ashore to get legless in the many bars of Gibraltar. I had finished cleaning the galley following tea and was standing on the upper deck in my cooks' whites fishing for mackerel.

I had only been there for ten minutes and the bucket next to me already had half a dozen fish in it, it was so easy to catch fish in Gibraltar harbour using my bent safety pin on the end of a long piece of string.

To attract the fish I again threw in a handful of cooked rice and the fish just queued up to be caught. I was looking forward to taking the fish back to the galley to cook myself a tasty treat of fresh grilled mackerel with a dash of soy sauce when an excited Sub Lieutenant ran up to me.

"Do you know how to use a Lee Enfield .303 rifle?"

His wild eyes demanded me to enlighten him and I noticed that his voice was high pitched and shaky. I told him that I was an ace shot when it came to shooting Germans and I started to recall my training at HMS Ganges.

"Yes, well never mind that now," he blurted out, rather a bit too dismissive of my attributes with a rifle I thought.

"Franco has closed the bloody border between Spain and Gibraltar and there's a buzz going around that he will anchor his ships outside the harbour and it looks like there's only a handful onboard to defend the ship if we are attacked."

I thought I would point out to him a couple of things, firstly that we were an experimental ship that didn't have any real guns so if we were attacked then any resistance would be futile and secondly the harbour was brimming with well armed proper British warships which would no doubt be able to handle the situation but he was in too excited a state to listen as he gave me the order:

"Go and get your number 8s on and report to the armoury as quick as you can."

I changed and reported to the armoury or more precisely a cupboard on the bulkhead with a small number of old Lee Enfield rifles locked inside. I was given a rifle and a small box.

"The rifle is unloaded but there are two bullets in the box," said the Duty Officer.

"You are to march up and down the upper deck and if we are attacked by the Spanish you are to put the two bullets in the rifle and defend the ship."

"One for them and one for me," I said jokingly but I just received a frosty stare in reply.

If only Franco knew that only a duty cook with an empty rifle onboard HMS Exmouth, a pacifist to boot, stood between him and taking back Gibraltar the history of the British Empire would have been completely different.

As it transpired the sight of my rifle either terrified Franco or the Spanish weren't really going to attack anyway. Also, the call had gone out to bring back some real seamen from ashore who took over my rifle duty after about twenty minutes so the chance of me seeing any real action was very remote, thankfully!

A decision was taken to put off the hot weather engine trials for the ship until some unspecified date in the future so HMS Exmouth left Gibraltar and set sail back to Chatham. On the journey back a mate of mine onboard named Jim told me that he had a girl friend in Plymouth and he wanted to leave the Navy and move in with her but his request for a compassionate discharge from the Royal Navy had been rejected. I talked a lot to Jim from then on about life in general and politics and he seemed at first to be a natural left winger. I was only allowed to talk to one person at a time so I decided to demonstrate to Jim the Great Money Trick that I had attempted on HMS Hecate one evening when we were at sea; this time I used matchsticks instead of pieces of bread as my raw materials. Unfortunately, Jim was no budding socialist, in fact he told me that he supported the Conservatives and my attempts to convert him cut no ice but my friend Neil had been listening to us from his hammock and he shouted down his support for me by saying that he hated the "fucking Tories."

That night Neil came up to me just as I was nodding off to sleep in my hammock and tapped me on the shoulder.

"Are you awake?" He asked.

"I bloody well am now," I said.

There was an excited tone to Neil's voice which indicated that he had something important to tell me so I swung myself out of the hammock in order that I could see him properly as he asked me to hear a story from the book he was reading.

I put on my number 8s and we went onto the upper deck to chat.

The lights were strong enough to read by and Neil said he wanted to tell me about a chapter from Jack London's book titled the "War of the Classes." [8]

It was a revelation, it described the moment Jack London became a socialist. Neil was a great fan of his as was I; we had both read some of his books but this one turned out to be a real gem.

He paraphrased some of the chapter and said that Jack London decided after working at sea for seven months to go tramping. On this adventure he found himself with people who had dropped down from the proletariat into what sociologists' call the submerged tenth. Jack London says he had shivered with these people in box cars and city parks, listening to life histories which began under auspices as fair as his own and talking to them he saw the picture of the "Social Pit" as vividly as though it were a concrete thing and at the bottom of the Pit he saw them. He was above them, not far, and hanging on to the slippery wall by strength and sweat when a terror seized him. Neil then told me that Jack London became a socialist when he thought how easy it was to fall into that Social Pit and we needed to collectively struggle against that happening to anyone.

I told Neil that I thought that I became a socialist when I was told that Labour had set up the National Health Service and the Tories had voted against it.

"I've become a socialist by reading Jack London!" proclaimed Neil proudly.

CHAPTER THIRTY EIGHT

A CONSCIENTIOUS OBJECTOR

As soon as the ship was berthed in Chatham Dockyard my Supply Officer came into the galley to tell me something:

"Next Monday you have to report to the Naval Chaplain in the Dockyard Church at 09.00."

I searched for Neil to tell him this news and we wondered why a Chaplain would want to see me. I told Neil that I had once received some very good advice from the Chaplain at HMS Ganges on how to clean windows using vinegar and old newspapers.

"Maybe there's an improved method of cleaning windows that's been discovered and he wants to update me," I joked.

Putting the intriguing assignation awaiting me on Monday morning out of my head I headed for Chatham Rail Station along with Neil to enjoy a weekend in London. Neil was off to Walthamstow and I was off to Finsbury Park but before we boarded the train we decided to celebrate his conversion to socialism by stopping off at a coffee shop in Chatham for a frothy coffee. The Juke Box was playing *"Something in the Air"* by Thunderclap Newman. We both joined in as Thunderclap sang out the lyrics about changing the world by revolution.

When I got back to London I met up with Jennifer and we discussed what we might do over the weekend.

We had spent a lot of our time going to political meetings and also to parties together in Crouch End, Stoke Newington and Muswell Hill over the period we had known each other but we wanted to do something on our own.

A decision was made to go to the cinema so we set off for London's West End and had an enjoyable evening watching *"The Virgin Soldiers,"* a very funny film about the experiences of young men performing their National Service in the British Army in Singapore. We walked all the way back from Leicester Square to North London just enjoying the pleasant evening and each other's company, it was wonderful.

**

On Monday morning after arriving back onboard ship I dressed in my best naval uniform and set off to see the Chaplain. The Church in Chatham Dockyard was an impressive building with doors at the side. I knocked on a door and a young and kindly looking man wearing a dog collar invited me in and sat me down at a table. A smiling woman entered and gave us a pot of tea and some biscuits and once the introductions and small talk were out of the way my interrogation began about why I held the views that I did. Over the next six weeks I was frequently required to have lengthy interviews and discussions with the Chaplain who had been designated by the Royal Navy to question me to see if I really was a Conscientious Objector. After my first meeting the Chaplain offered to show me around the Church and I noticed a sign on the wall that said:

"Honour thy Father and thy Mother that the days may be long in the Land which the Lord thy God giveth thee, Thou shalt do no murder."

At my second interview the Chaplain asked me if I had any hobbies. I told him that I enjoyed, poetry, swimming, football, politics and reading and that my favourite author was George Orwell.

"Well there you are," he said, "George Orwell wasn't a pacifist, he fought in the Spanish Civil War."

"Yes," I replied, "but he wouldn't fight in an unjust war in Vietnam on behalf of the USA."

I strongly argued about the unjustness of war and particularly the Vietnam War which Australia had entered to assist America and I told him that I was fearful that Britain might join in also.

Not for the first or last time, a country manufactured a story to justify going to war.

In the case of Vietnam we were later to discover that the Gulf of Tonkin incident, involving North Vietnam and the United States was a false flag operation to justify the USA going to war. The outcome of this incident was the passing by the United States Congress of the Gulf of Tonkin Resolution which granted President Lyndon B. Johnson the authority to assist any Southeast Asian country whose government was considered to be jeopardized by "communist aggression." The resolution served as Johnson's legal justification for deploying U.S. conventional forces and the commencement of open warfare against North Vietnam and it was based on a manufactured lie

As my interrogation continued the reasons why the Armed Forces were necessary were hammered home by the Chaplain and the reasons for not needing them were answered by a young cook in Her Majesty's Royal Navy, me! It all became so surreal and the phrase Thou shalt do no murder kept coming to mind. It seemed strange to me that a man of God should be arguing for violence and death but that was not for me to question. I just had to hold firm and tell him that I did not want to be a part of the Armed Forces.

"Pacifists turn the other cheek if they are attacked, would you do that if your Country was attacked?" asked the Chaplain.

I had to keep telling him that I would not fight in an unjust war and that I was a pacifist..

At one point the Chaplain said he was going to send me to Belfast to see how the Armed Forces were not really war makers but peace keepers and he wanted me to find out why we needed them. I declined his offer and I told him that no amount of argument would change my position and soon after this the meetings stopped. Onboard ship my Supply Officer, a nice man, also spent many hours quietly trying to talk me out of being a pacifist.

It was over a month later when a buff envelope with the words "On Her Majesty's Service" stamped on it was handed to me by the Supply Officer. I went onto the upper deck to read it but I looked at the envelope for a long time wondering what was inside. I guessed that it was the answer to my request for discharge but what would it say: yes or no? Tony Smythe had told me that there were three options:

1. They could refuse the request;
2. They could accept the request;

3. They could put me in prison.

Opening the letter with a thumping heart I discovered there was a fourth option: I was to be "Discharged on Grounds of Conscientious Objection;" elation! The discharge though was by purchase which would cost £200.

"Where the hell will I find £200?" I cried out loud.

I thought about this carefully, I had saved £80 over the past five years towards buying a restaurant, putting the money into a Post Office savings account, but no one else in my family had savings so I was buggered. A deep gloom came over me.

When I was next in London I asked around about how to raise £120 but I was getting nowhere until a couple of members of the International Socialists Group I was chatting to in the Queens pub came up with an idea.

"We will get everyone together and hold a fund raising party for you!"

So, on a Saturday night in October 1969, the socialists of Hornsey came together again, this time united in the cause of my freedom. At a house in Hornsey they opened the doors and charged everyone a minimum of £1 entry to what was billed as the: *Free Steve Mann Party*. I got the bus from Finsbury Park to the top of Crouch Hill that evening and listened as people chatted about a party they were on their way to where they were raising funds to help get a young sailor out of the Navy. They were talking about me! The party was really well organised and a host of people contributed to its success. The house was packed with socialists and anarchists who bopped away all night to the thumping music of the Rolling Stones and the Beatles. At the end of it my socialist pals Mike, Fergus and Wenda came up to me and handed me £120 in mainly one pound and ten shilling notes and loose change but there were a few five pound notes included too. Soon after I had deposited the money into the Post Office in Finsbury Park I withdrew the full amount of my savings in Postal Orders to the value of £200, these I took back to my ship and handed over to Jimmy the One who grumpily told me that I would be notified when I was to be released in due course.

In November I had still not heard and I met up with Tony Smythe who handed me the transcript of yet another debate about boy servicemen, the reluctant type that is.

There had been a Defence debate in the House of Commons [9] held on 13 November 1969 and the Minister of Defence for Administration, Mr. Roy Hattersley said:

"Boys in the forces cannot change their jobs in the same way as is possible in civilian life because the primary obligation of the Ministry of Defence is to make sure that manning levels are adequate to meet our needs. It is, however, our continuing enthusiasm to reconcile the demands of civil liberties with the need to maintain forces at an adequate level."

During a lengthy debate he went onto say:

"I am saying that the second Latey proposal – that young men should have the opportunity to leave the forces at or about their 18th birthday – is a risk which I do not feel it justifiable to take. I am going on to say, however, that there are other people who have urged, as well as a leap in the dark, a general relaxation and who claim that the general act of making engagement structures more flexible would in itself build into the system a compensation against future losses. They say that more flexible terms of engagement would encourage an increased number of boys to join the Service.

Some, of course, would drift off. I suspect that some would drift back, but there would be a net loss. That is a net loss which, I suspect, my hon. Friend and, no doubt, others would argue would be more than compensated for by the increased numbers of young people who would join the forces when they knew that they would not be committing themselves irrevocably for a long period.

If we adopted that system, there would, of course, be a substantial wastage of trained personnel. The creation of a trained adult Service man would be a great deal more expensive than it is today. For my part, however, I would not allow that financial problem to prevent a movement in that direction, but I would need to be convinced that things would work out in the way that these predictions suggest. Indeed, in the case of recruitment of young men, I believe that a strong case can be made for a general examination of their terms of reference, their organisation and the obligations they undertake.

I am, therefore, setting up a committee, which will include civilian as well as Service personnel, to examine these entire questions.

The exact terms of reference of the Committee have not yet been decided, but I can say that the committee will report to me and I shall report to the House.

I warn the House now, however, that whenever the committee's report leaves a question in doubt I shall come down on the side of safety; whenever there are two interpretations as to the outcome of a likely change, I shall feel it my duty to choose the alternative which ensures that the forces remain as large and as competent as we need them to be."

Speaking in the debate the MP for Barking, Tom Driberg, quoted the late Navy Minister, Gerry Reynolds, MP for Islington North who had said that:

"the compulsory 12-year service for a boy joining at the age of 15 was morally indefensible but that it had to be kept because of the risk of a mass exodus should it be relaxed."

Tom Driberg argued in the debate that the Latey Committee had recommended, but the Government had not acted on, a right for boy servicemen to be able to leave at the age of about 18 if they chose to. He argued that the Government are not morally entitled to keep them in the Navy or Army compulsorily without giving them that option to leave. He said:

"I do not like a Government I support defending an action which they say is morally indefensible."

He also said:

"We do not want to keep unwilling sailors in the Navy."

Unfortunately, the Defence Minister and his Government continued to keep unwilling sailors in the Navy and I was one of them!

There was a Broad Church of people fighting for the liberty of reluctant servicemen: anarchists like Tony Smythe; Bishops and Priests; progressive Liberals such as Eric Lubbock and people in the Labour Party like Tom Driberg and Fenner Brockway, the latter who I thought of as great socialists who had fought tooth and nail for my rights.

I was now proud to call myself a socialist too but I believed though that the way Government Ministers and the Conservatives had acted over the length of the campaign on Reluctant Servicemen was indicative of how some people see the world.

Take the issue of austerity, the ruling class preaches it but really it is for others not for them. For instance, in difficult economic times those with wealth and power say:

"We must tighten our belts; we are all in this together."

As poorer people lose their jobs or have their wages and benefits cut and go without the rich and powerful carry on with their lifestyle and indeed become richer and they will still go to expensive restaurants and discuss which champagne will go best with their turbot.

Freedom was a similar concept, it's what people preach but if a few thousand working class boys are denied their freedom it doesn't really matter. Members of Parliament can leave their jobs anytime they like regardless of the expense of a bye election to replace them. If you work in a bank or in any job in industry you can just chuck your job in and go off to somewhere else to work. In almost any job a week or sometimes a month's notice will suffice and you can leave, so why couldn't I?

At least the NCCL had convinced the Government to look into the issue and set up a committee that would include civilian as well as military members so maybe for others our Reluctant Servicemen campaign would make a difference.

**

Not long before Christmas I was having a talk onboard ship with Jim who had seen me visiting the Church in the Dockyard on a couple of occasions and wondered why. I told him about my request to leave the Navy and the interrogation by the Vicar and that I was hopefully soon getting out on grounds of conscientious objection.

Jim wished me luck and told me that after Christmas Leave he would not be coming back. He couldn't stand being separated from his girlfriend anymore. She had now moved up to London and into a flat in Ealing and had got herself a job in a department store in Oxford Street.

"I asked to leave the Navy but they wouldn't let me so I'm going to desert so that I can be with her," Jim told me.

"There's plenty of work I can do on the building sites in London where it's cash in hand with no questions asked about who you are."

CHAPTER THIRTY NINE

RED SOCKS AND LIBERTY

After Christmas leave I returned to Chatham Dockyard and again boarded HMS Exmouth to report for duty.

I was actually five minutes late as I had fallen asleep on the train from Charing Cross and had been woken up by cleaners in the sidings at Gillingham. Arriving back at the ship a Petty Officer saw me coming onboard and looked at his watch.

"Don't report me, I'm only 5 minutes adrift," I pleaded to his better nature.

The Petty Officer reported me and I was immediately placed on defaulters and had to appear straight away in front of the Officer of the day. I had changed quickly into my Navy clothes but had forgotten to put my Navy issue blue socks on and this was noticed.

"Why are you wearing red socks Cook Mann?" asked the duty Officer.

"Because I'm a communist Sir," was my flippant answer. Actually they were Arsenal Football Club socks with a little gun motif on the side I had been given as a Christmas present but I was now past caring.

"I was going to place you on a week's stoppage of leave and extra duties," said the Duty Officer.

"But for that remark I've increased it to two weeks."

I thought of mentioning to him the story of an Admiral I once met who wore red socks but I didn't think that would get me anywhere and so my punishment started with immediate effect.

I looked for Jim over the next couple of days but people in his mess thought he had gone on the trot, he had deserted.

"Good luck to you Jim, I hope you get away with it," I said to myself.

Before the two weeks of my punishment were up we were sailing through the Solent when the ship unexpectedly headed into and docked in Portsmouth Harbour. The Master at Arms appeared in the galley where I was working and told me that I had ten minutes to change into my number one uniform, pack my kit bag and leave the ship. I was to immediately report to Victory Barracks for discharge from the Royal Navy. I just made it down the gangway before it was whisked from under me and HMS Exmouth set off again for the open sea. I didn't even have time to say goodbye to my friends. It was January 16th 1970.

I stood on the side of the dock bemusedly watching the ship, my floating home for the past two years, sail away. I was thrilled that the long and traumatic process of getting out of the Navy was drawing to a conclusion but I would miss my ship mates. I had learnt great respect for them and for all the people who work in the ships of the Navy. I thought to myself how tough a profession it is and what a hard life people led at sea, if I had not been through it myself I would have difficulty understanding it. Then I remembered the lengths some had gone to trying to get out of the Navy. Basher had spent months pretending to be daft, Sparky had induced dermatitis and probably ruined his hands for life, Mad Man had punched Officers, Jim had deserted and I had become a Conscientious Objector.

I pondered on these thoughts for only a moment or two as I could see an Officer nearby giving me a strange look so I set off, marching quickly through the dockyard with my kit bag on my shoulder past HMS Victory, the real one, Nelson's ship that is, and into HMS Victory, the Navy Barracks. It suddenly occurred to me that I was becoming a free man and should get home that evening and might even be able to watch the Arsenal play Chelsea at Highbury the next day; what joy!

Once inside HMS Victory though I realised that the Royal Navy was still making things difficult for me. I was allocated a mess and told by a Petty Officer to report to the galley and start working straight away.

"Bloody Hell!" I said in response to this order.

I thought that I was being released from the Navy but over the coming days there was no word of my discharge as I was required to cook meals for the sailors of HMS Victory.

On Monday I was given a medical examination similar to the one I had when I joined the Navy. I was again made to strip off while my body was probed, examined and measured. At the age of fifteen I was deemed to be five feet, five and a half inches tall, my hair was fair, my eyes were blue, my complexion was fresh and my chest measured thirty one and a half inches. Now I was six feet tall and my chest measured forty one inches, my hair was still fair though, my eyes were still blue and my complexion was still fresh.

Following the examination I sat in the mess where I had a cup of tea and read the Daily Mirror that I had purchased at the NAAFI shop. I read that Arsenal had lost at home to Chelsea three goals to nil at the weekend so maybe going to that match wouldn't have been the best way to have celebrated my freedom after all!

The days dragged by and on the 23rd January I awoke from a nightmare I had been having. Everything in my dream was so vivid and in it I had been discharged from the Royal Navy but as soon as I had arrived home two policemen came and took me back to the ship again. I didn't know it then but it was to become the recurring nightmare I was to have for the next thirty years.

Sitting up in my bunk that morning I realised that my pyjamas were damp with sweat from my disturbed and restless sleep and as soon as I rubbed my eyes and became fully conscious the reality of my situation hit me like a hammer blow as I found myself still in Victory Barracks.

"Bollocks!" I shouted out loud, I had learnt how to swear in the Navy.

I got out of bed and showered and after dressing in my cooks' whites I made my way to the galley. I fried hundreds of eggs for breakfast and when everyone had been fed I sat down to have my own meal. I was feeling truly miserable.

"How much bloody longer do I have to wait, I've given them the money why won't they let me go?" I moaned out loud and received a few odd looks from my fellow chefs in return.

At that moment a door swung open and in marched a Master at Arms.

"Is there a Cook S. Mann here?" he enquired of the assembled chefs.

I jumped up and informed him that I was his man to which he ordered me to follow him outside. I left my half eaten eggs and bacon and hurried after him and when we got to a quiet spot in the open he stopped and addressed me.

"You will go to your mess and change into your civilian clothes. You will then pack up all of your uniforms and take them to the stores where you will hand everything in. At 11.00 you will report to my office which is in the main block."

He glared at me for a short moment after which he turned smartly on his heels and marched off.

I ran over to the mess to start packing, as I had been instructed, with a mixture of euphoria at the thought of my imminent release and fear as I remembered my nightmare. Once I had reported to the Master at Arms he took me to a small hall in Victory Barracks where they had set up a table at which sat an Officer of the Clerical Branch. Standing in a line were half a dozen sailors in their civilian clothes who were being discharged. The Officer explained that he would call out each name in turn.

"When I shout out your name you will march forward to the desk and state your name, number and reason for discharge and hand me your I.D. card."

The Officer at the table then shouted out: "Rooney!"

A well turned out middle aged man in a smart civilian suit but still wearing shiny navy footwear marched forward, stopped at the table with a crunch of his boots and saluted as he bellowed out:

"Petty Officer T. Rooney, P0112479, Discharge due to Completion of Service, SIR!" He then handed over his I.D. card and in return received a brown envelope with some money in it.

"Good luck Rooney," said the Officer.

Mr. Rooney, as he now was, turned and marched across the hall and down a corridor and off to Civvy Street.

I watched him and noticed that tears rolled down his cheek as he mumbled to no one in particular:

"Twenty six bloody years I've given to the Navy and now I'm turfed out, what the fuck will I do now?"

When my name was called I walked over to the table.

"Cook S. Mann P083270, Discharge by purchase on grounds of Conscientious Objection!" I sang out clearly and confidently.

Everyone stared at me in amazement but nothing was said. I took my brown envelope with £8 inside it and was conscious that the Officer didn't wish me good luck as I turned and walked across the hall picking up the bag I had left by the door. As I went through the gates of HMS Victory and back into the real world I did a little skip and a jump.

Breathing in the air of freedom I walked along the road to Portsmouth Harbour Railway Station where I called Jennifer's telephone number from a GPO red phone box and luckily she was at home and answered me so I excitedly said to her:

"I've got out of the Navy, I'm free at last! Can you meet me at Waterloo Station?"

**

On the train back to London I took stock of my life.

"So, what are the positives?" I asked my reflection in the window.

I had learnt how to keep most things clean, including my nose. I now knew how to scrape congealed fat off a cooker hood and importantly how to clean windows with vinegar and old newspapers. I also knew how to cook bloody good meals, even in a force eight gale. I thought of all the people I had met and concluded that most were decent people and many were good mates.

I never did get to go to Singapore though as the advert in the Daily Mirror had promised but I had been abroad and to some pretty exciting places. I was still only twenty and in four months time I would be twenty one years old and eligible to vote.

On the downside Her Majesty's Government had left me almost penniless apart from the £8 final wages. In the past five and a half years they had allowed me to be verbally and physically abused and they had denied me my freedom and my rights.

I had been punched, kicked, bullied, shot at, gassed and almost drowned. I had been placed at the mercy of some nasty sadistic individuals and I had been sea sick, often. I didn't have a job and I wouldn't be able to afford to own a restaurant.

But I was young, I was in love and I was free!

When my train arrived at Waterloo Station I was met by Jennifer at the end of the platform where we hugged and kissed and cried.

Daylight was fading as we boarded a number 4A Routemaster Bus to Finsbury Park. We took a seat on the upper deck to admire the view as we went across Waterloo Bridge and over the River Thames.

The words from the Kinks song, *"Waterloo Sunset,"* came to mind again and I quietly sang the lyrics as we looked out over the River. I had a broad smile on my face as we rode off into the sunset, well towards Finsbury Park Bus Station to be more precise, but I was indeed in Paradise.

In fact I had never been happier in my life!

THE END

BIBLIOGRAPHY

[1] Down and Out in Paris and London. George Orwell. Penguin Classics, ISBN 9780141184388

[2] Homage to Catalonia, George Orwell, Penguin Classics, ISBN 9780141911717

[3] The Ragged Trousered Philanthropists Robert Tressell, Flamingo Modern Classics, ISBN 0586090363

[4] Reluctant Servicemen, Published by Housmans and National Council for Civil Liberties 1967

[5] Hansard - BOY SERVICE IN THE ARMED FORCES– House of Lords Debate 16 March 1967 vol 281 cc488-516

[6] Hansard - ARMED FORCES - RELEASE RIGHTS OF BOY ENTRANTS – House of Lords Debate 23 April 1969 vol 301 cc431

[7] Hansard - Young Servicemen (Morale and Conditions) - House of Commons Debate 07 May 1969 vol 783 cc425-6

[8] War of the Classes, Jack London, Star Rover House, ISBN 0932458114

[9] Hansard –DEFENCE: House of Commons Debate 13 November 1969 vol 791 cc626-743

ACKNOWLEDGEMENTS

This book would never have seen the light of day without help and advice from my family; Martin Grimshaw and his Mum, and also Andrew Grimshaw, Norman "Dicky" Bird, Tony Attwood, Dave Charie, Robin Dunn and Gerard Harkin.

NOTE ABOUT THE AUTHOR

Stephen Mann joined the British Royal Navy at the age of fifteen. He has written the book "Sadism, Songs and Stolen Liberty" about his experiences in the Navy and how he tried for five and a half years to get out.

He has spent his working life first as a chef, then a postal worker before becoming a telecoms engineer. Stephen has been a lifelong trade union activist and now works as a health and safety officer for the Communication Workers Union. Stephen lives in North London and supports his local football team, the Arsenal and he is active in their Independent Supporters Association. Stephen is a member of his local Labour Party and he likes music, reading, writing and enjoys a nice cup of tea.

POSTSCRIPT

I will always feel proud to have been associated with the National Council for Civil Liberties "Reluctant Servicemen" campaign. The successes of the campaign by the NCCL and others including Fenner Brockway, Tom Driberg, the Bishop of Norwich and Eric Lubbock came too late for me and the reluctant sailors I served with but it did eventually result in some changes to the recruitment process of the armed forces. These though are not straightforward and anyone thinking of signing up should make very sure what they are letting themselves in for as they may still find that getting out is not that simple.

For boys and girls now enlisting under the age of 18 they have a right of discharge up until their 18th birthday but in practice I'm told they often are not informed of this right After the age of 18 they have the right to give twelve months notice after they have served their minimum time but, for those enlisting at 16 the service period could still be six years!

I was recruited as a child serviceman and deplorably many countries in the world continue to recruit children into their armed forces. This includes the United Kingdom where children aged 16 and 17 are still recruited and this is something I urge everyone to campaign against. I am delighted that organisations have been set up such as Child Soldiers International who campaign globally for an end to the recruitment and use of boys and girls under the age of 18 by armed forces or groups. I am also particularly pleased to have joined an organisation, Veterans for Peace, which is made up of ex servicemen who state that having served their nation they now affirm their greater responsibility to serve the cause of world peace.

The struggle continues!

Printed in Great Britain
by Amazon.co.uk, Ltd.,
Marston Gate.